WE COULD BE...
BOWIE AND HIS HEROES

WE COULD BE... BOWIE AND HIS HEROES

TOM HAGLER

CONSULTANT EDITOR: TONY VISCONTI

C CASSELL

To Elijah, Nathaniel, Petroc and Reuben

First published in Great Britain in 2021 by
Cassell, an imprint of
Octopus Publishing Group Ltd
Carmelite House
50 Victoria Embankment
London EC4Y 0DZ
www.octopusbooks.co.uk

An Hachette UK Company
www.hachette.co.uk

Distributed in the US by
Hachette Book Group
1290 Avenue of the Americas
4th and 5th Floors
New York, NY 10104

Distributed in Canada by
Canadian Manda Group
664 Annette St.
Toronto, Ontario, Canada M6S 2C8

ISBN 978 1 78840 272 9
A CIP catalogue record for this book is
available from the British Library.
Printed and bound in the UK

10 9 8 7 6 5 4 3 2 1

Editorial Director: Joe Cottington
Creative Director: Jonathan Christie
Senior Editor: Alex Stetter
Picture Research Manager:
    Giulia Hetherington
Senior Production Manager:
    Katherine Hockley

This FSC® label means that materials used for
the product have been responsibly sourced

CONTENTS

INTRODUCTION

"We are not a tribute band, we are the real thing," proclaimed the poster. It was right. After all, the band in question, Holy Holy, included not only Woody Woodmansey, the last surviving member of the Spiders from Mars, but also Tony Visconti, Bowie's most famous producer and original bassist. The band were playing at London's Roundhouse to mark 50 years since Bowie and Visconti had last appeared there in a gig, which went down in history as the first-ever glam rock performance. The date, the songs and the lineup made it a highly emotional evening; this was the closest that any of us would now get to a real Bowie concert. On a whim, I printed off an embryonic copy of this book, which I handed in at the door, along with a note suggesting that if Mr Visconti were short of reading material for the flight back to New York, it might raise a nostalgic smile.

I didn't expect to hear anything more, but a few days later I opened my email and there, written in capitals letters, was the name "ANTHONY VISCONTI". It was a name which stood out in every sense. Here was an email from Bowie's right-hand man. I later joked to friends that receiving this email was like being touched by the hand of the hand that had touched God.

"Hi Tom, fortunately, I had a tiny space left in my carry-on suitcase," it read. *Great!* "I have finished your very enjoyable book. It's a great idea and I bet it flies off the shelves and onto e-readers." *GREAT!!* "I have found many errors." *Not so great.* "I am happy to help, if you promise me you're going to finish it and get it published." *Are you kidding?!*

The emergence of COVID-19 closed off many avenues, but, paradoxically, it opened one crucial door for me. All Visconti's work had to be put on hold and he decided to use this window of free time to help someone he had never met. "All my corrections/suggestions are based on what David told me directly," he was to tell me.

After a month of correspondence, he emailed me one last time: "Okay. I'm moving on to creating some music. I'm very happy I got to work on your book. I'll be here for further assistance if you need me."

So, this book is in your hands thanks to COVID, Tony Visconti and a generous hand-luggage allowance.

Around that time, another Tony entered the fray. I was interviewing Tony Blair about the coronavirus. As our talk finished, and knowing that he was a Bowie fan, I asked him if he had any tales to tell. At the mention of Bowie's name, Mr Blair laughed loudly and enthusiastically. The one-time prime minister was transported back to being the wannabe rock star at Oxford who fronted his own Bowie-like band. He proudly told me that he had seen Ziggy Stardust not once but twice. Meeting Bowie, he said, had left him starstruck, something which had only happened three times in his life (Barbra Streisand and Paul McCartney were the cause for the other two occasions).

"One of the things I always used to say to people about being prime minister was that you got to meet the icons of your youth," he told me, revealing a motivation for office not often discussed in political biography.

Most people, like Mr Blair, were only too delighted to talk about their "Bowie moments". But there were a few exceptions. John Lydon told me he thought Bowie was a snob. He recalled one night when he and Sid Vicious deliberately lost Bowie and his passenger, Iggy Pop, who were following in the car behind to get to a party. A comical car chase across London ensued. Bowie and Pop never did make that particular bash.

This book is a compilation of such vignettes, all with one thing in common: they revolve around an encounter between Bowie and a fellow icon. Bowie lived through an era when icons were abundant and he appears to have met them all, from Dalí to Dylan, Lennon to Lydon, Princess Margaret to Prince. Who knew, for example, that Bowie and Frank Sinatra became such good friends that if you listen carefully to one of the crooner's Christmas records, you should be able to hear Bowie singing in the background? Or that Bowie, unknown at the time, was so annoyed at being snubbed by Jimi Hendrix that he penned an angry letter about him to a music magazine? And if you want to find out more about the time Bowie met Michael Jackson, you may be as astonished as I was to discover his seminal role in Jackson's moonwalk.

Each encounter is a story in its own right, but if the book is read cover to cover, a new picture of Bowie emerges. It is a picture that helps overturn the stereotypical image of him as cold, unemotional and aloof. There is humble Bowie, who is mistaken for a waiter by a band only to politely take their order, never once revealing his true identity. There is compassionate Bowie, who once helped save the life of soul legend Nina Simone. We all know cool Bowie, but how about naff Bowie? How else to describe the time he begged to write an album for teen heartthrob David Cassidy? And, in later years, there is homebody Bowie, who would ask to go on stage first so he could beat the traffic home. This is Bowie seen through his actions and not just his words.

This book is the result of interviews with dozens of people who knew Bowie, both friends and stars, and lengthy trawls through foreign-language newspapers, magazines and TV appearances to find interviews not published or heard in English. A big debt is owed to all the many great Bowie biographies out there, as well as the autobiographies of many of the stars he met.

But this book also represents a different approach to telling Bowie's story. Unlike the standard biography, which charts its hero's rise from humble beginnings to stardom, this book compiles some of his most surprising, amusing and revealing moments. In album terms, think of it as a Greatest Hits.

ABSOLUTE
BEGINNER
1947–69

Bowie formed his first band before the Beatles released "Love Me Do" in 1962. By the time the Fab Four broke up seven years later, he was still waiting for his first hit.[1] He was so spectacularly unsuccessful during this decade that no one nowadays even considers him a sixties artist. Despondent, he was to quit music twice in these years: once to be a Buddhist monk, once to be a mime artist. He was unsuccessful here, too. Even his younger school friend, a lad by the name of Peter Frampton, was to hit the big time first.

But during these years Bowie sang, played and experimented perhaps even more than he would do in the seventies. After all, he had no audience to lose. His bands changed as quickly as his styles. He was a rock and roller, a heavy rocker, a psychedelic rocker, a comedy novelty rocker, a mod, a folk singer, a crooner, a musical-hall wannabe and more. Then he wrote "Space Oddity" and he found his style – odd and from outer space.

This is the decade where he met future legends in the most ordinary of places: on coaches, at market stalls or in sleepy seaside towns. Elton gave him the advice which would launch his career, Freddie measured his feet for footwear, and a member of Herman's Hermits got Bowie stoned for the first time (that particular Hermit went on to form Led Zeppelin).

Queen Elizabeth II

From the very beginning, David Bowie appeared destined to rub shoulders with the rich and famous. After all, his first "celebrity" encounter, at the age of just five, was with the Queen.

Young David was in the Yorkshire town of Harrogate, where his father was working for the children's charity Dr. Barnardo's. For a day out, the family decided to go to the annual agricultural show, at which the guests of honour were Queen Elizabeth, who had just come to the throne, and Prince Philip. When the excited youngster spotted the royal couple, he evaded his parents' grip and dashed through the crowds.

"Oh, hello, little boy," said Elizabeth, as she looked down at him. Bowie later recalled that Her Majesty was somewhat bemused by his sudden appearance at her waist. The moment was unusual enough to be snapped by a photographer from the local paper. Sadly, no copies have survived.

Bowie's desire to meet royalty dampened with the years. He twice turned down the offer to receive honours, including a knighthood, and he was to boot the Queen's sister out of a party (see page 210).

Tommy Steele

A Royal Variety Performance provided the occasion when nine-year-old David met the singer who would inspire him to enter the world of entertainment. The name of Tommy Steele may stick out like a sore thumb alongside the likes of Lou Reed, Iggy Pop and Kraftwerk, but the fifties cheeky chappie with a cockney image was to become a primary role model for the young Bowie.

It may seem incongruous that the light entertainer was to inspire one of rock's great iconoclasts, but the parallels between the two are notable. Steele had rejected the fake American accents in vogue at the time to keep his own broad south London accent. He was also an all-round entertainer in the English music-hall tradition, a style that influenced Bowie's desire to make rock more theatrical. Coincidentally, photographs of Steele in his prime, with his Teutonic good looks and tombstone teeth, show him looking uncannily like a Berlin-era Bowie.

David's father, John, was keen for his son to be an entertainment star and had access to the celebrity world through his role organizing charity events. His job allowed him entry backstage where he would introduce his son to some of the stars. Bowie's cousin Kristina Paulsen was there when the young David met Steele, and recalls the conversation thus:

"My son is going to be an entertainer, too," Bowie's father said. "Aren't you, David?"

"Yes, Daddy," David squeaked, his face flushed and beaming with pride.

The Royal Variety Performance had been initially postponed because of the Suez Crisis, but when it finally took place, Steele was accused of "extending the limits of acceptability" by some newspapers for asking the crowd to clap along. Audience participation had never been a feature of a royal show, and it was not until the Queen Mother started to clap that the crowd felt comfortable enough to join in. David would have noted this challenge to convention, as did the young John Lennon, who quipped a few years later when on stage at the same event, "The people in the cheaper seats, clap your hands. And the rest of you, if you'd just rattle your jewellery."

Arthur Haynes

Not every star was as accommodating as Tommy Steele. Bowie had always adored comedy, and one of his first loves in this area was another working-class Londoner. The name of Arthur Haynes is now largely forgotten but, in the late fifties, the tubby, trilby-wearing comic was Britain's highest-paid TV performer. So, young David was delighted to discover while holidaying in a caravan at the Pontins resort on the south coast that his neighbour was none other than Haynes himself.

Excitedly, the young boy went over to ask his hero for an autograph. "I went over three mornings running and he told me to fuck off every day," Bowie recalled in *Dazed & Confused*. "That was the first time [*sic*] I met a celebrity and I was so let down. I felt if that's what it's all about…They're just real people." Bowie promised, then and there, that, if he ever became famous, he would never treat his fans that way.

Brian Jones

Bowie's first encounter with the Rolling Stones was only marginally less antagonistic. The teenager was an early fan of the band and, hanging around after one gig, he fawningly offered to carry Brian Jones's guitar. The musician was in no mood to humour his hanger-on.

"Piss off!" he said. Those were the first words spoken by any Rolling Stone to David Bowie.

Despite the rejection, Bowie and the Stone, whom he idolized above all the other band members, became friends. "I am Brian Jones," a young Bowie once proudly declared to his girlfriend.

The two began to hang out together, sharing a love of music and a desire to look like Keith Relf in the hope that they too could pick up the Swedish groupies, who were smitten by the Nordic looks of the Yardbirds singer.

"I made a better Keith Relf than Brian Jones," Bowie said. "He was too short and fat."

Peter Frampton

When the 12-year-old Peter Frampton enrolled at Bromley Technical High School for Boys, the first thing he did was to ask his father, the art teacher, who was worth getting to know when it came to rock and roll. "There's this Jones chap," replied his dad. So, the young guitarist made a beeline for the older boy and together they would jam on the art-block stairs at break, with Bowie teaching the newcomer songs by Eddie Cochran. As was the case with many of his school friends, Bowie would stay pals with Frampton until his death.

Despite being younger by three years, Frampton was the first to hit the charts. When a surprised Bowie one day saw his young friend performing on TV, he was heard to say, "Wait a minute, that's Peter. He should be in school!" Frampton then went on to become a member of one of the first "super groups", Humble Pie, formed by Small Faces frontman Steve Marriott. Bowie was humbly and gratefully the group's support act. The young guitar wizard Frampton would then go on to compose "Show Me the Way", a forerunner of the stadium-filling pop rock to come. Bowie must have looked on with a mixture of fraternal pride and envy.

But when Frampton became unfashionable and his career nosedived, Bowie did not forget his friend. Despite their musical differences, he asked Frampton to join his tour band. "I can never thank him enough for believing in me, and seeing past the image of satin pants and big hair to the guitar player he first met at school," said Frampton.

Bowie not only saved his friend's career, he arguably saved his life, too. While on tour, the band sometimes travelled in a small charter plane. Once, just before take-off, Bowie noticed fumes filling the cabin. "Smoke! Smoke!" he shouted. The pilot brought the plane to an emergency stop and an attendant flung open the door. "I'm in my seat and David literally lifts me up and carries me down the chute," said Frampton. "He could have run but he wanted to make sure I was okay."

Little Richard

Standing atop his piano and midway through a song, Little Richard suddenly came to a halt. He clutched his chest, fell to his knees and toppled lifelessly to the floor. His horrified bandmates dropped their instruments and rushed to his side, as the compere appealed to the stunned audience for a doctor. In the audience, a panic-stricken 15-year-old named David Jones turned to his friend and, ashen-faced, said, "I think he's going to die!"

But then, the prostrate singer lifted his head up, grabbed the microphone, screamed "A-wop-Bop-a-Loo-bop, A-wop-bam-boom!!!" and bounded to his feet. The band launched into "Tutti Frutti" and the crowd went berserk. That piece of classic showmanship was to be forever burned onto the mind of the flabbergasted Bowie. "I'd never heard anything even resembling this," he said of the song. "It filled the room with outrageous energy and colour and outrageous defiance."

19

"Little Richard," Bowie would reply when asked who he most wanted to be. "He was my first idol." His most prized possession was a cellophane-wrapped photograph of the singer in a red Cadillac, which he would place on the mixing desk for inspiration. Little Richard, after all, was rock's first makeup-wearing gender-bender with a towering hairdo. Come the nineties, Bowie not only got to meet his hero but to jam with him, too. "I did get to play piano with him one night," recalled Bowie. "That was fun. He was a real hero of mine for years and years."

The oddest thing, said Bowie, was that Little Richard was the only other person he knew who had different-coloured eyes.[2]

Stevie Wonder

Bowie formed his first band at the age of 15 and, over the next few years, would meet not only many of his heroes but also those who were to become future legends. One evening, his band was booked to appear on Radio London's less than inspiring-sounding *Inecto Show*, named after a brand of shampoo. Bowie and the Lower Third were squeezed into a backstage room at London's Marquee along with all the other acts. Among them was an even younger lad. He was from the United States and blind, and Bowie took note of the daring stage name.

Stevie Wonder was to live up to his self-titled billing. Ahead of the show, the young American, already several years into his career, was led to an upright piano in the corner of the room. He began to play and, as his female backing band started singing along, all the other bands fell silent and watched.

"We were all stood together listening intently to the amazing Stevie Wonder," recalled Bowie's drummer, Phil Lancaster, in his book *At the Birth of Bowie*. It was made even more wonderful because Wonder and his singers appeared to have improvised the song on the spot.

Ray Davies

In the early sixties, tour buses were often as packed as dressing rooms. Record companies would squeeze half-a-dozen or so bands onto one coach and send them off on a circuit around Britain. One tour in1964 was typical of the time. On board were Marianne Faithfull, who would usually sit beside her new boyfriend, Gene Pitney, headliners Gerry and the Pacemakers, who would keep everyone entertained, and the Kinks, who would keep themselves to themselves. In the midst of it all was the 17-year-old Bowie, then billed as Davy Jones. The teenager's attempts to strike up a conversation with the glamorous Faithfull had fallen on deaf ears, but, somewhere between Wigan and Stockton, he managed to get the attention of his idol, Ray Davies, the Kinks' lead singer, who had just had his first number one with "You Really Got Me".

The two became friends, and Bowie started to visit Davies's north London home. "He used to hang around with us," recalled Davies's girlfriend at the time, model Jeanette Ross. "We used to live in Park Avenue, Golders Green, which became well known for people just turning up. We had a studio there as well, and everybody would come around and jam."

The Kinks had a greater influence on Bowie's writing in the sixties than any other band, and he covered their songs throughout his career, from "Where Have All the Good Times Gone" to "Waterloo Sunset".

"I've never heard a Kinks song that I didn't like," Bowie said.

"The Kinks have come to stand for some of the most enduring and heart-clutching pop of all time. They are in the gut of every British songwriter who followed them and are indisputably a cornerstone of everything pop and rock. I love 'em. The world loves 'em."

The two mainstays of quintessential English rock finally got to perform together at Carnegie Hall, New York, in a 2003 benefit concert for Tibet. As Davies recalled, "We did 'Waterloo Sunset' and David said, 'Who's going to take what line? How shall we sing this?' I said, 'Let's imitate each other.' So that's what we did. David was a great mimic. That ability gave him his diversity as a performer. He was a smart kid." In the audience was Caryn Rose, a journalist at *The Village Voice*, who described their duet as "one of those amazing, transcendent moments. The affection and shared emotion between the two has you holding your breath."

Davies was so affected by Bowie's death that the day he heard the news, he travelled to London's West End where the Kinks' musical, *Sunny Afternoon*, was playing. Unannounced, he took to the stage to tell the audience that he needed "to say a few words about my friend". Davies spoke about touring together in the early days and recounted his fondest memory: that day in New York when they finally got to sing together. At that point, the house band struck up "Waterloo Sunset" and Davies joined the cast for an emotional rendition, which left many in the audience in tears.

James Brown

The tour bus was eventually replaced with a van, not that it would make touring any easier. Davy Jones and the Manish Boys were on their way to support James Brown in 1965 in the unlikely surroundings of Portsmouth when their notoriously unreliable vehicle broke down once again. Bowie was deeply disappointed. He was such a fan of the soul man that he would travel to Brixton at weekends to go to the only club guaranteed to play Brown's records.

In the mid-seventies, the two singers once again came close to meeting. This time, it would have been facing each other in a court room. Brown is one of the most copied artists of all time, but now it was the turn of the American legend to be accused of plagiarism. Bowie's guitarist, Carlos Alomar, had heard a record that sounded uncannily like "Fame". It was "Hot" by James Brown. The similarity was no coincidence, as Brown had played "Fame" to his band ahead of his recording and told them to recreate the sound.

Alomar suggested suing Brown, but Bowie was flattered by his hero's imitation and suggested they wait to see whether "Hot" charted; otherwise they wouldn't get any money, anyway. The song was a flop and Bowie was spared having to decide whether or not to take one of his biggest heroes to court. No doubt, Brown's lawyers would have argued that "Fame" was a classic James Brown sound in the first place.

It was not until 2001, and a New York fashion show, that the two singers finally met. The soul singer had just finished performing. Bowie was next up and did a classic James Brown foot shuffle as he walked to the microphone. The shimmy was so accurate, it drew a round of applause and appreciative laughter from the audience. A photograph taken backstage afterwards showed the two singers embracing and pointing at each other like two goofy fans.

Pete Townshend

If Portsmouth was an unlikely place to meet James Brown, Bournemouth seems just as incongruous a location for Bowie to meet guitar smasher Pete Townshend. It was 1965, and Bowie's band, the Lower Third, were supporting the Who in the seaside resort beloved by pensioners. Bowie was trying to sound like the London outfit at the time, and recalled how Townshend had watched their sound check. "You're trying to write like me!" remarked a peeved Townshend. "I don't think he was very impressed," recalled Bowie.

Nonetheless, the two became friends, so much so that Townshend would even ask Bowie to babysit his kid brother. "I took my eight-year-old brother Simon and left him in David Bowie's care," said Townshend of a 1969 concert at the Royal Albert Hall, where the Who played songs from their concept album, *Tommy*. Even by the Who's standards, it was a raucous night; this time, the audience started rioting before the band. The group was banned, but Bowie and Simon were thrilled. "They both said the same thing: 'I am going to do this,'" said Townshend. "David, I think, meant, 'I'm going to do concept albums that have an underlying artistic story.'"

Bowie was to hand over a song he had recently written, telling Townshend, "Play that and let me know what you think of it one day." That day came a decade later, when Bowie asked the guitarist to play on his *Scary Monsters* (1980) album. "I've been meaning to tell you," Townshend said, "that single should do alright." The song was "Space Oddity".

Bowie would ask Townshend to join him again in 2001 on his new album, *Toy*, at the New York studios of Philip Glass.

As an introduction, the minimalist composer proudly pointed out the studio's defining feature: a window that looked directly out onto the city's symbol, the Twin Towers. When Townshend returned six months later, the towers were gone. So was the album. "David had completely dumped everything he'd been working on," said Townshend. "The new album [*Heathen*, 2002] was darker, grimmer and more about what had changed on that extraordinary day. That event changed him, it made him darker and I don't know that he ever really snapped out of it."

Sonny Boy Williamson

Despite still living at home and having saxophone lessons, the 17-year-old David was confident enough to take his alto to the Marquee Club, on London's Wardour Street, which had a tradition of allowing any musicians in the audience to join in a collective encore. One band he is said to have played along with was the High Numbers, who would change their name to the Who. Another artist Bowie is believed to have briefly joined on stage was Sonny Boy Williamson, a big influence on the Rolling Stones, Eric Clapton and Robert Plant.Legend has it that a young Plant was so obsessed that he stole Williamson's harmonica, although the reality appears to be that the blues legend told the 14-year-old fan to "fuck off" after being approached at a urinal, and that the spurned Plant nicked his hero's harp in revenge.

Soon after the Marquee concert, British police issued an arrest warrant for Williamson in connection with the stabbing of a man during a street fight. The 52-year-old musician quickly returned to the United States. Within months, he was dead from a heart attack.

John Lee Hooker

Bowie's television debut provided him with the chance to meet another blues legend and one of his earliest musical heroes. "Everybody was picking a blues artist as their own," said Bowie. "Somebody had Muddy Waters, somebody had Sonny Boy Williamson. Ours was Hooker." Bowie had even named one of his short-lived bands, the Hooker Brothers, in tribute.

Bowie and his group at the time, the King Bees, were preparing for their appearance on the nation's top pop show, *Ready Steady Go!*, when the thrilled singer discovered that the blues guitarist was in the next dressing room. "I've seen him close up!" an awestruck Bowie told his bandmates. "Look at those hands, those fingers!" he marvelled.

Bowie also owes one of his biggest hits to Hooker. A bandmate was strumming one of the bluesman's riffs while on the top deck of the bus. "Hand the guitar over here," said Bowie, who converted the riff into a song he later called "The Jean Genie".

Marc Bolan

The two future stars of glam rock first met not with guitars in hand but with paint brushes. The teenaged wannabes had been set to work whitewashing the office walls of their record manager, Les Conn. The 17-year-old Bowie started the conversation.

"Are you a mod?"

"Yeah. I'm king mod. Your shoes are crap."

"You're short."

"I'm going to be a singer, and I'm going to be so big you're not gonna believe it."

"Well, I'll probably write a musical for you one day because I'm going to be the greatest writer ever!"

The two talked so much that the painting was forgotten and the manager had to convince another young wannabe to finish the job.

Despite being a year older, Bowie was the one in awe. "David would say, 'Well, Marc says this,' or 'Marc says that,' wrote Bowie's manager Kenneth Pitt. "He considered him an authority." Bowie described it as a "sparring relationship", but the rapport was instant and the two started going out to the clubs or Carnaby Street, where they would "dustbin shop", as they searched for free cast-offs.

Bolan was the first to hit the big time. "We were all green with envy," admitted Bowie. "We fell out for about six months. But we got over that." Bolan stayed loyal and gave his pal a support slot, despite Bowie, fed up with his lack of success with music, having switched to being a mime act at this point.

When Bowie became famous, however, the bitterness crept in. "I don't consider David to be even remotely near big enough to give me any competition," Bolan told the writer Cameron Crowe. "I don't think that David has anywhere near the charisma or balls that I have. He's not gonna make it, in any sort of way." That was in 1973, a year after Ziggy Stardust.

Producer Tony Visconti insisted that David continued to adore Marc, but he remembered an often visibly upset Bowie walking through the door after the diminutive singer had taken "one too many digs at him". According to Visconti, "David never saw him as a rival as much as Marc saw him as a rival." But Bowie could be snide and superior about his friend, too. "Marc only has his music," Bowie said. "He knows my areas stretch out."

Bolan and Bowie share a stage for the last time in September 1977.

"The little imp opened the door," Bowie said much later in a backhanded compliment. "What was so great, however, was that we knew he hadn't got it quite right, sort of Glam 1.0."

In September 1977, Bolan asked Bowie to guest on his TV show, memorable for a drunk Bolan falling off stage. A week later, Bolan was dead, killed in a car crash.

Bowie truly loved his friend. The fact that there was no proper will meant that Bolan's partner and son were left destitute. It was Bowie who helped them out financially. "David's generosity helped my mother and me to survive," said Bolan's son, Rolan.

At the funeral, Bowie was in tears. "He was fabulous, one of the funniest guys I've ever met. We would be on the floor rolling with laughter most of the time. I really miss him. He was stellar."

John Peel

- - - - - - - - - -

"Crap." That was the rather un-BBC-like verdict handed down by the Corporation's audition panel upon first hearing Marc Bolan sing. Bowie was to fare little better. "A singer devoid of any personality. Sings wrong notes and out of tune," declared the panellists in 1965. Given that the BBC had a radio monopoly, their verdict appeared to deal a fatal blow to his fledgling career. But then John Peel stepped in to the rescue.

The DJ was a powerful voice within the Corporation and insisted Bowie be given a second chance. "With your inimitable manner and tremendous enthusiasm, you got me back on for another audition which I passed second time around, and which gave me freewheeling access to a lifetime of singing all the wrong notes," the singer told a *This Is Your Life* tribute to Peel. Bowie continued to rely heavily on Peel, who remained the only DJ to play his records. "We kept Bowie alive for a couple of years," Peel recalled.

As success continued to prove elusive, Bowie decided upon the most bizarre career choice ever made by a future rock god – he became a mime artist. But things got worse and Bowie ended up at the foot of the bill or, as Peel described it, "below that lowliest of God's creatures, an Australian sitar player". Peel was close friends with the top-billing Bolan and was often in the star's dressing room on concert nights. The DJ's main job come showtime, he said, was to get things started by sticking his head out of the door to shout down the corridor, "David, you're on!"

One night, Peel decided he could take no more of his friend's struggles. Bowie had just finished a lengthy mime routine depicting China's occupation of Tibet, and the audience had again reacted with a mixture of perplexity, indifference and disdain. For the second time, Peel stepped in to rescue Bowie's career. "Go back to songwriting," he told his friend.

"You didn't like mime," Bowie told Peel later. "You were right. Nobody in the world likes mime."[3]

Bowie's involvement in that TV homage genuinely touched the DJ. His previous memory of trying to have a word with "my old mate" involved Bowie's muscle-bound, karate-trained minder stepping in: "Hey, asshole! Where the fuck you think you're going?" "Just going to have a word with my mate David," said Peel timidly. "Like fuck ya gonna have a word with David," the minder replied.

"Since then," wrote Peel, "and surely way beyond the New York karate expert's intention, I've not had a single word with David."

Jonathan King

Another influential future BBC figure who helped Bowie's early career was Jonathan King. King was a rotund, bespectacled singer-songwriter and music producer who would eventually be found guilty of child sexual abuse. David Bowie was David Bowie, a man once described as "always the most beautiful person in the room". And yet it was the DJ who rejected a sexual advance from the singer. At least, according to King himself.

An early convert to Bowie, King raved about the 1966 single "Can't Help Thinking About Me" in his music magazine column. The delighted singer got in touch and was invited round to King's place. "He was desperately trying to be a star," King was quoted as saying in Wendy Leigh's *Bowie: The Biography*. "I thought he was very sweet and I think he fancied me. But I didn't fancy him because of his different-coloured eyes. I just had the vibes that if I wanted to..."

Bowie's view of the encounter is not recorded, but 15 years later King, now a TV show host, was scheduled to interview the singer after a concert. Thinking back to their early friendship, King told his crew, "This is going to be great!" After a lengthy delay, they heard a commotion outside and then in walked Bowie, followed by a large entourage. The singer sat down opposite King, looked him in the eye, said, "You are a fat shit," then stood up and walked straight back out again.

Simon Napier-Bell

Jonathan King was to promote a number of acts that made it in the seventies, but the Svengali of the music business in the mid-sixties was Simon Napier-Bell. The Simon Cowell of his day, Napier-Bell was so famed for finding and manufacturing pop acts that outrageous offers were sometimes made to obtain his patronage.

Once such incident occurred in 1965, when Napier-Bell was contacted by an up-and-coming manager named Ralph Horton, who insisted he had a hot new act destined for stardom. Horton was desperate; a creditor was asking for the return of a £4,000 loan and the electricity in his basement flat had been cut off. Napier-Bell, then managing the Yardbirds, went over to Horton's "grubby" apartment in Pimlico to find, as he recalled, "a not especially attractive" young man called Davy Jones sitting quietly in the corner. After a brief conversation, Horton told Napier-Bell that he could have sex with the singer on condition he become co-manager. "The sheer sleaziness of the proposal was enough to make me run – which I did," Napier-Bell wrote on his website. He never did find out if the 17-year-old Bowie was in on the proposal or not, although those close to Bowie maintain that the singer would never have agreed to such a transaction under any circumstances.

Mandy Rice-Davies

Bowie did, however, seriously countenance some highly unlikely and unglamorous proposals. In 1966, for instance, he almost threw away his chance at rock stardom to become a nightclub singer in Tel Aviv. The offer was made to him by Mandy Rice-Davies, one of the models at the centre of Britain's biggest political scandal of the sixties, the Profumo affair, which involved illicit sexual liaisons and alleged leaks to a communist spy.

Following her part in the government's downfall, Rice-Davies had reinvented herself as a music impresario and opened a nightclub in Israel. On the lookout for a resident singer to entertain the tourists, she bumped into Bowie at Soho's La Giaconda café, a musicians' hangout. Swept away by his looks and charisma, she offered him the job there and then. Bowie, down on his luck and desperate for money, accepted. Romance may also have played a role. "If I hadn't been married at the time, I may well have fallen for David," said Davies.

Drummer Phil Lancaster recalled the two dancing so close together that when the ex-model's beefy boyfriend walked in, Bowie was forced to do a runner. "Her fiancé not only looked like a champion boxer, he actually was one," said Lancaster.

When Rice-Davies returned to La Giaconda two weeks later with contract in hand, fate intervened. "I'd love to come, but I can't," Bowie said. "I've just got a recording contract."

Elton John
- - - - - - - - - - - -

La Giaconda was to play a key role in Bowie's development. It was here, for example, that teenagers Reg Dwight and Davy Jones would discuss over a cup of coffee how they were going to conquer the world. Reg would walk the few doors down from the music publishing house where he worked as a mail boy. Davy only needed to roll out of the bed in his converted ambulance, parked semi-permanently right outside, so close that the café staff would sometimes simply pass the coffee through the vehicle's window. Come the evening, the two singers would regularly bump into each other at the Marquee or some other music venue.

As their careers progressed, Davy became David and Reg became Elton. Then, one day, David played a song to a publishing company. He was sure it was his best song yet, but it was peculiar. His demo was greeted sceptically. His first choice as producer, Tony Visconti, dismissed it as a novelty song and passed the project on to someone else.

According to Angie Bowie – the American model and journalist who was Bowie's wife from 1970 to 1980 – Elton happened, by chance, to be present and could tell that his friend was worried that the song was about to be swept under the carpet.

"Gus [Dudgeon] is a great producer, David. He'll do you right," she recalled Elton saying. Bowie was placated and agreed to give the producer a chance. Dudgeon loved the demo and decided to use an array of innovative studio techniques which were to prove a perfect fit for a strange song about a spaceman called Major Tom. Angie later described the conversation as being the turning point in Bowie's career.

The song certainly turned out to be a turning point in Elton's career. The boy from Pinner was floored upon hearing "Space Oddity" on the radio. "It was the most incredible record I'd ever heard," he said. Elton immediately contacted Dudgeon and arranger Paul Buckmaster and begged them to work with him as well. It was a union made in heaven. The very first track they were to work on was "Your Song", and their long-lasting relationship was to provide the bedrock upon which Elton would become the biggest-selling artist of the seventies.

But that was not the only time Bowie influenced Elton's career. Just over two years later, Elton was in the audience at London's Rainbow Theatre for Ziggy Stardust. Astounded by the theatricality, costume changes, lights, dry ice and songs, Elton emerged with his throat raw from screaming. "That was a turning point," he later said. "It was like, fuck, the bar's been raised. His stage presence was quite extraordinary. David was so beautiful, so glamorous, so androgynous and so sexual."

The two were still friendly at this point. Elton remembered going out for a "fabulous" dinner with Angie and Bowie, when the latter insisted his ultimate dream was to be Judy Garland. But the rivalry was turning bitter. Elton quickly adopted the glamorous costumes and theatricality of Ziggy, and by the time he released "Rocket Man" in 1972, Bowie was fuming. Seeing her husband seethe as he watched Elton on *Top of the Pops*, Angie told him, "Other people can sing about space travel too." She also dryly noted that no one had ever mentioned Elton's influence on the piano-based *Hunky Dory* (1971).

The relationship between the singers never recovered. Come 1976, one interviewer recalled Bowie and Mick Jagger laughing about "fat Reg". Bowie went on publicly to accuse his former friend of being at the vanguard of "a whole new school of pretensions" who were copying him, before dismissing Elton as a Liberace, rock and roll's "token queen".

"That was a cunty thing to say from somebody like that," Elton responded bluntly. "But then, he's a cunt anyway." Bowie was, said Elton, "a pseudo-intellectual, and I can't stand pseudo-intellectuals". Later, he said, "He wasn't my cup of tea," before pausing to add, clearly hurt, "No, I wasn't his cup of tea."

When Bowie died, Elton put all of that to one side and paid a glowing tribute to Bowie's music, influence, dignity in death and mystique. "We know David Bowie the figure, the singer, the outrageous performer," he said. "But, actually, we don't know anything about him. And that's the way it should be."

Dana Gillespie

One Bowie incarnation of which we certainly know very little came well before the Thin White Duke, Ziggy Stardust or the Berlin years. It was Bowie's "Robin Hood" period. Although next to nothing has been written about this brief part of his career, the singer Dana Gillespie remembers it vividly. She was at London's Marquee Club when she noticed a singer dressed in a tunic, leather waistcoat and thigh-high suede boots with tassels, looking like he had just stepped out of Sherwood Forest.

Gillespie went to the bar after the set but, too young to order a drink, occupied herself by brushing her hair. She felt someone take the brush and gently continue to comb her locks. Bowie, it seemed, had found his Maid Marian. Within minutes, he had convinced Gillespie to take him back to her parents' place for the night. It was the beginning of a long friendship which would, with help from Bowie himself, see Gillespie become a well-known

Bowie's "Robin Hood" period: Davie Jones and the King Bees, c.1964.

actress and singer. The two became so close that Bowie would seek out Dana to get her views on his latest compositions. One time he called to say, "I've just written this song half an hour ago. I'm coming over to play it to you now." So it was that Dana became the first person to hear "Space Oddity".

Looking back at the night they met at the Marquee, she confessed that Bowie may have had other things than sex on his mind. One reason he asked to go home with her, she said, was that the trains didn't run all the way to Bromley at that hour.

Lindsay Kemp

The young Bowie was to leave a string of broken hearts, and not only women's, in his wake. His mime instructor, Lindsay Kemp, was so devastated when he discovered that his protégé was two-timing him that he rode his bicycle into the sea off Whitehaven in a suicide attempt. But Kemp quickly ended the bid to kill himself because, he said, he found the water too cold. Defeated and bedraggled, the dancer returned to the hotel and was on stage with Bowie within hours. As the performance progressed, blood from his wounds seeped through his costume. "It was a fabulously dramatic effect," Kemp fondly recalled.

At least, that is how the mime artist described the episode later. The truth was slightly less dramatic: Kemp had half-heartedly tried to slash his wrists in his room after hearing Bowie and costume designer Natasha Korniloff having sex next door.

If one person could be credited with turning Bowie into a theatrical performer, it was Kemp. Bowie had gone to see him perform in 1967. Impressed, the singer went backstage to pass on his praise. According to Kemp, it was "love at first sight". The mime artist took the young man back to his Soho flat which was filled with strippers, druggies, pimps and prostitutes. "He was completely at home," recalled Kemp.

"His day-to-day life was the most theatrical thing I'd ever seen," said Bowie. "It was everything I thought Bohemia was. I joined the circus."

When it came to mime, Bowie did not do things by halves, going to France to study under the greatest of them all. Keyboard whizz-kid Keith Emerson recalled how, while he was playing at London's Marquee in the mid-sixties, a youngster came straight

37

up to him as if they had known each other for years. "I've just come back from Paris having lessons with actor Marcel Marceau," Bowie told him. "My first thought," said Emerson, "was why would he want to do that?" But Emerson was impressed enough to remember the encounter when Bowie later became famous. "I was intrigued at the depth he would go, to discover art in all its forms," said the prog rocker.

Lionel Bart

In the late sixties, rumour had it that Lionel Bart and Bowie were having an affair. "Lionel had the hots for David and turned up one day, making it very clear my presence wasn't welcome," recalled Bowie's one-time girlfriend Mary Finnigan. The composer of *Oliver!* disdainfully threw the keys to his Rolls-Royce in her direction and ordered her to "go away and play". He then turned to Bowie and suggestively said, "Please, sir, I want some more." It left Finnigan in no doubt that their relationship went beyond friendship.

Bart was the colossus of the West End, and his patronage would have been very useful to Bowie, according to Finnigan's cynical view. Other friends described the fur-coated Bart as often being seen around town "with a rent boy in tow, or snuggled up to David".

But Bart had a profound musical influence on Bowie's career, too. In writing hit songs for Bowie favourites Tommy Steele and Anthony Newley, Bart was the first to reject the fashion for fake American accents and create songs with what was described as "the evocative aroma of the chip shop". His impact is also seen on Bowie's first stab at writing his own musical, the unproduced

Kids on the Roof, almost a direct copy of Bart's street urchins hiding out in the city's lofts. Bowie turned the idea into the album *Diamond Dogs* (1974) and described his young protagonists as "vicious Oliver Twists". He finally got to follow in Bart's footsteps towards the end of his life when he achieved his dream of staging his own musical, *Lazarus* (2015).

Electric Light Orchestra

It was 1966, at a small venue in Birmingham called the Cedar Club, when a young drummer named Bev Bevan got the advice that was to launch his future band on the road to global superstardom. A London outfit by the name of Davy Jones and the Lower Third was playing. Bevan was so impressed by the singer that he went up to have a word. "It's obvious you are going to make it," he said. "What advice would you give us because that's just what we want to do?" "Just find the best musicians in the city, rehearse like crazy until you are as tight as a drum, then go to London, find a manager and get yourself a record deal," Jones replied.

Bevan would stick to the advice with his bands The Move and, later, ELO. "So, Bowie played a big part in our careers," recalled Bevan. "I will always be really grateful."

Paul McCartney

Paul McCartney was used to finding dozens of fans waiting outside his London home throughout the sixties but one, with his permed locks and floppy hat, stood out. On seeing the youngster outside his door again, McCartney invited him in for a cup of tea. The fan revealed that he was a musician and handed over a demo disc. McCartney happily played the song and was impressed. He wished him well, and Davy Jones left.

Years later, history repeated itself in New York. This time, a now-famous Bowie wanted to play his latest record to the ex-Beatle. McCartney was in the city to discuss the legal dissolution of the band with John Lennon, and they had dropped in on Bowie, who was renting a hotel suite nearby. Bowie insisted on playing his guests his new LP, *Young Americans* (1975), not once but twice. The atmosphere was already tense because of the lingering rancour between the two Beatles, so when Bowie looked like he was about to play his own record a third time, McCartney asked if there was anything else they could hear.

Bowie ignored the request, at which point Lennon felt compelled to say, "It's great. Do you have any other albums that might be of interest?" Bowie put on another record and then walked out in a huff. When Lennon later returned to his own apartment, the phone was already ringing. On the end was a distraught Bowie, worried that the Beatles hated his music.

While Bowie never developed as close a friendship with McCartney as he did with Lennon, the two did hang out together given the opportunity. The ex-Beatle recalled one evening when the two of them pored through an old *Billboard* chart book, intrigued to find out where some of their lesser-known singles had ended up. McCartney certainly respected Bowie's opinion. He sent him a pre-release version of the Wings album *Back to the Egg* (1979) to get his initial thoughts (Bowie loved the most experimental track, "Broadcast", and suggested that it be the single), and McCartney added crowd-favourite "Love Me Do" to his solo set list on Bowie's recommendation.

But there was also a spikiness to their relationship. Bowie and his girlfriend Ava Cherry once popped round to McCartney's apartment in New York in the seventies only to be greeted by a wall of silence (Bowie, once again, stormed off). While in 1990 McCartney telephoned to say he had finished a painting of Bowie vomiting which he wanted to call "Bowie Spewing". Would his pal be offended by the title?

"Of course not," Bowie replied. "But what a coincidence – I am currently working on a song that's called 'McCartney Shits'."

As for that very first encounter, McCartney must have been at least a little impressed: he still has that disc by Davy Jones.

Alfred Lennon

Bowie was also to meet Lennon early on. Not John, but Alfred. The 52-year-old estranged father of the Beatles' singer had briefly made up with his son. Such was the hysteria surrounding anything to do with the band, Lennon Snr was even given his own recording contract.

Pye also happened to be Bowie's label, so when the company held a promotion party in 1966 for Bowie's "Can't Help Thinking About Me", Alfred was one of the guests. Drummer Phil Lancaster spent much of the evening with Alfred, who spoke at length about his difficult relationship with John and how he wanted to make up. "I know John must have wondered if I was after this or that," he told Lancaster, putting a hand behind his back to mimic a handout, "but I wasn't." Others present remembered the older Lennon being in a "highly inebriated" state, tragically asking anyone he could buttonhole, "Do you know who I am?"

Bowie, though, appears to have kept his distance. "He quietly steered away from Lennon that night, making it clear he didn't want to be in any photos with him," said Lancaster. "Maybe he thought it would be disrespectful to John Lennon if he did pose with his father."

John Paul Jones

Bowie had been popping pills and taking speed since he was 13. Then one day a hippy bass player in a minor pop band called Herman's Hermits said to him, "Come over and I'll turn you onto grass." That person was John Paul Jones, the future Led Zeppelin bassist.

"Sure, I'll give it a whirl," replied Bowie. Three spliffs later and stoned, Bowie got his first taste of the munchies and consumed two loaves of bread. When the telephone rang, Jones was too stoned to answer, so asked Bowie to pick it up. But Bowie himself was so high that by the time he had got downstairs, he had forgotten the instruction. He walked straight past the ringing phone, out the door and all the way back home.

Years later, Bowie underwent his one and only drugs bust. It was for possession of marijuana. "What a dreadful irony," Bowie said. "The stuff sickens me. I haven't touched it in a decade."

Eric Clapton

One of the most momentous events in Bowie's life happened while watching Eric Clapton. Bowie had taken his mentally fragile older brother, Terry, to a rock concert. Terry was thrilled but Cream's deafening sound quickly disturbed him. Seeing something was badly wrong, Bowie took his brother outside, but by the time they reached the street Terry was hallucinating. He threw himself down onto the floor, shouting that he was being sucked into space and that flames were leaping out of the cracks. It was the first time Bowie had seen his brother have a schizophrenic episode. Terry's condition worsened, and he was later sent to a psychiatric unit, where he would spend much of the rest of his life.

Although the episode cast a heavy shadow over Bowie's life, he retained fonder memories associated with Clapton. When Bowie and his band the Lower Third toured in 1966, their support act was a new outfit called Cream. The roles were soon reversed, and Bowie's group ended up backing the rock trio. Never one to settle for second best, Bowie even convinced Clapton to give him some guitar lessons, according to future bandmate Woody Woodmansey.

The favour was returned decades later. Intrigued by all the media hoopla surrounding the release of Bowie's *The Next Day* in 2013, Clapton listened to "Where Are We Now?" "This song took me by the scruff of the neck," the guitarist said. "The construction gave me cold chills." Clapton sent an email to Bowie's office praising such "a beautiful song". Bowie emailed back: "Thanks for the shout-out, old sock."

Clapton loved the phrase so much that he named his next album *Old Sock* (2013).

Jimi Hendrix

Bowie was also to meet the greatest rock guitarist of them all. Jimi Hendrix played a concert in London in 1967, and Bowie was in the crowd. Amusingly, the youngster had turned up to see not the American but the support band, a Scottish prog rock outfit called 1-2-3. The group, who were his pals, had promised to play one of Bowie's songs, "I Dig Everything", albeit in true prog fashion with the verses chopped up and a Bach fugue inserted. Not that Bowie wasn't a fan of the guitarist. He had turned up early at the Saville Theatre to help set up. The band remembered a delighted Bowie grabbing the chance to carry Hendrix's own guitar into the venue.

The concert was typical Hendrix fare, with the guitarist battering the amplifier. The audience went wild, but 1-2-3's organist, Billy Ritchie, recalled laughing. "What we could see from the side of the stage and the audience couldn't, was Jimi's five-foot-nothing roadie standing behind the Marshall amps, struggling to keep them from collapsing in a heap!"

After the set, Ritchie took Bowie backstage to their dressing room, and there, in the middle, was the gangly figure of Hendrix himself. The Saville Theatre may have been able to fit in 1,400 punters, but it only had one space for all the bands. "I introduced David to Jimi," recalled Ritchie. "It seemed no big deal at the time. David was just a bloke then, not the famous Thin White Duke."

But the meeting did not go as hoped. "Jimi at that time was very shy and quite introverted off stage, he was withdrawn and ill-confident with strangers," said Ritchie. "He shook David's hand and muttered something I didn't quite catch. I could see David was a bit miffed: even though he was unknown, he liked to be taken seriously and certainly not be misjudged."

Later that week, a review in the weekly music newspaper *Record Mirror* was critical of 1-2-3 for failing to match up to the might of the American guitarist. Bowie penned an angry response, defending his friends. But, for Ritchie, it was also because Bowie was angry at his perceived snub. "David was annoyed with Jimi, offended that he hadn't been given a bit more enthusiasm and respect as he saw it," said Ritchie. "I told David it was not personal, it was just Jimi's shyness but I think he thought

I was trying to placate him rather than tell him the truth. He was pissed off with not being taken seriously."

Bowie did have one reason to thank the flamboyant showman. Like everyone, he had been thrilled when Hendrix played the guitar with his teeth and he suggested taking that display a step further. "One person gnawing the guitar was one thing," he said, "but two people, well, that was two things." The photograph of Bowie "giving head" to guitarist Mick Ronson on stage was to propel Ziggy into the stratosphere.

Vince Taylor

But when it came to Ziggy and his antics, the fundamental inspiration came from a rocker closer to home. Draped in bed linen and looking like Jesus, Vince Taylor walked out on stage, proclaimed himself the Messiah and proceeded to sack his band in front of the audience. If that sounds familiar, it should do.

The singer was briefly "Britain's Elvis", a leather-clad rock and roll rebel. Bowie was a big fan of his unpredictable, odd-ball iconoclasm and remembered one particular encounter outside London's Charing Cross tube station. An agitated Taylor was convinced the end of the world was nigh. He unfurled a map on the pavement and, using his magnifying glass, pointed out to Bowie all the secret locations where alien spaceships had gathered to prepare for the invasion.

"He was out of his gourd," Bowie told the BBC presenter Alan Yentob. But Taylor's madness enthralled Bowie. His flipped-out vision of a rock and roll Messiah was to become "part of the stew" of his most famous creation. "I thought of Vince Taylor and wrote Ziggy Stardust," Bowie said.

Taylor spent many subsequent years in prisons and psychiatric units, before moving to Switzerland where he ended up getting married and working as an aircraft mechanic ("The happiest days of my life," he said). He was still working there, living anonymously, when he died in 1991, aged 52.

Syd Barrett

Another ingredient of the Ziggy stew was an English eccentric whose career would burn briefly and end in tragedy. "Wow!" was Bowie's response on first seeing Syd Barrett. The Pink Floyd frontman's theatrical space rock, complete with English accent and heavy eyeliner, was unlike anything that had gone before, and Bowie was taking notes.

"He's a bohemian, a poet, and he's in a rock band. His impact on my thinking was enormous," recalled Bowie, who named Barrett as one of his three major influences alongside Iggy Pop and Lou Reed. "He was the first I had seen in the middle sixties who could decorate a stage," said Bowie. "This strange mystical look to him, with painted black fingernails and eyes fully made up...Syd wasn't altogether of this world."

One reflection of Barrett's influence was that Bowie named his prototype Ziggy Stardust band Arnold Corns in homage to the Pink Floyd song "Arnold Layne". Another, less celebrated, link is that Barrett is the only rock star other than Bowie to write a song about a gnome.[4] The two English eccentrics would appear, on paper at least, to be destined to hit it off. After all, if anyone had decided to "turn and face the strange", it was Barrett. But the opposite was the case. "I only met him on a couple of occasions, and then we didn't get on all that well," Bowie recalled. Perhaps it was because

Bowie was feeling sensitive after Barrett's disparaging review of his single "Love You Till Tuesday". "He [Barrett] began to laugh with delight until I played him David Bowie's latest pop platter," wrote Chris Welch of *Melody Maker*. "Syd stared at me with a haunted look and launched into a cold, angry diatribe: 'Yeah, it's a joke number. Very chirpy. But I don't think my toes were tapping.'"

However, it is also likely that Barrett was already suffering the side-effects of heavy drug use. The man who became known as "rock music's first acid casualty" underwent regular mood swings and would often descend into catatonic bouts of silence. Sometimes, he would strum just one chord throughout an entire concert. Or he might stand there, stationary, and not play at all.

Pink Floyd were eventually forced to replace him. In came Dave Gilmour, and Barrett turned to a reclusive life of painting and gardening. Bowie's biographer David Buckley believes that Barrett's removal from the limelight left the stage to Bowie. "Had Barrett continued, there might have been less room for Bowie to manoeuvre in the 1970s," he wrote.

Despite Barrett's lack of interest in Bowie, the latter did him one enormous favour. The royalties accrued from Bowie's cover of "See Emily Play" allowed the former Floyd man to continue living on his own in London rather than move back in with his mother in Cambridge.

If Barrett's presence was there at the beginning of Bowie's career, it was there at the end, too. In 2006, two years after his heart attack, Bowie accepted an invitation to appear on stage with Gilmour at the Royal Albert Hall to sing "Arnold Layne". The evening was Bowie's last-ever performance in Britain. He had come full circle, replacing the singer whom he had once emulated. "A major regret is that I never got to know him," Bowie said. "A diamond indeed."

Bob Harris

"Whispering Bob" had become shouty. "Remember this night. Remember the name, David Bowie. You're all going to regret this!" That was the DJ's furious admonishment after a group of college students had just booed Bowie off stage.

Harris had been asked to DJ at a London college one night in the late sixties. Wanting some backup, he asked his young friend along to perform. When the DJ handed over the reins to Bowie, the dance floor was packed. But, unable to plug into the main sound system, Bowie was left with a tinny-sounding cassette player for the backing tracks and an acoustic guitar which could hardly be heard in the large ballroom. The crowd became restless, and the boos and slow handclaps soon followed. Jumping to the defence of his beleaguered friend, Harris grabbed the mic and said, "Mark my words. He is going to be absolutely huge and you just sent him packing."

Ridley Scott

Such reactions made Bowie sometimes question whether he was ever going to make it in music. One career avenue he considered was acting, and one of his first cinematic outings was directed by none other than Ridley Scott. This was to be no sci-fi epic, though: this was a commercial for ice cream.

In 1969, Bowie was struggling. To make ends meet, he worked part-time as an office clerk whose main job was to monitor the photocopier. An offer to appear in a black-and-white ad for "Luv" ice lollies was definitely a move up the ladder. The commercial featured Bowie sitting on the top deck of a bus holding a lolly before finding himself transplanted to a stage where he played guitar. When asked years later if it were true that he had been directed by Scott, Bowie replied, "Apparently, yeah. I didn't know it was Ridley, though. I found out only last year. I'm sure he's as embarrassed about it as I am."

Bowie was once asked for his biggest regret when it came to acting. Declining an offer from Scott, he replied. It is tempting to think the part may have been connected to *Blade Runner* (1982). Not only did Scott and Bowie share a fascination with future dystopias, but the director also decided to give his Bowiesque "replicant", eventually played by Rutger Hauer, a birth date of 8 January – the same birthday as Bowie.

Lionel Blair

Even getting bit parts in commercials was not easy. Around this time Bowie tried out for a KitKat ad and failed the audition. He also tried to get into musicals but again faced rejection. Dancer, singer and all-round entertainer Lionel Blair remembered turning down a young man "with bum-fluff on his chin" for a role in a sixties West End musical. "I told him he'd be better off as a solo artist," recalled Blair of the singer then known as David Jones.

Years later, the two met up again on the set of the musical film *Absolute Beginners* (1986). "You don't remember that day, do you?" said Blair. "We always remember our rejections, you know," replied Bowie, who did not speak to the dancer after that.

Freddie Mercury

Noddy Holder of Slade remembers the day he bought his trademark mirror hat from a cocksure young trader at Kensington Market. "One day, I'm gonna be a big pop star like you," the toothy salesman told him. "Fuck off, Freddie," replied Holder.

The Slade frontman was not the only celebrity to come across that particular trader. In 1969, a broke David Bowie would regularly trawl the capital's markets, bargain-hunting. One day, he turned up at a shoe stall, also in Kensington Market, run by his friend, a Scottish bass player called Alan Mair. "I asked him if he wanted a pair of boots," said Mair. "He said no, he'd just popped in to say hello, but that he didn't have any money, anyway. 'But you've just had a Top 20 hit!' I said. And he replied, 'You know what the music business is like, Alan.'" Feeling sorry for the penniless singer, Mair offered to give Bowie a pair of boots for free and called over his assistant to do the measuring. "Freddie will fit you up," he told his friend.

"I only wish I had taken a picture of Freddie on his knees fitting David's boots," Mair added.

Mercury never mentioned this episode to Bowie. But it seems they may have encountered each other even earlier. According to Queen biographer Mark Blake, in 1968 Bowie was booked to play a small lunchtime set at Ealing Art College. In fact, it was such a small set that the concert was to be held in the canteen, without a stage. Undaunted, Bowie asked one of the students, an eager fan who was hanging around, to help shift some tables and build a makeshift platform. The student was Freddie Mercury. Likewise, Mercury was never to speak to Bowie about his brief stint as his "roadie".

While Mercury was "fascinated" by Bowie, Bowie was once asked if he was influenced by Mercury. "I doubt it," he haughtily replied, "since Freddie asked me to produce his first album." Bowie was, however, impressed by Mercury's stage presence. "Of all the more theatrical rock performers, Freddie took it further than the rest," he said. "And of course, I always admired a man who wears tights."

The two memorably collaborated on the 1981 single "Under Pressure". Both were nervous about singing in front of the other, so Bowie suggested that Mercury go first and promised not to listen. When Mercury later questioned how Bowie's vocal track seemed perfectly to counterpoint his own vocals, the sound engineer revealed that Bowie had listened in. "The bastard," Mercury replied.

Although they never recorded together again, it was Bowie who had the unenviable task of following Queen on stage after their "performance of the century" at Live Aid in 1985, and it was Bowie who brought about the show-stopping moment at the Freddie Mercury Tribute Concert in 1992, when he dropped to one knee to recite the Lord's Prayer.

HADDON
HALL
1969–73

Flat 7, 42 Southend Road, Beckenham, in the London Borough of Bromley, may not be an address that screams rock and roll, but Haddon Hall does. The Victorian Gothic mansion with its stained-glass window, sweeping staircase and minstrel gallery is the place where Bowie composed some of his greatest tunes, jammed with Mick Ronson and hosted notorious partner-swapping sex parties. The name of this strange building in the London suburbs was to become synonymous with a period of rapid change for Bowie.

He was to meet Lou Reed, Iggy Pop and Andy Warhol all in the space of a week. Then came Ziggy Stardust, and Bowie became the most untouchable rock star on Earth, a planet that he did not appear to originate from.

Teenagers dreamed of emulating him by becoming their own Rock God of Misfits. Young singers like Ian Curtis, Chrissie Hynde and Marc Almond were to meet their hero in encounters that were to change their lives. While Bowie was busy shaping the seventies, he was already influencing those who would define the eighties.

Mick Ronson
- - - - - - - - - - - - -

Mick Ronson had just made one of the most left-field career moves ever made by a musician: he had quit music to become a shepherd. Tending to sheep was just part of the job requirement of being a groundskeeper for Hull City Council, who also paid the former rocker to look after its sports fields. So when his old drummer, John Cambridge, drove up from London with an offer to join a new band, he found Ronson marking out the boundary lines on a rugby pitch.

"I'm not sure about this, John," said a reticent Ronson, who was delighted to be earning a regular weekly wage for the first time in years. Cambridge's persistence eventually paid off, although Ronson insisted on one condition before leaving – that he be allowed to finish the paint job.

Within minutes of arriving at Haddon Hall, the two future bandmates began jamming and Bowie knew he had found his guitarist or, as he put it, "That's my Jeff Beck!" Bowie had a BBC gig booked that weekend, but Ronson was far from ready. "I didn't know anything, none of the material," he said. "I just sat and watched [Bowie's] fingers." The show was rough, and the compere, DJ John Peel, asked Bowie if they were intending to do more gigs. "Well, looking at them…no," he replied, largely joking.

Ronson not only played guitar and arranged piano and strings for Bowie; he was also a key part of his new image. It was Bowie's on-stage "encounter" with Ronson's guitar, famously photographed, that launched the band into the upper reaches of stardom.

When Bowie disbanded the Spiders from Mars in 1973, the two men drifted apart. Ronson was, by all accounts, hurt. But they had an emotional reunion in 1992 for the Freddie Mercury

Tribute Concert. Ronson knew by then he had liver cancer, and the two began working together on each other's albums. "They were going to do all sorts of things together in the 1990s," said filmmaker and friend Jon Brewer. "But they just ran out of time." Ronson was dead within a year.

The reunion had meant a great deal to both men. But Ronson's easy-going nature was such that he tended to approach whatever happened with a calm acceptance. "There was something about cutting grass, pruning roses," he once said, looking back at those early years. "I had sheep to look after too! Really enjoyed it."

Peter Gabriel

Mick Ronson was one of those on stage on a Wednesday evening in March 1970, when a strange and, frankly, motley-looking group of individuals performed at London's Roundhouse. Imagine the Village People having gone to art school. Ronson, renamed Gangsterman, appeared as a 1930s hoodlum dressed in a gold lamé suit; bassist Tony Visconti was Hypeman, a superhero in crocheted knickers; John Cambridge was Cowboyman; and Bowie, who was dressed in white tights, pirate boots and swirling, diaphanous scarves, went by the name of Rainbow Man. The playful seriousness of glam had made its first colourful bow.

On the stage were a bucket of amyl nitrate and a flannel. At various points through the evening, someone would soak the flannel in the tub and walk around the audience, wiping their faces. Not that it improved the band's reception. "They were yelling at us, calling us faggots and whatever filthy homophobic name you could think of," said Visconti. The only person in the audience to clap was Marc Bolan, who was at the front taking mental notes.

It is possible that Bolan was not the only singer to be influenced. The opening act that night was a relatively new band called Genesis, led by their 20-year-old singer, Peter Gabriel. The band's keyboardist, Tony Banks, a follower of Bowie from early on, was certainly paying attention. "Bowie and the band were all wearing costumes and I hadn't really seen that kind of thing before," he said. "It was pretty interesting."

"The stage was very small and there wasn't much atmosphere," recalled Genesis guitarist Anthony Phillips. "I do remember David wearing a space suit [*sic*] but there was always a rush. We were always like ships in the night."

What is true is that Gabriel soon began to cover his own face in makeup and wear flamboyant outfits. The music press suggested he had been influenced by Bowie, much to Gabriel's annoyance. "Just because I was dressing up, people assumed I was imitating Bowie, but the characters I play are things talked about in the lyrics," said the Genesis frontman. "I don't think Bowie's costumes are relevant to his music."

Thirteen years later, the two singers were to perform on the same stage again, this time in Vancouver, Canada. Gabriel was fortunate to be there at all. That morning, he had gone windsurfing in nearby English Bay. The winds had picked up quickly and had swept the inexperienced Gabriel far out to sea. Luckily, an eagle-eyed coastguard spotted the distant figure and sent out a lifeboat. The grateful singer told the audience later that evening that the only reason he was alive, let alone performing in front of them, was because of the coastguard's vigilance. The crew, whom Gabriel had invited along to the concert as a thank-you, were given a rapturous round of applause.

Alice Cooper

- - - - - - - - - - - - - -

Frocks, makeup, glitter, glam, an alter ego and a backing band called the Spiders. This was not Ziggy Stardust but Alice Cooper in 1969. It is unsurprising, therefore, that America's shock-rock star believes Bowie followed in his platformed footsteps.

"I remember him coming to one of our shows early, early on, before he was David Bowie," said Cooper. "He was just an average boy who wore jeans and shirts. I remember him looking at us with his eyes and mouth wide open when he was a nobody." The American rockers "opened that door", Cooper believed, for Bowie to become Ziggy.

The press saw the similarities and quickly created a "feud", but, in fact, the two were good friends. Cooper recalled one particular dinner with Bowie and sci-fi writer Ray Bradbury, where the conversation lurched from UFOs to quantum mechanics. "It was really interesting because these guys were in outer space somewhere," recalled Cooper.

Bowie said he loved the American rocker's sound but thought the stage act was "blood-and-guts pantomime". "Not long after seeing Alice, I started wearing the drag queen feather boa as a rather feeble visual pun," said Bowie. "So, an inspiration of a sort – but not in the way that Alice seems to think."

But Bowie can thank Cooper for getting his own Spiders into spandex. The T-shirt and jeans-wearing lads from Hull were wary about wearing "girls' clothes" until they saw the American glam rocker perform. "It looked good, so we went along with it," recalled Bowie's bassist, Trevor Bolder.

Perhaps the oddest encounter of all, though, happened on the golf course. According to Bowie biographer Christopher

Sandford, in their older years Bowie and Cooper would team up with Iggy Pop to head off to the course to form, surely, the world's most unlikely golfing threesome.

Gene Vincent

But if Ziggy had a birthday, it was the day Bowie jammed with the original rebel rocker, Gene Vincent, on 13 February 1971. Still on his first trip to America, Bowie flew to Los Angeles to stay with record executive Tom Ayers in his plush Hollywood Hills home-cum-recording studio. Ayers also happened to be the manager of Vincent, and the leather-clad rockabilly himself turned up.

"Gene was very impressed with him," said Ayers. "That was quite amazing when you think that David was virtually nobody then." Bowie was going through a highly creative period. According to his biographer Kevin Cann, the singer would wake up Ayers at 4am most days and insist on going straight to the studio to record his latest ideas, one of which would make it onto *The Rise and Fall of Ziggy Stardust and the Spiders from Mars* (1972).

"Tom asked whether I would like to jam or sing something with Gene," recalled Bowie. "We settled on 'Hang on to Yourself' and made a ghastly version of it, which is floating around somewhere on eBay, I expect."

The music might not have gelled, but Bowie was in awe of Vincent and was especially taken with his unique singing posture: eyes rapturously fixed heavenwards as he trailed his steel-braced leg, the result of a car crash, awkwardly behind him. That stance became "position number one for the embryonic Ziggy", said Bowie. It was not lost on Bowie that his other Ziggy prototype,

Bowie was initially deflated, but he soon put the experience to good use. The idea of a rock star who wasn't real but in whom the audience believed was taking root in his mind. A few weeks later, when he met Gene Vincent, he started putting flesh on Ziggy's imaginary bones.

Lou Reed

Bowie returned to the United States later that year for what would be the most significant week in his career. On the evening of Thursday 9 September 1971, he was sitting down for dinner in a New York restaurant. In a few hours' time, he would meet Iggy Pop. The following Tuesday, he would be introduced to Andy Warhol. But first, he was about to encounter the real Lou Reed. These five days were to define not just Bowie's future but the decade.

Bowie had long bragged that he was Britain's first Velvet Underground fan, having been given a pre-release copy of their first album, *The Velvet Underground & Nico* (1967). "I played it and thought, 'Oh my God. This is it. I just want to be in this band,'" he said. Now the two were being introduced by rock writer Lisa Robinson at a "really straight" eatery in New York called the Ginger Man. Bowie was garrulous and polite; Reed was taciturn and sharp. Bowie's career was on the up, Reed's had nosedived. The New Yorker was back living with his parents and had "retired" from the music business.

"Lou was going through an incredibly bad patch when I met him," recalled Bowie, who tried to convince the American to relaunch his career. Reed was swayed. "I knew there was somebody else living in the same area I was," he said. "It was almost like the beginning of a romance," recalled the actor and writer Tony Zanetta, also present. "They were kind of sizing each other up."

"He's the only interesting person around," Reed told *Melody Maker*. "Everything has been tedious, rock and roll has been tedious, except for what David has been doing." He went on to describe Bowie as the best white performer he had ever seen.

Most critics have written about Reed's influence on Bowie, but it was Bowie who produced Reed's best solo album, *Transformer* (1972), and who transformed those songs. "Walk on the Wild Side" was turned from a skeletal, acoustic number into Reed's first hit; "Satellite of Love" lifts off with Bowie's backing vocals in the rousing final chorus; while "Perfect Day" ranks as the album's third classic with its majestic piano and strings arrangement by Bowie and Mick Ronson. "Bowie's imagistic lyrics display barely a trace of Reed's pared simplicity," wrote author Simon Reynolds. "The truth is that Bowie had far more influence on Reed than the other way round."

Without the constant praise by Bowie, who was to become the definitive cultural scene-setter of the seventies, the Velvet Underground are unlikely to have become regarded as rock's most seminal band. Reed, often dismissive of *Transformer*, later became grateful for its commercial success. "Without it, who knows, maybe I'd be digging a ditch somewhere," he said.

But along with the highs, there were lows and there were blows. At a London restaurant one night in 1979, Reed asked Bowie to produce his next album. Bowie agreed on condition the singer cleaned himself up and quit drugs. According to *Melody Maker*'s Alan Jones, a furious Reed launched himself across the table at Bowie, saying, "Don't ever say that to me. Don't ever fucking say

Bowie, Iggy Pop and Lou Reed at the Dorchester Hotel, London, 1972.

that to me." Minders had to haul Reed off. Later that evening, a furious Bowie was heard banging on Reed's door calling him a coward and ordering him to "come out and fight like a man". Reed never reappeared, and Bowie never produced that next album.

Despite Reed's combustible temperament, the pair made up, if cautiously. "David and I are still friends...amazingly enough," said Reed in 2004, aware that he could be "difficult". The pair would meet up with their partners, artist Laurie Anderson and supermodel Iman, and go to art shows and museums together. They also performed together at Bowie's 50th birthday celebration at Madison Square Garden, singing "I'm Waiting for the Man" and Bowie's homage to the Velvet Underground, "Queen Bitch".

"He is a very dear friend of mine," said Bowie. However, when asked to comment on a photograph in which it looked as though the two were about to kiss, Bowie said, "I'm not actually kissing him. No, I think Lou Reed is the last person in the world I'd want to kiss."

Iggy Pop

Pop had been stealing food to survive and sleeping in a garage with a male hustler. Even by his standards, he had reached a new low. And now, he was under arrest for the second time. The first detention had been for "impersonating a woman". This time, it was for "drooling aggressively" at diners in the Hamburger Hamlet, a burger joint in LA. Pop was given the choice of going to jail or to a psychiatric unit. He chose the latter. It was a decision which would not only cement his greatest friendship, it would change the musical landscape.

"Nobody came, nobody," said Pop of his stay on the ward in the mid-seventies. "Not even my so-called friends. But David came."

Discovering Pop was in a mental hospital, Bowie turned up with pal Dennis Hopper in a spaceman suit. Forgoing the traditional grapes and flowers, they brought something more appropriate. "We trooped into the hospital with a load of drugs for him," recalled Bowie. "This was very much a 'leave your drugs at the door' hospital. We were out of our minds, all of us. He wasn't well, that's all we knew. We thought we should bring him some drugs because he probably hadn't had any for days!"

The two had first met in New York at the famously hip hangout Max's Kansas City in 1971. Pop's manager, Danny Fields, was told there was a British musician keen to meet his client. Fields was delighted. "Thank you for mentioning Iggy. It's the only time he's been mentioned in England," he told Bowie. Despite Fields's efforts to rouse his client back at his apartment, Pop remained engrossed in an old black-and-white Jimmy Stewart movie and refused to budge. Fields allegedly even threw some water over him. Sometime well past midnight, the American musician walked into Max's to meet Bowie.

Pop had not eaten in close to four days. The first thing he did was order two breakfasts, which immediately perked him up. Declaring that the only good rocker was a dead rocker, he proceeded to smash himself over the head with a beer bottle to prove the point. He then spoke about being on a methadone programme to wean himself off heroin. "Man, I'm on my way to being clean," he told Bowie, who was transfixed by the larger-than-life character. Bowie's manager, Tony Defries, was equally smitten. "What do you need?" he asked. "Everything," Pop replied. Defries asked if he wanted to sign a new record contract and go to England with them. "Sounds terrific," Pop said before leaping up, grabbing another roll and rushing off to his appointment at the methadone clinic.

"Bowie talked about Iggy for a full week," recalled record exec Bob Grace. "It was definitely all-consuming." Bowie's style changed immediately. Bringing out his internal Iggy, he created Ziggy. When he returned to the studio the next week, he told producer Ken Scott, "You're not going to like the album. It's much more like Iggy Pop."

The first thing they worked on together became the sound template for punk. Bowie was called in to remix Iggy and the Stooges' *Raw Power* (1973). Pop hated it. "That fucking carrot-top ruined my album," he said. In truth, the original tape was so badly recorded that Bowie could do little more than slide a few faders up and down.

But while everything Bowie touched turned to gold in his professional life, his private life was increasingly desperate. Having been brought back from death's door several times after overdosing, he realized that his only hope was a new start in a new country. He chose Berlin and he chose to go with Pop, partly for companionship and partly to help his friend. "We have to do something for Iggy," Bowie would regularly tell his bandmates. Although trying to kick drugs by going to the heroin capital of the world with a notorious addict was not the most sensible choice, the offer came at the right moment for Pop; he had recently picked up a job application form for McDonald's.

As it was, the two not only survived, they went on to record some of their best work. They leapfrogged punk, which they can claim to have partly invented anyway, and went straight to what would later be termed "post punk". "Not since Van Gogh and Gauguin were together at the Yellow House in Arles, have two artists of such stature cooperated so closely with such influential results," wrote Iggy and Bowie biographer Paul Trynka.

That first year in Berlin, they did everything together. They lived in the same apartment, watched *Starsky and Hutch* on television, shopped at antique markets, went to museums and generally drove around the city. Iggy sat in the passenger seat, inspiring the lyrics to his song "The Passenger". Pop was broke, but Bowie was also in financial straits thanks to a disastrous management contract. Even so, every morning Bowie would hand over ten Deutschmarks to his friend for food and essentials.[5]

Bowie has been accused by some critics of being a vampire who fed off Iggy. But what is clear is that the two not only helped reinvent each other's careers, they saved each other's lives. Without Pop, Bowie may not have had the courage to go to Berlin or the support needed to make it through his withdrawal and depression. For Pop, Bowie was the reason he was not dead. "This guy saved me from annihilation, simple as that," he said.

Andy Warhol

Excruciating silences, a ritual disembowelling and a temper tantrum – the meeting between the King of Pop Art and the King of Art Pop was both bizarre and eventful.

Bowie had become friends with the Warhol crowd in 1971, after seeing a London performance of *Pork*, the artist's play about masturbation, fornication, vomiting, douching and "plate jobs" (the act of defecating onto a glass table while someone looks up from underneath). He was enthralled, if more by the outrageous transgender cast than by the play itself. Bowie went in a long-haired hippy and came out a gender-bending iconoclast.

So, when the singer went to New York, he was invited into Warhol's inner sanctum, The Factory. Upon Bowie entering the large open space, a cameraman started filming and asked the new arrival to "not perform". This was Warhol's idea of a "natural" screen test, designed to see if his guests possessed star quality. The video shows a perplexed Bowie standing there at a loss, while a mute Warhol, dressed in jodhpurs and carrying a riding whip, looks on. Eventually, Bowie performs a "man-trapped-in-a-box" mime routine before "disembowelling" himself and placing his intestines in a neat row, perhaps in reference to the awkwardness of the situation. After a couple of minutes, and greeted by total silence, Bowie says, "I've had enough" and walks off.

Warhol, Bowie and the rest then decamp to a room, but the awkward silence continues. "Warhol was not a great talker, you had to talk and entertain Andy, and David wasn't a great talker either," recalled Tony Zanetta, one of the Warhol crowd. In an effort to break the ice, Bowie handed over a copy of his song "Andy Warhol", the lyrics of which described the artist as looking like "a scream" and being "jolly boring". The record was listened to in uncomfortable silence. When it finished, Warhol got up and walked out. "Andy didn't say anything but absolutely hated it," said Zanetta.

"He walks away and I was left there," Bowie told writer Bill DeMain. "Somebody came over and said, 'Gee, Andy hated it.' I said sorry, it was meant to be a compliment. 'Yeah, but you said things about him looking weird. Don't you know Andy has a thing about how he looks? He's got a skin disease and he thinks people see that.'"

After some minutes, Warhol returned and, as if nothing had happened, started snapping away on his Polaroid, although again in complete silence. Finally, he looked down and saw Bowie's patent-yellow women's shoes (a gift from Marc Bolan). "Gee, I like your shoes," he said. "That's where we found something to talk about," said Bowie. "He absolutely adored them. I found out he used to do a lot of shoe designing when he was younger. He had a bit of a shoe fetishism. That kind of broke the ice."

"Andy noticed David's shoes and that spurred a sequence of neurological reactions resulting in, of all things, volubility," said Angie Bowie. "Everybody relaxed. You could tell because their eyeballs twitched more slowly."

Bowie was often dismissive of Warhol. "Like anyone else, I never knew him," he told Mike Jollett of *Filter* magazine. "I mean, what was there to know? To this day, I don't know if there was anything going on in his mind." Elsewhere, he described the artist as an "insecure queen" who was funny, albeit unwittingly. He could even sound bitter, describing Warhol as "reptilian" for shying away from a handshake. "Everything he said was like, 'Wow, did you see who's here?' And it was never any deeper than that level," said the singer. "Lou [Reed] knew Andy much better and he says that there was an awful lot happening in his mind. But I never saw it."

Bowie also dismissed the idea that Warhol had been a significant influence on him. "I've always felt more emotive than Andy. I know I've been read as cold but it's not true. Andy was more interested in the cold reality of the surface image, what you see is very much what you get. My work has always been attached to multiple interpretations because I like to build up in layers. We really are the antithesis of each other."

When asked what had he liked about Warhol, he replied, "A few of his quotes. Everything could be reproduced. The idea of that was great." In fact, that first encounter was truly Warholian. Alongside the genuine Andy, there were three copies: Tony Zanetta, who had performed as Andy in *Pork*; lookalike Allen Midgette, who was Warhol's stand-in on lecture tours; and Bowie, who would end up playing Warhol in the film *Basquiat* (1996).

As for Warhol's view, upon seeing Ziggy Stardust at Carnegie Hall, he described Bowie as "the best thing since Kitty Hawks". It was typical Warhol, leaving just about everyone asking, "Who?" Hawks was a well-known interior designer in New York at the time, not that this helps to explain what Warhol meant. It may well be he just said the first thing that came into his head, as he often did, when asked a question by a journalist.

The meeting between Warhol and Bowie remains fascinating not because it represents an exchange between two of the most original minds of the century, but because it is so banal. As Warhol said of himself, "Just look at the surface and there I am."

As Bowie turned to leave, Warhol called out, "Goodbye, David. You have such nice shoes."

Rick Wakeman

Imagine "Life on Mars?" with a comedian on piano. That almost came to pass when Bowie asked Dudley Moore to play on his new song. Moore would often play humorous songs as part of his comedy act with Peter Cook, and Bowie believed the diminutive comic was just the man to accompany him on his greatest song of the early seventies. But Moore never returned the call. Rejected by his first choice, Bowie turned to a session musician.

The singer invited Rick Wakeman to Haddon Hall to listen to some new songs, picking up a borrowed 12-string guitar before moving onto piano. According to the pianist, Bowie ran through embryonic versions of "Oh, You Pretty Things", "Changes" and "Life on Mars?" "They were the finest selection of songs I've ever heard in one sitting in my entire life," said the stunned keyboardist. Or, as Bowie more modestly recalled of that evening, "I played my plodding version and Rick wrote the chords down, then played them with his inimitable touch."

Wakeman's playing was to define *Hunky Dory* (1971). Bowie was so impressed that he asked him to join a band he was thinking of naming "The Spiders from Mars". But that same night, Wakeman received a call from a guitarist named Chris Squire, with an offer to join a new prog-rock band. Worried about his mortgage, with a child on the way, and thinking that Bowie would forever remain an obscure genius, Wakeman said yes to Yes.

But the musician always remembered Bowie with great fondness, not just for his talent but for his generosity. When Wakeman's folk club in north Acton, London, ran into financial trouble, it was Bowie who offered to play for free. "We took these ads out plugging Bowie," recalled Wakeman, "and about four people turned up. Everyone thought it was a wind-up." By the next week, word had belatedly got around. There was no Bowie but the place was packed. For the first time in ages, Wakeman was debt-free.

Ian Curtis

The debt Joy Division owed to David Bowie was large: the band's original name, Warsaw, was taken from a track on *Low* (1977); their music was modelled on his austere Berlin soundscapes; and their doom-laden vocals were based on Bowie's baritone. Poignantly, the record that was still spinning on the turntable when singer Ian Curtis was found hanged in his kitchen was Iggy Pop's *The Idiot* (1977), on which Bowie closely collaborated.

Curtis and Bowie met in 1972, when Ziggy-mania was hitting Britain. The Spiders from Mars performed 92 concerts that year and Curtis went to three of them. According to his sister Carole, he tried to copy Bowie's look by wearing blue eyeshadow, black nail polish and "awful" red satin trousers to go with his spiky mullet. "I remember thinking, 'Oh my God'", she said, recalling her reaction on first seeing her brother's garish outfit.

After one Manchester gig, the 16-year-old fan managed to inveigle his way into the dressing room, where he silently passed around blank sheets of paper and a pen for autographs. Curtis proudly told Joy Division drummer Stephen Morris that Bowie had asked him if there were any clubs nearby that played northern soul. Curtis was certainly a fan of that style of music ("Interzone" was to be based on a northern soul record), but whether he had the courage to reply to his hero, he never did tell Morris.

The year Curtis died, 1980, Bowie released *Scary Monsters*. For the title track, he told his musicians to play "like a British punk group". "The punk group in question was almost certainly Joy Division, a Bowie favourite at the time," claims music writer Bill Cummings, who says the song was influenced by "She's Lost Control". If so, it is a tribute that would have delighted Curtis.

Marc Almond

Fifteen-year-old Marc Almond was on the train to Liverpool to see Bowie in concert when, dolled up in glitter and makeup, he attracted the attention of some thugs. Their taunts soon turned to violence, and the homophobic hooligans smashed a glass bottle over Almond's head, knocking him briefly unconscious. Dazed and bruised, he staggered from the station to the venue. "I was bleeding but I refused to let it stop me from enjoying the show," said the Soft Cell singer.

When Bowie made his entrance, the wounds were forgotten. Almond climbed over several rows to get to the front. "Give me your hands," Bowie called out. A thousand arms, all hoping to be touched, stretched out in response.

"I reached up my hand," said Almond. "Blood, makeup and glitter were running down my face. He reached down and took it. I was in a state of near-religious ecstasy. It was a glam rock epiphany. I didn't feel the bruises. It was one of the most magical things that has happened to me."

Boy George

- - - - - - - - - - - -

Eleven-year-old George O'Dowd had been waiting for this moment for much of his young life. As was his wont on a Sunday afternoon, he was hanging around outside Bowie's residence in Beckenham with a small crowd of Bowiephiles. Nothing of note had ever happened, but one day a window opened and a face appeared. The face seemed to look directly at O'Dowd before shouting, "Why don't you fuck off?" It then disappeared and the window was slammed shut. The face belonged to Angie Bowie.

Far from being chastened, George was thrilled. This was the first acknowledgement of his existence by the celebrity couple. "We adored Angie just as much as David," said George, who once claimed his only qualification upon leaving school was "A-level Bowie".

Years later, the Culture Club singer was invited inside a Bowie household. After a conversation about *EastEnders*, George recounted his Haddon Hall episode to an amused Bowie, who said dryly, "That's probably Angie's greatest line from the seventies."

Steve Jones

- - - - - - - - - - - -

No Bowie, no Sex Pistols. Not because of Bowie's musical influence, but because Steve Jones stole Bowie's gear to form the band.

Jones and his pal Paul Cook were wannabe musicians but were too poor to buy any instruments. Fortunately for them, Jones lived around the corner from the Hammersmith Odeon. "I was like the Phantom of the Opera for that place – I knew it like the back of my hand," recalled Jones, who had watched a Ziggy Stardust show in 1973 and then snuck his way back in around 2am. "I didn't know what any of the stuff was. All I knew was that I had to have some of it because I was a massive fan." He took a couple of cymbals, a bass amp and Bowie's microphone, which still had the singer's lipstick on, and carried them to his van, also stolen. "Out of respect" to Mick Ronson, he refused to touch the guitar.

"We got a full range of equipment before we could even play," recalled Pistols drummer Paul Cook.

Years later, Jones admitted the theft to Bowie himself. "I get on very well with Steve, now," Bowie said. "But at the time I was extremely angry. Of course, we had no idea who actually stole the stuff." Jones felt guilty enough that, when Bowie's old drummer, Woody Woodmansey, appeared on his LA radio show almost 50 years later, he gave him $200 to cover the cost of the cymbals.

Hall & Oates

Hall & Oates were a long-haired folk duo whose idea of a rousing encore was to bring out the mandolin. But everything changed when they were the support act to Ziggy Stardust one night in 1972 in Memphis.

"I saw him backstage with the shaved eyebrows and the orange hair and the giant platform shoes," recalled John Oates. "I was like, 'What is this?'" After their politely received support set, Oates took a Quaalude and went to watch the main attraction among the audience. The theme to *2001: A Space Odyssey* started up, the strobe lights flashed and Bowie walked on to the proto-punk sounds of "Hang on to Yourself".

"I had never seen anything like that in my life," said Oates. "It was a totally life-changing experience."

"We thought we better change our act," said Daryl Hall. "Yeah, we better get some amps!" added Oates. "This guy put the live performance bar up to another level. We immediately did a 180."

Sylvester

Bowie was unusual, but when it came to his androgynous persona he was not unique. When he performed at the Winterland Ballroom in San Francisco in 1972, he was to find he was not the only gender-bending singer on stage. His support act was a flamboyant drag artist called Sylvester. Still a few years away from his falsetto disco anthem, "You Make Me Feel (Mighty Real)", Sylvester was incongruously doing covers of "A Whiter Shade of Pale" by Procol Harum and songs by Neil Young. "He was fun, campy, sometime diva-ish and totally glam and glitter way before David Bowie," recalled his friend Ruth Pointer, of the Pointer Sisters.

Local DJ Paul Wells was in the audience and recalled that, despite Sylvester's colourful look, everyone was stunned when Bowie walked out. "I enjoyed watching the jaws of Sylvester's fans drop. Bowie's band rocked!" Less flatteringly, the renowned music critic for the *San Francisco Chronicle*, John Wasserman, wrote of Bowie's performance, "The man is not talentless. Not Carl Sandburg perhaps, but also not Neil Diamond." Sandburg was a popular American poet of the era, known for his stage recitals.

Bowie was clearly a fan of Sylvester. When asked why more people in San Francisco hadn't turned out for the concert, he replied, "They don't need me. They have Sylvester." The American singer would later tell reporters that he would hang out with Bowie when he visited London in the late seventies.

As for that night when they played together, the most

memorable moment came not from Bowie or Sylvester but from the other band on the bill, the Turtles. During their opening song, the tambourine player became so excited he missed his footing and fell off stage. He was taken to hospital where doctors diagnosed a broken hand and gave him a sling. In true rock and roll fashion, he demanded to be taken back to the concert and returned in time to join his bandmates for the encore.

Chrissie Hynde

Chrissie Hynde was a 21-year-old waitress when she decided to "borrow" her mother's car to drive the five hours to Cleveland, Ohio, to see Bowie's first concert on American soil (1972). A devout fan with her own Bowie scrapbook, she waited outside the venue all that cold afternoon, listening to the sound check. Then, from out of the back entrance, appeared the singer. This was not the pretty blond, feminine thing from *Hunky Dory* but an alien in platform boots sporting a shock of red hair. Ziggy and his minder looked around, seemingly lost, before spotting Hynde and her friend. In need of directions and a car, and assuming the girls were locals, Bowie's minder crossed the street and asked if they wouldn't mind driving the lost pair back to the hotel.

"Ziggy waited for me to pull the seat forward and then climbed into the back of my mother's Oldsmobile Cutlass," recalled Hynde in her autobiography, *Reckless*. "I was gaga."

"This is a nice car," Bowie said politely.

"How embarrassing to be driving my mom's car!" recalled Hynde. Bowie invited the teenagers to his room where his young fan suggested the audience would love to hear his cover of "I'm Waiting for the Man" by the Velvet Underground. Sure enough, when Hynde watched the concert that night, Bowie played her request.

More than a decade later, the Pretenders singer bumped into Bowie again. Desperate to see if he remembered the girl who gave him a lift that day in Cleveland, she recounted the story. "He just went, 'Is she taking the piss?'" said Hynde. "I was begging him to remember because it was the most important day of my life!"

Placido Domingo

When the Cleveland concerts ended, Bowie and his band went out to celebrate. They happened to choose the same restaurant as Placido Domingo and his entourage. When the Spanish tenor looked over to Bowie's table, his eye was drawn not to the red-headed singer but to his stylist, Suzi Fussey, the woman responsible for the Ziggy cut.

"You have to introduce me to this girl," he told record executive Gustl Breuer, seated next to him. "The boobs!" Domingo gushed.

Breuer, aware that Fussey was the girlfriend of guitarist Mick Ronson, told the tenor to forget her, but Domingo was insistent. Under duress, Breuer grudgingly approached the table. After exchanging pleasantries with Bowie, he turned to Fussey and told her "the greatest opera singer ever" would like to speak to her.

"What?" she replied, looking over. "That fat slob?"

Kansai Yamamoto

Suzi Fussey may have been responsible for the Ziggy cut, but the person behind the style itself was the flamboyant Japanese designer Kansai Yamamoto. Bowie had seen a photograph of a

Kansai Yamamoto and Bowie in the designer's Tokyo studio, April 1973.

Yamamoto model with a shock of red, spiky hair in a magazine. He not only stole the haircut, but also started wearing Yamamoto's brilliantly coloured kimonos and platform boots. The designer's *basara* style, which translates roughly as "to dress freely", was a vivid mix of the kooky and the kaleidoscopic. The look that was to revolutionize rock in the West came from the East.

The first time the designer heard Bowie's name was in the middle of the night when he was woken up by an "urgent" call from a friend in New York. "If someone calls you at 4am telling you to get on a plane, it must be for something pretty interesting," said Yamamoto. He took his insistent friend's advice, cancelled his appointments and caught the first flight out of Tokyo to catch Bowie at New York's Radio City.

The designer was stunned – here was a Western rock star not only wearing Japanese outfits but wearing outfits made for women. When Bowie had his costume dramatically ripped off to reveal an even more exuberant Yamamoto outfit underneath (a technique from Kabuki theatre called *hikinuki*), the crowd rose to its feet. "Some sort of chemical reaction took place," Yamamoto recalled. "My clothes became part of David, his song and his music." The relationship between the fashion designer and the rock star was to change the face of pop music.

At some Ziggy shows in the UK, there were reports of the audience openly having sex and masturbating. But Angie Bowie remembered the reaction of the fans in Japan as being, if anything, wilder. That was down in part, she believed, to Yamamoto's clothes. "Here was a real Western rock star dressed in Japanese outfits, digging them! They almost couldn't stand it," she said. Bowie was appreciated "so ecstatically" by fans after the show, she added, that the costumes had to be painstakingly repaired each night.

While in Japan, the Bowie and Yamamoto families spent much time together, with the designer pointing out aspects of Japanese culture. That included indulging Bowie in one of his favourite pastimes – shopping in markets. "He was delighted to find an over-the-shoulder bag, which he bought, but actually it was a type made for Japanese bus drivers," the amused Yamamoto told *Elle* magazine.

In turn, the designer was influenced by Bowie's advances in theatrical rock when he created the fashion world's first "super shows" – Olympic-scale extravaganzas of more than a hundred thousand people involving music, dance, theatre, fashion and fireworks. For Yamamoto, Bowie not only changed music and fashion, he changed Japanese society. "What he did in terms of bridging the male–female gap continues to this day," he said.

Bandō Tamasaburō V

Bowie's revolutionary use of makeup came from traditional Japanese theatre, and the man who taught him how to apply it was the country's most famous kabuki actor.

Tamasaburō was renowned as an *onnagata*, a male actor who played female roles (female actors had been banned from the stage since 1629). Like all *onnagata*, Tamasaburō was expected to lead his whole life in character, never once being allowed to drop his female stage persona or be seen without makeup. Meeting Tamasaburō, one of Bowie's crew recalled, was like being in the room with an exotic animal.

Bowie was feeling stuck in his Ziggy Stardust character, so, on his first trip to Japan in 1973, he was enthralled to meet someone equally trapped in their stage persona. Tamasaburō offered to give Bowie a crash course in how to apply kabuki makeup. There were no subtle shades or outlines here; this was makeup boldly and thickly applied onto a stark white base. Bowie used the lesson to create the visual image for his next alter ego, a character who had a lightning bolt across his face.

Chris Difford

Before forming Squeeze, Chris Difford had a hand in the creation of Aladdin Sane. The young south Londoner was a roadie with Bowie in the mid-seventies, responsible not just for moving equipment but also for painting the trademark zigzag bolts onto a giant canvas backdrop. Despite seeing the singer at close quarters daily, Difford said Bowie came across "like someone from Mars", even to his own crew.

The Squeeze frontman, who was to copy Bowie's accent when he became a vocalist, did not get the chance to chat to Bowie until a decade later, when Squeeze had become his former boss's support act. The two were sitting next to one another on a flight to New York. Bowie was scared of flying and, this time, it turned out he had good reason.

"I remember the plane having to divert very quickly, as we had just missed another plane leaving the runway at JFK," said Difford. "I looked at him across the aisle and he had become 'the thin, very white Duke'. I was the slightly tubbier version."

Elvis

Despite his aerophobia, Bowie was such a fan of Elvis that he once flew to New York in between gigs, just to catch the King perform. But the tight turnaround meant that, by the time he arrived at Madison Square Garden, the concert was already under way. All eyes turned as the space-suited figure with the towering red hair took his front-row seat.

"I hobbled down in my high-heeled shoes as fast as I could," said Bowie. "But we nearly stopped the show." Among those who had noticed the latecomer was Elvis himself. "If looks could kill!" recalled Bowie. "I could see him thinking, 'Who the fuck is that? Sit the fuck down!' I felt like a right cunt." Elvis carried on and gave what Bowie described as an "unmissable" show.

Bowie had been promised the chance to talk to his hero after the concert. He jokingly talked about it being a meeting between the King and Queen of Rock and Roll. But, whether Elvis felt aggrieved or unwell, the offer to go backstage never materialized.

Bowie was deeply disappointed but remained infatuated with the rocker. He let it be known that he would like to write for Elvis and sent him a version of "Golden Years". Elvis told his manager, Colonel Tom Parker, "I really want to sing songs like that," and Parker arranged a meeting. Again, the fates conspired against Bowie. Unable to go in person, he entrusted his wife Angie with taking the tape to Las Vegas. But when an assistant came to her hotel room to take her to Elvis, she declined to go, claiming to be laid low with a sore throat. She later said she did not want to meet "the poor, sad travesty" of a man she had just seen perform, but rather remember Elvis as he was before the drugs. It was a big blow to Bowie, and the fact that he never got to meet Elvis remained one of his major regrets. "I would have loved to have worked with him," he said. "God, I would have adored it."

But it now appears they may have got to talk after all. Country singer Dwight Yoakam recently said that Bowie once told him that Elvis had called out of the blue, just six months before the Memphis singer's death. Elvis wanted to discuss the possibility of Bowie producing his next album. "I thought, 'Oh my God,'" said Yoakam. "1977 Bowie producing Elvis! It would have been fantastic. It's one of the greatest tragedies in pop music history that it didn't happen."

Although it appears that he only told Yoakam that story, Bowie certainly did receive a telegram from Elvis. "Good luck on your tour. Looking forward to meeting you when you get back," it read. Bowie added, "I was very, very excited about that."

Bowie had felt mystically connected to Elvis since they were both born on 8 January (it was a link that Bowie's mother did her best to encourage). If they were linked at the beginning, they were certainly linked at the end; Elvis also recorded a song about dying. It, too, was called "Black Star".

Bryan Ferry

Bowie nicked plenty from the man he described as "my only real rival". He took his sounds, his bandmate, his idea for a covers album and even his girlfriend. Unsurprisingly, Bryan Ferry remained wary of Bowie throughout his career. From the start, it seemed destined that Bowie would arrive just as the Ferry had left.

In 1972, Bowie asked the newly formed Roxy Music to support him on his Ziggy Stardust tour. Keen to meet the singer, Bowie popped backstage after the show, but Ferry had already gone. According to Bowie, "Ferry had a splitting headache and a smashing-looking bird, so had to rush home for a quick aspirin." All was not lost, though, as the person Bowie did meet that night was Ferry's bandmate, Brian Eno.

Bowie continued to shower praise on Ferry, describing him as "one of the most gifted and talented of British artists" who was trying to "expand the vocabulary of rock music". Ferry, though, seemed intent on keeping his distance, not just literally but musically, too. "I don't really like the idea I'm part of a movement," he responded when pigeonholed alongside the "too poppy" Bowie. "What was interesting in Roxy Music is that we had so many sounds at our disposal. Bowie is another story."

Ferry had grounds to be suspicious. When Bowie saw a woman in a skin-tight leather outfit on Roxy's album cover, he asked her out, despite the fact that she had been Ferry's partner. Ferry was further aggrieved when Bowie "ripped off" his idea of a covers album, stealing what he felt was his own original idea of "breaking with the cult of originality". Eno jumped ship, and Roxy's Phil Manzanera even claimed that Bowie stole their idea of wearing catsuits. "We got our own back, though," the guitarist said. "We stole his lighting man."

The idea, popular on fan websites, that Ferry told Bowie about his covers album idea while the two were playing tennis seems highly fanciful. In fact, when Bowie was asked on his own website about meeting Ferry, he seemed genuinely surprised by how few times they had encountered each other. "I have met him on a number of occasions," Bowie answered, before correcting himself by adding, "Actually, this is not true."

Ferry gave his own revealing response in 2010 when asked if

he would ever consider collaborating with Bowie. "If Bowie had said in '73, 'Oh, can we write together?' I'd have said no, I'm not interested," he replied. The interviewer persisted: what if Bowie asked tomorrow? "Ah...that could be...ah...maybe, yeah. I'd be interested in anybody that I liked," said Ferry. His hesitancy felt like an answer in itself.

Brian Eno

Bowie told friend Kate Moss that, if he had to single out one moment when everything changed, it would be a meeting with Brian Eno in 1972 in the Greyhound, a dowdy-looking pub in Croydon, south London.

Bowie had gone backstage looking not for Eno but for his bandmate. Believing Bryan Ferry to be one of the country's greatest lyricists and a fellow rock revolutionary, Bowie was desperate to meet him. But when he walked into Roxy's dressing room, Ferry had already gone, leaving behind, as Bowie memorably said, "a short, balding brain with a feather boa and remarkably silly clothes". Eno might have been the runners-up prize, but their encounter was to revolutionize music or, to use Bowie's phrase, "change the vocabulary of rock".

The two talked for hours about existentialism, the minimalism of Philip Glass and the death of rock. Bowie was impressed not only with Eno's ideas but also with his role on stage; Eno was putatively the synth player but, in reality, more of a knob-twirling sonic force, who saw himself as "a non-musician", a job description he once tried to get inscribed into his passport. Bowie was equally captivated by Eno's attire. "He was dressed even more glamorously than I was," recalled the singer.

Five years. That's what it took before the two got to work together. This time it was Eno going backstage to meet Bowie. The latter said he had been listening to Eno's *Discreet Music* (1975) non-stop. "I thought, 'God, he must be smart!'" the former Roxy Music man said. The fire was rekindled and within weeks the two began working together on a series of albums which were to re-ignite Bowie's career. "The Berlin trilogy" included new sounds and new ways of composing thanks to Eno's Oblique Strategy cards, which included instructions such as "If given a choice, do both." There was also, with ambient music, a new intention behind the music itself. Eno had become the driving force behind yet more Bowie incarnations.

Ian Hunter

Bowie was just one sure-fire hit away from becoming one of the world's biggest rock stars. And then it came to him. The song was not only his most commercial yet, it had the transatlantic appeal to break the American market. Moreover, the chorus was set to make it an anthem for a generation. In short, it was a song that would still be played in 50 years' time. It was exactly what Bowie needed, and he gave it away.

Bowie's gift of "All the Young Dudes" to Mott the Hoople remains one of rock music's greatest acts of charity. Even Mott's singer, Ian Hunter, could not believe his luck. "He just walked in and played it on an acoustic guitar," said Hunter. "I've never been so grateful for anything in my life."

Bowie had surprisingly taken a shine to the macho pub rock group and, when he heard they were about to disband, decided to help. The band remembered Bowie trembling as he knocked on their dressing-room door to tell them that, if they stayed together, he could make them successful. He played them a song he had just written on acoustic guitar. "Very seldom in your life do you get to sit behind a hit and know it's a hit," said Hunter. "I would never have given that song away to anybody."

Bowie later told the *NME*, "I thought, 'This will be an interesting thing to do, let's see if I can write this song and keep them together.' It sounds horribly immodest now but you can go through that when you're young. How can I do everything? By Friday?'"

Years later, Bowie appeared baffled by his own largesse. "Don't tell me about it," he laughingly replied to a reporter when asked why he had given away one of his best songs. "When I finished writing the song, I knew it would be a hit and I could not believe that I was about to give it to somebody else."

Hunter has sometimes sounded less than grateful towards Bowie. "He sucks like Dracula and then he moves on to another victim" is one typical quote. But he also admitted that the working-class band would have been forced "back to the factory" without Bowie. "He helped a few people along the way."

Jethro Tull and Steeleye Span

Folk rockers Steeleye Span were putting the finishing touches to their 1973 album *Parcel of Rogues* when they decided they not only had to have a sax solo, they needed it to be played by David Bowie, whom they had recently seen on *Top of the Pops*. The trouble was that neither the band nor their producer, Ian Anderson of Jethro Tull, knew him. Unperturbed, Anderson put in some calls, and a few days later, much to everyone's surprise, a stretch limo turned up and out climbed Bowie and a gaggle of colourful acolytes.

"He had an incredible aura around him," recalled drummer Nigel Pegrum. "You had to think, 'This guy is a special human being.'"

Bowie went straight to the studio, played the solo perfectly and left almost as quickly, departing with the words, "See you later." It was some 25 years later that Anderson got to see Bowie again. This time it was on the set for a German TV music show.

"I managed to push my way past some heavies into his dressing room," said the Tull singer. "I thanked him for playing on the song and, more importantly, for serving as a role model to me in regard of offering the gift of music for no fee, something I have always done since."

Bowie looked at Anderson thoughtfully. "I'd forgotten about that," he said. "I suppose it's too late to send an invoice?"

Cliff Richard

Cliff Richard once accused Bowie of being behind the disintegration of "society's moral fibre". "He upsets me as a man," the Christian rocker responded when asked about Bowie's androgyny. "What will those ten- or eleven-year-olds think of someone who's a man dressing up as a woman on a pop show?"

When the two did briefly meet backstage at an awards ceremony in 1970, the awkward moment was captured on camera. A bespectacled Richard is caught looking into the middle distance, nervously fiddling with the ring on his finger and biting his bottom lip, while at his side is a smiling and seemingly oblivious Bowie. Years later, when asked to comment on that photograph, Bowie said, unsurprisingly, "I was never a great fan of his."

Richard was later to ameliorate his view. "What a terrible loss," he said after Bowie died. "I admired his extreme talent. He made so many contributions to so many areas of life."

Jacques Brel

"I couldn't give a fuck about meeting that faggot" was Jacques Brel's response on hearing that David Bowie would like to meet him. Bowie had become fascinated by Brel's melancholic balladeering early in his career, and ended up covering two of the Belgian chansonnier's songs. In fact, the anthemic line in "Rock 'n' Roll Suicide" ("Oh no, love, you're not alone"), is taken from a Brel composition. For Bowie biographer Chris O'Leary, Brel's moody "Amsterdam" is the template for everything from "Five Years" (1972) to *Station to Station* (1976). So, when Bowie was in Paris in the spring of 1973, he tried to arrange a meeting with his great inspiration. The request was passed on by Jérôme Soligny, a singer-songwriter and journalist for *Le Soir*, but resulted in a crude brush-off (Brel used the term *tapette*, a derogatory term for a homosexual).

The meeting never transpired, but the parallels between the two continued. Brel, also a heavy Gitanes smoker, dropped out of the limelight for a decade and then recorded a final album knowing he was dying of cancer. Likewise, a superhuman effort was required just to get to the studio each day. The recording was also kept a secret until its release. But perhaps the most eerie coincidence was a series of photographs taken of Brel's last weeks, which showed him wrapped head to toe in hospital bandages. It was an uncannily similar look to the one Bowie was to use in his final video, "Lazarus".

The B-52's

"Faggot!" the crew shouted at a colourful figure who was walking up the gangplank. Fellow passenger Kate Pierson looked up ahead to see what all the fuss was about. There, boarding the SS *Canberra*, was a man dressed in thigh-high, red leather boots and a lurid jacket. "I go to the boat and who should be getting on right in front of me, but David Bowie!" recalled the B-52's singer. Pierson, who had just finished a lengthy vacation around Europe, was thrilled to discover she would be sharing the voyage back to the States with one of her favourite rock stars.

That evening, some of the passengers spontaneously arranged a small party for the handful of misfits and oddballs on board. Among them were Pierson and Bowie. "It was amazing," recalled Pierson. "He sang 'Space Oddity'."

Pierson's hopes of getting to know Bowie more intimately were cut short when seasickness confined her to cabin for the rest of the voyage. But her female cabin mate stoically refused to let her friend's nausea get in the way of a good time. "I remember her saying, 'Ooh, I've got the wind in me [*sic*] sails and now I'm going to dance with David Bowie,'" recalled Pierson. "She did. And I was lying there, groaning."

Her fellow B-52 Cindy Wilson met Bowie a few years later. The newly formed Atlanta band had just finished their set in a small, trendy New York club when someone popped their head around the dressing-room door to say Bowie had been seen dancing in the audience. "David BOWIEEEEEE!!!" screamed Wilson, beside herself with delight. Then, literally beside herself, was David Bowie, himself. Wilson went red with embarrassment, but Bowie simply laughed. He confided to the band that he found touring such a bore that he had been considering packing it in, but, inspired by their zany, high-octane show, he now felt inspired to carry on.

New York Dolls

When Bowie arrived by boat in the States in 1972, the first thing he did was see New York Dolls in concert. The band were not only the most self-destructive group in rock, they were to provide the link between glam and punk, and Bowie loved them.

"He arrived like an alien abduction," recalled guitarist Sylvain Sylvain. Drummer Billy Doll and his girlfriend subsequently disappeared into Angie and Bowie's suite at the Plaza Hotel, "only to re-emerge several long nights and short days later," said the guitarist. Bowie was fascinated by the band's outrageous look and their sheer voltage. "They have the energy of six English bands," raved Bowie. He would ask them where they bought their shoes and, most importantly, who cut their hair. "Johnny Thunders," replied David Johansen truthfully, pointing to the band's other guitarist.

One night, Bowie went to meet the band at their favourite bar. Afterwards, Johansen took Bowie on a late-night stroll hoping to entertain him, but instead just frightened him. "It was a pretty rough spot and Bowie does not want to be there," Johansen said in Nina Antonia's biography of the band, *Too Much, Too Soon*. "Then a big truck stopped at the light and the driver leans out and says to me, 'Hey baby, I want to eat your cunt,' and I'm going, 'Well, you're just going to have to suck my dick.' Well, Bowie's knees are going, and he's like, 'David, don't, please don't provoke him, David, please,' and I'm yelling at the truck driver, 'C'mon, get out of that truck you muthafucker!'" Johansson and Bowie became so close they even ended up sharing a girlfriend, Cyrinda Foxe.

Billy Doll died a few months later, asphyxiated by coffee which friends had forced down his throat in an attempt to stop him from falling asleep on barbiturates. Bowie's tribute was the song "Time". There is also a belief in Dolls' fans circles that "Rebel Rebel" was about Billy Doll, too, after Bowie had seen the way the drummer's mother had lovingly reacted to her son's androgynous outfits.

Cyrinda Foxe

The Andy Warhol "Superstar" who partly inspired "The Jean Genie" remembered going with bated breath to see her new boyfriend perform as Ziggy Stardust. Having heard all about his outrageous and androgynous outfits, Cyrinda Foxe was prepared to be surprised. She was.

Bowie and Cyrinda Foxe shooting a video for "The Jean Genie", 1972.

"Look at those pants! Those earrings!" she told her friend as Bowie walked out on to the stage. "They're just like mine!" They were. Bowie had gone into her wardrobe just before the show and taken her clothes and jewellery.

Bowie, she said, never wanted to be left alone and always needed someone to talk to, even at the seemingly most inopportune moments. "He once called me into the room while he was fucking a girl because she was so stupid all he wanted to do was fuck her, and he needed someone to talk to," she wrote in her autobiography, *Dream On*. "I'd be watching the TV and talking with David, and he'd be screwing the groupie. Very nonchalant."

Sweet

"The Jean Genie" was kept off the number-one spot in 1973 by Bowie's RCA glam rock stablemates, Sweet, and their hit "Blockbuster". Both tracks had coincidentally copied their riff from the Yardbirds' "I'm a Man", so when Sweet first heard Bowie's track, they were mortified. Nicky Chinn, who wrote "Blockbuster", recalled nervously coming across Bowie at an RCA meeting. Bowie had also noticed the similarity. He gave Chinn a steely look and then said, "Cunt!" Chinn was horrified, but then Bowie burst out laughing, jumped up, gave Chinn a warm hug and congratulated him on his chart topper.

Sweet were the critically disdained side of glam, more macho pub rock drinkers than arty androgynes. But Sweet's Andy Scott recalled sitting next to Bowie in the *Top of the Pops* makeup room when the guitarist was having his nails varnished by a manicurist.

"Do you mind putting that on the other side, as I don't smoke?" he said, pointing to Bowie's cigarette. Bowie politely complied and looked over at Scott's nails. "Good idea, that," he said and promptly asked the BBC makeup woman to put the same white pearl varnish on his nails. "I was a trendsetter!" recalled Scott.

Todd Rundgren

A sharp-tongued exchange, tears and a stolen girlfriend: David Bowie and whizz kid Todd Rundgren got off to a bad start.

Bowie was in the ultra-hip Max's Kansas City club in New York when he spotted the eclectic American singer, also known for his space suits, wild-coloured hair and theatrical performances.

"I've heard of you," Bowie said. "You're supposed to be pretty fucking smart."

"Yes, I am," Rundgren replied, "and I hear you're supposed to be ripping me off."

Rundgren glared at the supposed upstart, while his girlfriend, Bebe Buell, recalled a shocked Bowie looking at her boyfriend "as if he were out of his mind". "I do remember someone crying," Rundgren said of his encounter with Bowie, "and it wasn't me."

But Bowie was not to be outdone. He phoned up Buell and asked her to show him the city. According to her, they spent the time sightseeing and kissing. Bowie not only stole Rundgren's girlfriend, he was also later to take Rundgren's band (Roger Powell, Tony Sales and Hunt Sales were all to play for him).

"I have to be quite honest and say that I was not always impressed with him artistically," said Rundgren. "The constant gadding about and experimenting sometimes came up with something interesting but just as often came up with something that was no more than what he had invested in it in the first place." He was also dismissive of Bowie's cut-up technique: "That leaves the audience open to their own interpretation but it also means the artist doesn't mean anything when he's doing it. So, a lot of that stuff just never reached me."

Funnily enough, when Rundgren instigated the altercation, he was a fan of Bowie. Buell remembered the two of them lying in bed listening to *Hunky Dory*. "It was a much more vulnerable and revelatory album than a lot of the ones where he's playing a character," Rundgren said.

Any hard feelings had long since gone by the time Bowie died. When the news came out, Rundgren was on tour. He finished his concert with "Rebel Rebel".

Jim Morrison

Bowie was used to having relationships with girlfriends of other rock stars. He even had a brief flirtation with Jim Morrison's wife.

Bowie's "creative contact" at RCA was Patricia Kennealy, who wed Morrison in a pagan Celtic ceremony in 1970. After one particularly successful session together with Bowie recording radio adverts, Bowie kissed Kennealy. "I can't really say more than that, and I'd rather keep the rest private in any case," she later said. Kennealy, though, did describe Morrison and Bowie as having the same charismatic wattage palpable on first meeting. "It was the same kind of shock that I had the first time I met Jim," she said. "I could feel history swing past."

Astoundingly, Bowie was also once considered as a replacement frontman for the Doors. After Morrison's death, drummer John Densmore was adamant that Bowie be their new singer when the three survivors decided to reform for a reunion tour. But while the other band members admired the singer, they vetoed the suggestion. "I cannot see Bowie singing 'Light My Fire' or the Doors doing 'Beep, Beep Fashion'," said Ray Manzarek. "It's one of my favourite songs but I don't want to play it." Densmore was so annoyed with their decision that he refused to re-join the band.

Bowie loved the Doors and admired Morrison, describing him as a "commanding performer" after seeing the band perform in the sixties. After writing "Hallo Spaceboy" in 1995, Bowie said, "I adore that track. It was like Morrison meets industrial. I thought, 'Fuck me, it's metal Doors!'"

Michael Palin

Michael Palin remembers the time that Bowie kept him awake all night. The singer had just finished a Ziggy Stardust concert in Edinburgh and was holding a party in his hotel suite. Down the corridor was Palin, whose Monty Python crew were performing their *First Farewell Tour* in the city. "It felt like trying to sleep through the invasion of Poland," wrote Palin.

Despite the late-night noise, the easy-going comic was delighted to find Bowie and his colourful entourage in the lobby come morning. "What a relief from roomfuls of grey suits," Palin wrote. "Tall, gangling men dressed in denim moved through the room like a dozen Jesuses, sharply dressed chicks sat around smoking – everyone wore a relaxed air of confidence – they were, after all, part of the hottest road show in Britain. With our Sunday papers and our conspicuous lack of hangers-on, we looked very dull and anonymous."

It was another 25 years, though, before the two men got a chance to talk at length, when they ran into each other at a launch party in New York. Bowie, Palin recalled, spoke admiringly about the daring of English painter Walter Sickert and *The Camden Town Murder* (1908) – a series of four explicit paintings focusing on the real-life brutal killing of a young prostitute, a murder that became the cause célèbre of its day in 1907. "Who would do that nowadays without howls of outrage from the newspapers?" Bowie asked Palin rhetorically.

As for Bowie, Palin was impressed by how he handled all the attention. "He was very relaxed, adept, I suspect, at creating around him an oasis of ordinary, everyday life, whilst being the goldfish at the centre of the bowl," wrote the comedian.

Bob Hope

The Python was not the only comedian to be kept awake by Bowie. The singer had been performing in Hollywood's Universal Amphitheatre when police received a call from a local resident complaining about the noise. Officers were sent to the venue. Bowie was ordered to turn down the volume for the following night despite there being just the one complaint. After all, the person who made the call was Bob Hope.

Peter Cook

A game of footsie under a rug in the back of a limo. That's what Peter Cook's wife recalled of their evening with the Bowies.

It was a cold winter's night in New York. David and Angie had come around in their chauffeur-driven car to take the Cooks out for dinner. All four sat on the back seat, and the chauffeur draped a rug over their laps for warmth. Almost immediately, someone started rubbing their foot slowly up and down the leg of Judy

Huxtable, the comic's wife. "There was deliberate footsie going on but I'm unsure whose foot it was," she said.

At the club, Cook and Bowie got into "an intense conversation", Huxtable recalled in her autobiography, *Loving Peter*. Angie asked her to dance. "It was quite sexy and we carried on for a few dances," she wrote. When the women returned to the table, Cook said he had to leave because he was performing the next day. The foursome piled back into the limo, and the game of footsie began all over again. "But it didn't go any further," stressed Huxtable, who never did find out who the foot belonged to.

Bowie was once asked whose death had affected him more, Cook's or Cobain's. "Peter Cook's, without a doubt," he said. "I knew him a little and there was a real sadness in his life." The comedian's satire, he said, had changed his outlook on the world. "His lessons in irreverence were really important to my generation."

Mick Jagger

Bowie may have lionized Lennon, idolized Iggy and revered Reed, but the rocker he perhaps most wanted to emulate was Mick Jagger.

Bowie saw the Stones in 1963. He was impressed by their attitude as much as by their music. "The Stones were so funny," he recalled. "They had, like, four fans at that time, who rushed down the aisles to the front. And some bloke – I'll never forget this – some bloke in the audience looked at Jagger and said, 'Get your hair cut!' And Mick said, 'What – and look like you?' We just collapsed in our seats."

The first Stone Bowie befriended was guitarist Brian Jones,

whom he considered the band's leader alongside Keith Richards. But it was to be several years before the Stones's singer was to notice the young fan. "David was thrilled when the mighty Mick first paid attention to him," said Angie, who added that the two subsequently became inseparable. The first thing that struck Bowie, according to manager Simon Napier-Bell, was that Jagger had cash in his pocket. "David, of course, had nothing but cocaine," said Napier-Bell.

Friendship quickly blossomed. "They were always talking on the phone together like teenagers. 'Shall I meet you at Tramp's?' became the million-dollar question of many a day," recalled Angie, who famously opened the door on the two men naked and asleep in bed.

Angie was convinced the relationship was more than platonic, though Bowie and Jagger laughed off the suggestion. However, Bowie's other partners also believed the relationship went beyond a shared love of music. "They used to pick up beautiful black girls and take them back to the hotel and have mad sex with them," recalled Bebe Buell, briefly one of Bowie's flings. For Amanda Lear, another girlfriend, the relationship was more fundamental: "I believe David was madly in love with Jagger."

"I used to dream of being Mick Jagger," Bowie admitted. He was so obsessed that, at one point, he believed Jagger was sending him messages in Rolling Stones songs. Around the time of "Rebel Rebel", he even copied the Stones' sound, confiding to a fellow musician that he wanted to "piss Mick off a bit".

When Jagger showed him paintings by a new artist the Stones wanted to use for their album cover, Bowie immediately called the designer and got him to design his own *Diamond Dogs* (1974) sleeve. Jagger was not pleased, but Bowie was unapologetic: "Mick was silly. He should never have shown me anything new. He will never do that again. You've got to be a bastard in this business."

Jagger was aware of the rivalry and of Bowie's magpie instinct to pick up anything to hand. "Be careful of the shoes you wear around David because next time you see him, he'll be wearing them, and he'll be wearing them better than you," he said.

Pete Townshend believed the rivalry cut both ways: "Mick wants to do new things. He would much prefer to be David Bowie than to work with Keith Richards who wants to be like Muddy Waters and grow old and die playing the blues." For Bowie, though, there was one notable difference: "Mick believes in music as music, as a source of uplift, of enjoyment. I see it as a vehicle for ideas, as vocabulary."

They finally performed together for the Live Aid single "Dancing in the Street". "My favourite memory is the time we did that together," said Jagger. "We enjoyed camping it up. It's the only time we really collaborated on anything, which is really stupid when you think about it." Bowie adored the online "shreds" (spoofs) of the video, which made fun of Mick and him.

At this time, the two also vacationed together, with Bowie again following his friend's lead by buying a house on the exclusive Caribbean island of Mustique. It was here that Bowie revealed another side of his character, helping on local health care projects and at schools. "He was so relaxed there and so kind to everyone," recalled Jagger. "He'd do story time with the local kids, it was really sweet."

Marianne Faithfull

"One night we were all a bit drunk at David's house and David began coming on to me," recalled Marianne Faithfull in her autobiography. "We went into the corridor, I unzipped his trousers. I was trying to give him a blow job but David was scared to death of Oliver [her partner]...Oliver does have this Gestapo-officer vibe to him...so he couldn't keep it up."

The two singers had first encountered each other almost a decade before in 1965 while on the same record-company bus (see page 21). But the young man at the bottom of the bill left no impression on the older woman. "I remember the Hollies and Freddie and the Dreamers and all sorts of other funny people, but I don't remember David at all," said Faithfull. Bowie's bandmates, however, would rib the long-haired, effeminate-looking Bowie that he was Faithfull's secret sister.

Despite her being Mick Jagger's partner, Faithfull and Bowie did not get to meet properly until around 1973. Faithfull became interested in Bowie because of what she called his "beautiful" sixties covers on *Pinups* (1973). Bowie was at the height of his Jagger obsession and was more than intrigued by her public interest. The offer was there from both Bowie and wife Angie to be more than friends.

"They seemed very close but their relationship obviously did deteriorate because of infidelity and drugs and orgies," said Faithfull. "I'd had enough of that kind of shit in the 60s." As for Bowie being worried about being caught in flagrante delicto by "Gestapo Oliver", he need not have. "This was not the sort of thing that would have upset Oliver," Faithfull said.

Twiggy

David Bowie was set to become the first man to appear on the cover of *Vogue*. The magazine had commissioned a photoshoot of the singer together with Twiggy, the face of Swinging Sixties London. Bowie was delighted, as he had sung about the model in "Drive-In Saturday", while Twiggy was so thrilled upon hearing her name sung on the radio that she immediately went out and bought a copy of the record.

The photographer Justin de Villeneuve, who was also Twiggy's manager, was initially concerned by the stark contrast between the two. Twiggy had just come back from Bermuda with a deep tan while Bowie was still very much the Thin White Duke. Deciding to play with the image, de Villeneuve had the makeup artist whiten Twiggy's face and darken Bowie's. But by the time the photograph was sent back to London, the magazine's editors had got cold feet. "They said we love the picture but we can't put a man on the cover," recalled Twiggy. "I said are you crazy? You'd sell more copies than ever!"

The two stars were to have the last laugh. Bowie used the photo as the cover of his covers album, *Pinups*. "So, it's had a much longer life," observed Twiggy.

Carrie Fisher

Carrie Fisher had struggled with addiction since adolescence. When an autopsy was carried out following the *Star Wars* actress's death from a heart attack aged 60, a cocktail of drugs including cocaine, ecstasy and heroin was found in her system. Her descent into the world of hard drugs had begun more than 40 years earlier.

In 1973, the 17-year-old Fisher was studying at the Central School of Speech and Drama in London. She and her mother, Hollywood actress Debbie Reynolds, were invited to a party hosted by Mick and Bianca Jagger. Introduced to Bowie, Fisher found herself drawn to a person, she said, who "made the world a better place for rebels, oddballs and misfits like me". It was the beginning of a six-week relationship which, she would later say, marked the start of her drug addiction.

"I took drugs with him," she was quoted as saying in *Carrie Fisher & Debbie Reynolds: Princess Leia and Unsinkable Tammy in Hell* by Darwin Porter and Danforth Prince. "I have no one to blame but myself for my future addiction but he certainly led me to the water to drink."

It was a dark period for both. "Some nights were torture for him as he sank into a cocaine pit of hell," said Fisher. "He could be ruthless, mean, jealous. At other times, he conquered his demons and could be sweet and tender, wanting and needing love." She described how he would cry for hours on end after bouts of excessive drinking or drug taking, and say that he felt he was standing on the edge of a crumbling cliff.

One morning she woke up naked in the same bed as Bowie, with fleeting memories of a night of passion. She later confided to a friend that she had consumed so much alcohol and so many drugs, she was no longer sure what had happened. "I think we had sex, or did I fantasize about it?" she said, making her, surely, one of the few to forget sleeping with Bowie.

Lulu

"I'm not going to sing with Lulu," Jimi Hendrix once said. "I'd look ridiculous." No such qualms affected Bowie, who not only recorded with the diminutive Scottish singer, but had an affair with her, too.

By 1973, Lulu was a household name as a Eurovision Song Contest winner and a light-entertainment star. But cool she was not. The two singers bumped into each other at a hotel in Sheffield. Lulu recalled that she was in the lobby discussing her new TV series when in walked a "stick-insect man" with bright orange hair. Bowie went over and invited her to his concert that night. During the after-show party, the two disappeared into the bowels of the hotel, leaving an angry Angie knocking on doors into the early hours in a fruitless bid to find them.

"The odd couple", as they were known, soon became an item, with Bowie taken not only with Lulu's bubbly character but also with her powerful, rasping voice, which had made "Shout" such a hit. "People laugh now, but you'll see," Bowie told *Rock* magazine at the time. "She's got a real soul voice, she can get the feel of Aretha." They worked on two songs together, including Lulu's hit single and Bowie cover "The Man Who Sold the World" (1974). Bowie convinced Lulu to go for an androgynous look and her performance on *The Morecambe & Wise Show* dressed as a 1930s gangster unnerved many of the prime-time audience. "He was uber cool and I just wanted to be led by him," Lulu said.

Touchingly, she introduced Bowie to her mum and dad, who described him, with classic understatement, as "a bit odd". Lulu went further, describing some of her conversations with Bowie as outright "insane", although she added he could be down-to-earth and funny. A plan to record a whole album together in Memphis never materialized, but Lulu credits Bowie with saving her from being typecast as a light entertainer.

Arrestingly, one of the abiding images she retained was of Bowie's thighs: "long and slim but muscular," she eulogized, "not pumped up, but really powerful."

Salvador Dalí

When Bowie started dating It Girl Amanda Lear in the mid-seventies, he discovered he had competition. Each morning, his rival would phone the model's London flat on the pretext that it was a wake-up call. Not only did Bowie ensure he answered the bedside phone but, adding insult to injury, he parodied the caller's limited English and thick Catalán accent. The fact that his rival was one of the century's greatest artists proved no deterrence.

"Ggguudda morrrrning, Maestro Dah'Leeee," Bowie would say in his cartoon Spanish before stretching across the bed to hand over the phone.

"Of course, Dalí didn't like him," Lear told writer Stan Lauryssens, author of *Dalí and I*. "He was jealous. He liked Alice Cooper more."

The painter had become transfixed by Lear on first meeting. She quickly became his artistic model, muse and confidante. Bowie was equally attracted to the flamboyant model with polymathic knowledge, partly because of her relationship with another rival, Bryan Ferry, and partly because he was fascinated by Lear's ambiguous gender.

Lear once took Dalí to see a Ziggy Stardust show in New York. According to Bowie's friends, the fact that the artist was present sent a frisson through the performance. She offered to introduce the painter to Bowie, but Dalí feigned disinterest, saying he thought Bowie looked "ridiculous", which could be seen as a compliment, perhaps, from the master of the absurd. He did grudgingly admit, though, that Bowie moved "like a cat".

They met once, in passing, in a New York elevator. The two most outlandish artists of their respective generations eyed each other warily like cautious peacocks before leaving without saying a word. "He stayed on one side looking at me, I stayed on the other side looking at him," Bowie told his friend Kevin Cann. The painter, who loved to show off his Elvis socks, was fascinated by rock and roll stars but, Cann believes, would have felt aggrieved that there was someone as weird as him.

Certainly, Bowie was transfixed by the outrageous Spaniard. He would quiz Lear on everything to do with him. He even began subsequent tours with the screening of the Dalí–Luis Buñuel short film *Un chien andalou*, which included a notorious eyeball-slicing scene.

Despite Dalí's jealousy or indifference, Bowie remained a long-term fan. He told *Life* magazine in 1992 that his greatest heroes were those who "transgressed the norm". Alongside Lennon, Little Richard and Marcel Duchamp, he mentioned the name Salvador Dalí, this time without a spoof accent.

William Burroughs

On 17 November 1973, Bowie had an encounter which changed his approach to songwriting. William Burroughs was one of the Beats, a group of writers whose iconoclastic attitudes to sex, drugs, literature and authority defined the sixties counterculture.

Burroughs became the most notorious, partly for his unapologetic look at drug addiction, and partly for shooting his wife dead at a party, allegedly in an attempt to demonstrate their "William Tell act". But what made him stand out as an author was his radical "cut-up" style. Burroughs believed true communication through existing language was impossible, as it locked people into conventional patterns of thought and cliches. His answer was to randomly rearrange words and phrases in a bid to break the cycle and release true creativity. So when, in 1974, young *Rolling Stone* writer A. Craig Copetas decided to bring together the two greatest cultural transgressors of the time, he turned to Bowie and Burroughs.

Before the meeting, Copetas set them both "homework". He suggested that Bowie read Burroughs's novel *The Wild Boys* (1971), whose guerrilla gang of boys in a dystopian world had parallels with the Ziggy Stardust myth, and that Burroughs listen to some of Bowie's records, including "Five Years". The writer was intrigued enough to read all of the singer's lyrics. "Bill was certainly more interested in the lyrics than the chords," said Copetas. As for Bowie, the singer later described *The Wild Boys* as influencing Ziggy, but it seems that his view may have been coloured by time, because his alien character was an established phenomenon well before he had read the book.

Burroughs was taken to Bowie's London house. Two flamboyant Bowie acolytes brought in prawn cocktails and a bottle of Beaujolais Nouveau, which caused Burroughs a wry smile. The two men embarked on a conversation about art, prompted by Bowie's paintings hanging in the front room. "There was an immediate liking and respect," said Copetas.

Burroughs veered from grand statements about the need

for artists to seize control from politicians to plans for a mind-
expanding centre in Scotland that would, he said, allow people to
mutate into higher life forms. Commuting would not be an issue,
insisted the writer, because adherents would get to work using
the centre's "astral air force". By comparison, Bowie came across
as positively down-to-earth.

The singer had started using cut-up techniques at the
beginning of his career, long before his encounter with

Bowie and William Burroughs photographed by Terry O'Neill, 1974.

Burroughs. Back in 1965, Helene Lancaster, the wife of Bowie's then drummer, Phil, recalled the singer cutting words out of a newspaper while in a café. "This is how I write," Bowie told her as he proceeded to rearrange the words randomly. But his face-to-face with Burroughs reignited his interest in the technique and, having struggled to write lyrics, he found that the approach sped everything up. Years later, Bowie computerized the technique and used a randomizer program.

For Bowie, Burroughs was the man who allowed him to become truly modern. "He was really a mentor as far as how to write in a late 20th-century fashion," he said. As for Burroughs, Bowie's constant and public adulation turned him from a marginal figure into a writer ranked alongside the giants of 20th-century literature.

The author was responsible for one other notable encounter for Bowie. Burroughs had enthused about a device called the Dreamachine invented by his friend Brion Gysin, the sixties originator of the cut-up technique. Intrigued, Bowie arranged with Copetas to meet Gysin in his Paris flat to experience the effects of the device first-hand.

Gysin took them to a room and pulled aside some curtains to reveal a turntable on which was placed a tall cylinder with slats and, inside, a light bulb. "Would you like to try it?" Gysin asked. The men nodded.

Gysin told the men to sit in front of the machine and close their eyes. He then switched on the turntable, and flickering images danced across their eyelids as the cylinder spun around. The idea, he explained, was that the brain would start to turn these flashing images into patterns and they would enter a higher consciousness, or "alpha wave", state. Gysin was so thrilled by his idea that he believed his Dreamachine would eclipse television as the new form of mass entertainment.

"It was supposed to open up your mind," said Copetas. "It just gave me a headache."

Jean Genet

William Burroughs also had a hand in Bowie's efforts to meet Jean Genet, the French writer whose name has long been famous in Bowie circles as the inspiration behind the punning song title "The Jean Genie". But when Bowie reached out to the enfant terrible of the Parisian literary scene, it was nothing to do with his song, but to save a friend's play.

Lindsay Kemp had been having trouble with the London police ever since staging, in 1974, an adaptation of Genet's debut novel, *Our Lady of the Flowers* – as *Flowers. A Pantomime for Jean Genet*. The novel was described as "an epic of masturbation" by Jean-Paul Sartre, and the Kemp play, too, was an explicit and defiantly homosexual show. The frequent raids gave the production notoriety but also threatened its existence. Moreover, Genet's English-language agent said the production violated Genet's copyright. Bowie thought that, if anyone could save the play, it would be the author himself. Burroughs gave the singer the name of the hotel where Genet resided, and Bowie dispatched a couple of friends to Paris.

"You're a journalist," Bowie told his friend Copetas. "Go to Paris and see if you can get his permission."

Despite Genet's reputation as a flamboyant outsider, which had seen him serve time in prison and be dishonourably discharged from the French Foreign Legion, he was quiet and reclusive.

Bowie's helpers tried his hotel, his favourite café and his publisher but there was no trace of Genet. They even got hold of Sartre but the French Existentialist was in the middle of a bitter feud with Genet and was unable to help, so the pair returned empty-handed.

Somehow, though, the message did get through. Genet's friend Paule Thévenin, quoted in Kevin Cann's *Any Day Now*, recalled that "Genet and Bowie agreed to meet in a restaurant in London. The others in Genet's group looked around for Bowie in vain, but sharp-eyed Genet spotted an attractive-looking woman sitting by herself and went up to her and said, 'Mr Bowie, I presume.' His presumption was correct."

The production survived and went on to inspire one 15-year-old member of the audience to ask Kemp for mime lessons. Her name was Kate Bush.

George Orwell

Burroughs was not the only dystopian author to influence Bowie. George Orwell was to have a profound impact on him, and although the singer never got to meet the writer, he did come into contact with his hero's wife.

The English novelist had died from tuberculosis in 1950 aged 46, and left his literary estate in the hands of his young spouse, Sonia Brownell. Bowie approached her with the idea of turning Orwell's novel *Nineteen Eighty-Four* into a musical. Certain of her approval, he had already written several songs for the project when news of the rejection came through. Bowie dispatched some colleagues to win her over, but she sent them packing, telling them that the previous dramatization had been such "a disaster" that she would never let the work slip out of her grasp again. She also had a personal interest: Julia, the novel's heroine who offers a rare vision of love to its doomed protagonist, Winston Smith, was based on her.

To try to save the project, Bowie intervened personally but was told no amount of money would change her mind. He remained, however, sceptical of her motives. "For someone who married a socialist with communist leanings, she was the biggest upper-class snob I've ever met in my life," he said. Making the best of a bad deal, Bowie quickly wrote some more songs to create his own dystopian future and the *Diamond Dogs* LP and tour were born.

When Brownell died in 1980, Orwell's new executors jumped at the chance to turn *Nineteen Eighty-Four* into a film. Ironically, the first person the director, Michael Radford, turned to for the music was David Bowie. By then, the singer had cooled on the idea, although the film's producers suggested his wage demands were beyond their budget anyway. Radford turned to a cheaper option: Eurythmics.

Arthur C Clarke

Arthur C Clarke was not just a science-fiction author, he was also a respected physicist who predicted the advent of the satellite, the smartphone and the Internet. So, the scientist must have been surprised to find himself seated opposite David Bowie one night in the mid-seventies, discussing the latest New Age fad for "aura", or Kirlian cameras.

Angie Bowie had invited Clarke to her London home for what she termed a civilized soirée. Bowie was over the moon. He so loved *2001: A Space Odyssey* (1968), Stanley Kubrick's film developed in tandem with Clarke's novel, that he had seen it several times. Famously, it was to inspire "Space Oddity". The conversation turned to a peculiar device that had been invented by a Russian scientist, Semyon Kirlian, and his wife in 1939 and which was later claimed to capture people's "auras". The Kirlian camera worked by resting an object, often a person's hand, on a photographic film while a small electric current was passed through a metal plate underneath. The result was a fuzzy outline of the object or, in those Aquarian times, "an aura". Despite the device's link to mysticism, Clarke proved both knowledgeable and enthusiastic about it, and Bowie was impressed that such a scientific man was open to such ideas.

Later, Bowie was to acquire his own Kirlian camera. It was given to him by the Department of Parapsychology at the University of California, Los Angeles, which, incredible as it may seem now, received funding from the Pentagon to investigate ghosts, clairvoyance, telepathy and extra-terrestrials. Bowie would use the device to record differences in his aura after taking cocaine, convinced it showed the drug sapping his energy.

Shortly before his death, Arthur C Clarke was asked, with a nod to Bowie, "Is there life on Mars?" As "out-there'" as any rock star, the sci-fi author replied, "There are large areas of vegetation, like banyan trees. And if there is vegetation, it seems probable there are other life-forms as well."

Ray Bradbury
- - - - - - - - - - - - - - - -

While Clarke's *2001* is credited as the major sci-fi influence on "Space Oddity", Bowie's fictional character Major Tom also owes a debt to another sci-fi writer, Ray Bradbury. Bowie was a fan of the author and of one story in particular, "No Particular Night or Morning", in the collection *The Illustrated Man* (1951), which featured an astronaut exiting an airlock to kill himself. It was the fate which was to befall Major Tom.

Bradbury and Bowie met after the author's daughter convinced her father to use his star power to get tickets for the singer's sold-out concert in Los Angeles in 1974. A rather sheepish Bradbury was put directly through to Bowie's agent. When the writer insisted he was not after free tickets, the agent replied, "Are you kidding? David Bowie's your number-one fan. You're gonna come, and you're gonna see him after."

Bradbury later recalled a comical backstage encounter with various stars that left his daughter flummoxed: "David Bowie comes out and embraces me, and then he introduces me to Ringo Starr. Ringo falls over a chair getting to me. Neil Sedaka, Bette Midler and John Belushi are all there too, and they swarm. My daughter was standing there like, you know, 'This is just my father.'"

The two men got on so well that they had dinner the next night. Alice Cooper, also invited, remembered the conversation spinning from quantum mechanics and UFOs to Francis Bacon and the occult. "These guys were in outer space somewhere," said Cooper.

Bowie wasn't the only glam rock star who used Bradbury's stories in his music: Elton John and Bernie Taupin wrote a song based on another Bradbury short story, also collected in *The Illustrated Man*, "The Rocket Man".

Rod Stewart
- - - - - - - - - - - - -

Bowie's relationship with Rod Stewart mirrors the one he had with Elton John. While their early encounters were warm, a chill was to creep in.

"Rod Stewart and Ronnie Wood have been frequent visitors of late and we usually sit around listening to music until the wee hours, turning each other onto our favourite sounds," was one published entry from Bowie's diary from the early seventies. According to Rolling Stones legend, the three musicians were once hanging out at Mick Jagger's place when they decided to see what a vodka pancake might taste like. The rockers headed to the kitchen to refine the recipe. As they got drunker, things got out of hand. "The four got into a heated argument about what should or shouldn't be put in the batter and how long the pancakes should be cooked for," an associate of the Stones revealed to the band's fan site, SHIDOOBEE. As tempers rose, the rockers battered each other with batter and "roaring with laughter, they rolled through the milk, flour and vodka". Early the next morning, Jagger's wife Bianca found all four on the kitchen floor covered in dough and fast asleep.

But rivalry and cattiness took over. Stewart took offence at Bowie's "snottiness", believing Bowie had snubbed when they came across each other in a London studio in 1973. Asked shortly after that encounter if he owned any Bowie records, Stewart replied, "I don't think I even know any of his tunes." Certainly, Stewart felt that he was treated differently by the press despite his career having also undergone many changes. Bowie, he said, had always been the darling of rock critics. "They look at him as an intellectual writer and me, just the opposite," he said.

George Harrison
- - - - - - - - - - - - - - - - - - -

George Harrison was another who never saw eye to eye with Bowie. In fact, thanks to Bowie's fedora, Harrison could not see his eyes at all. Meeting the singer backstage after a concert in Memphis in 1974, Harrison pushed up the brim of Bowie's hat and said, "Do you mind if I have a look at you to see what you are, because I've only seen those dopey pictures of you?" Bowie was stunned into silence.

The guitarist later attempted a semi-apology on American radio, but simply ended up repeating the slur. "I hope he wasn't offended by it because all I really meant was what I said," said Harrison. "I mean, every picture I've ever seen of David Bowie or Elton John, they just look stupid to me." Seated next to him was John Lennon, who was sufficiently taken aback to counter, "I thought they looked great."

Mutual friend Eric Idle tried to get Harrison to change his mind about Bowie, but to no avail. "I even got David as far as Henley [where Harrison lived], but George would not admit him."

After Harrison died in 2001, Bowie covered one of his songs, "Try Some, Buy Some" (1973). But it turned out that the homage was inadvertent, as Bowie thought the song to be a Ronnie Spector number. "It's rather fitting and quite lovely that it is an unwitting tribute to George," said Bowie, who admired the ex-Beatle's writing. "It's one of the greatest, most under-rated popular songs ever written and recorded," he added, not letting his view be coloured by their frosty meeting. "I wish I could write a tune that is one tenth as foreboding and spectacular."

FEAR & FOAMING IN LOS ANGELES

1974–76

The drugs, the divas, the discs and the demonic, dark stains at the bottom of a foaming swimming pool...Bowie once described a fellow singer who inspired Ziggy Stardust as "out of his gourd", and that's what Bowie was for most of this period. His encounters with fellow stars reveal him as insecure, desperate to please and paranoid. He believed Aretha Franklin had it in for him, and that Jimmy Page had put a curse on him. But if his initial friendship with Led Zeppelin seems odd, what are we to make of his best-pals relationship with Deep Purple?

Despite copious amounts of cocaine, his work rate remained prodigious. He put out two great albums and got his first US number one. He met the A-listers of A-listers: Dylan hated him, Springsteen was baffled by him but Liz Taylor adored him. It's touching to see how nervous he was when he met Lennon, who became one of the few who could poke fun at Bowie without triggering a nervous breakdown. It is surprising to see Bowie and Sinatra become best buddies. It is even more surprising to discover his role in Michael Jackson's moonwalk. But it is stupefying to see his love of David Cassidy. Did he and Lou Reed really offer to write an album for the clean-cut teen heartthrob? Ah, those drugs.

Elizabeth Taylor

No one keeps a diva waiting. And absolutely no one kept the "Queen of Divas" waiting. Except, that is, David Bowie.

When the singer met Elizabeth Taylor, he was not simply fashionably late, he was five hours late, and high on drugs. As befits any diva worth her diamonds, Taylor threw a fit and threatened to leave. "We managed to persuade her to stay," said photographer Terry O'Neill, who was there to do a photoshoot of the two of them. When Bowie finally arrived, the two stars hit it off and the resulting photographs show them flirting with each other. They were to become "phone" friends, with Taylor calling him daily to update him on her latest illness, her latest hairdo, her most recent marriage (she was on number five of eight) and her latest round of colonic irrigation.

By 1974, Taylor's golden years were behind her, but the two-time Oscar winner was keen on remaking one film that had fascinated her since childhood, a *Wizard of Oz*–type fantasy called *The Blue Bird*. Her ideal lead was Bowie. With that in mind, a lunchtime meeting had been arranged at the Beverly Hills home of director George Cukor. It was late afternoon before Bowie showed up.

"No one had ever made her wait five hours before," said O'Neill. If anything, it was Taylor who kept people waiting. The photographer calmed things down by getting the two stars to pose for the camera, and the mood quickly lifted. The shots show them cuddled up together, flirtatiously sharing a cigarette. Taylor told a flattered Bowie that he reminded her of her friend James Dean. "That endeared me to her," he later said. (Bowie had once said it was impossible to consider himself good-looking because his older brother, Terry, had looked just like the American actor.)

For the next couple of months, the 42-year-old actress would call Bowie at his hotel just after she had woken up at 3pm. The conversations tended to be one-sided, with Bowie listening as Taylor went into detail about her daily routines. But it was not just a one-way street. Taylor was a mother hen-type figure, who was intimately familiar with the world of superstardom Bowie had recently entered, and who could relate to his fragile, lonely and drug-addled state of mind. The phone calls and their mundane subject matter were almost certainly attempts to keep Bowie tethered to planet Earth.

As for the movie script, she told Bowie, "Read this and make it with me. Be my leading man."

"I was so excited when she handed it to me," Bowie said. "I went through it and it was absolutely awful." Bowie made his polite excuses. He made the right call. On the set in Russia, Taylor suffered from dysentery and dehydration, and Cukor had to use sign language to be understood by the crew. The film was promoted with the less than snappy slogan, "The First Joint American–Soviet Fantasy Film". Unsurprisingly, it bombed.

There is little evidence for the rumours that Taylor and Bowie were more than friends. But the actress did have at least one significant influence on Bowie's life. It was at one of her high-society parties that Bowie was to meet one of the most significant figures in his life.

Bowie kept Elizabeth Taylor waiting for this photo shoot in 1975.

John Lennon

- - - - - - - - - - - - -

Bowie tried not to panic. Ahead of him stood the most revered rock star on the planet. Attempting to compose his thoughts, he told himself, "Don't be sycophantic and don't mention the Beatles, you'll look really stupid." Steeling himself, he edged his way through the party guests and approached a small group consisting of hostess Liz Taylor, Elton John, a former record-company secretary named May Pang and her boyfriend.

"Hello, Dave," said the boyfriend amiably.

"I've got everything you've made," said Bowie, "...except the Beatles." In one brief sentence, Bowie had managed to put his foot in it. Twice.

Bowie would always remember his first awkward encounter with John Lennon with a mixture of horror and humour. But it wasn't to matter. A few days later, they found themselves together again, this time at the Grammys. Backstage, once again nervous and high, Bowie poured out his insecurities to Lennon, claiming America did not understand him. He then went on stage to present an award to Aretha Franklin, who unceremoniously snatched the Grammy from his hands and proclaimed to the audience, "This is so good, I could kiss David Bowie." Bowie was crestfallen. Not only did he feel humiliated by his favourite soul singer, he felt his fears about being misunderstood had been vindicated.

Lennon spotted the dejected figure slink backstage. "He bounds over and gives me a theatrical kiss and a hug and says, 'See, Dave, America loves ya!'" recalled Bowie. "We pretty much got on like a house on fire after that."

The two singers became so close, they would even go on holiday together. Bowie recalled them once being kicked out of a Chinese restaurant in Hong Kong for being drunk. "John is frothing at the mouth, shouting, 'Let us back in! We've paid out money. We want to finish our drinks!'" said Bowie. "They said, 'No, you fuck off.' And he said, 'Do you know who I am? I'm a fucking Beatle!' and we started laughing. We were on the floor, it was so funny."

On the same trip, Bowie recalled a young Beatles fan running up to ask, "Are you John Lennon?" "No," replied the ex-Beatle, "but I wish I had his money." Bowie loved the response so much he decided to use it at the first opportunity back in New York. Sure enough, one day when he was peering into a shop window, he heard someone behind him ask, "Are you David Bowie?" "No, but I wish I had his money," he responded smugly. "You lying bastard!" came the reply. "You mean you wish you had my money." He turned around to find John Lennon.

The two would often hang out at each other's apartments. Tony Visconti recalled the three of them staying up into the early hours with several bottles of cognac and a mound of cocaine "the size of the Matterhorn" on the table. The straight-talking Liverpudlian would continue to say what he thought, even if it meant poking fun at his often overly sensitive friend. "What the hell are you doing, Bowie?" Lennon is filmed as saying on one of Bowie's homemade movies, while playing hit songs of the day on guitar. "It's all so negative, your shit. All this Diamond Dogs mutant crap! Ha! Ha! Ha!" "I loved John," said Bowie wistfully. Then came the revelation in a book by Lesley-Ann Jones called *Who Killed John Lennon?* that the two men's relationship had gone far further than previously thought. Speaking about one night in Los Angeles, Bowie told Jones, "There was a whore in the middle of us and it wasn't either of us. At some point in the proceedings she left. I think it was a she. Not that we minded."

The friendship between these two figures, revered as rock gods even by those within the rock pantheon, was unique. Bowie looked up to Lennon with something akin to worship, describing him as "my greatest mentor". "I don't know why you're interviewing me, when you've got someone like Lennon," Bowie told a young Tina Brown of *The Sunday Times*, who had spent months tracking Bowie across the United States for an interview. "He's the last great original." It was a similar story when the BBC's Andy Peebles went to New York to interview Bowie and then Lennon, in what was to be Lennon's last interview before his death. When Bowie found out who the DJ was to speak to, "all he wanted to talk about was the Beatles," said Peebles.

There was great admiration on Lennon's part, too. Bowie was the only one of John's friends, according to Yoko, who was his equal in terms of talent and intellect. Lennon told his friend his music was just "rock and roll with fookin' lipstick on", but when he returned after a five-year hiatus to record *Double Fantasy* (1980), he told the BBC, "I wanted to do something as good as *Heroes*." Even before their friendship, Lennon had jumped to Bowie's defence on an American radio show after George Harrison had begun to criticize Bowie's personas (see page 117). Although the Beatles singer did laughingly add later, "You never know which one you're talking to."

The two famously collaborated on "Fame", Bowie's first US number one. Bowie was "like a little kid" awaiting Lennon's arrival, recalled backing singer Ava Cherry. Yoko handed out some sushi, then left. Lennon played a bit of "Across the Universe", a song Bowie loved, and then began to shout out, "Are we having a good time?!" The atmosphere was breathtaking, recalled Bowie. Guitarist Carlos Alomar started to play a funky riff he had written. Lennon adored it and started playing along on his 12-string guitar. He began to scream and shout what sounded like "Fame", and Bowie, inspired, rushed to get his notepad to scribble down lyrics. Another version of the story, again by Bowie, has Lennon playing "Shame, Shame, Shame" by Shirley & Company, with Bowie switching the lyric to "fame". Either way, the song was finished by the end of the day.

"John was so up, he had so much energy," Bowie told *Musician* magazine. "It must have been so exciting to always be around him." Despite the song's success, "Fame" was to be the only time they would collaborate. "I can't believe we didn't try to write more things together," said Bowie. As a gift, Lennon drew a caricature of his new friend, which the latter put in a gold frame and kept in pride of place on his mantelpiece.

When Lennon was assassinated, Bowie was devastated. Lennon's former girlfriend May Pang recalled going around to Bowie's apartment on hearing the news to find the singer pacing up and down, shouting, "What the hell! What the fuck is going on with the world!" Details began to emerge that Bowie had also been a target. Killer Mark Chapman later told his girlfriend that, if he had not encountered Lennon that night outside the Beatle's apartment, he intended to kill Bowie. After a search through the killer's possessions, police found Bowie's name ringed in black on a programme for the play *The Elephant Man*, in which the singer was appearing. Chapman had bought a ticket for the following night. Bowie was asked whether he wanted to cancel the show, but he said no. He was asked whether he wanted extra security, and again he declined.

So, the evening after the murder of his friend, Bowie went back on stage. Directly in front of him were two empty seats. They had been reserved by John and Yoko. A few seats further along was one other empty seat. This one had been reserved by Chapman.

"So, the night after John was killed, there were three empty seats in the front row," said Bowie. "I can't tell you how difficult that was to go on. I almost didn't make it through that performance."

The fear of also being killed by a deranged fan led Bowie to spend less time in New York and more time at his chalet on Lake Geneva. He hired a former Navy Seal as a bodyguard and took self-defence lessons specifically designed for celebrities. Yoko and her son Sean had similar thoughts and also began spending longer in their Swiss getaway. Sean was just five years old, and Bowie, sensitive to the fact that the boy had lost his father so young and in such a brutal and public fashion, took him under his wing.

"There was nothing that didn't interest him," Bowie said of John Lennon. "He had a real appetite. 'What's that? (adopting a Liverpudlian accent). I love that! It's big, red and I want it!' A lot of us wanted to be that way."

Aretha Franklin
- - - - - - - - - - - - - - - - - - -

David Bowie was left crushed when his idol Aretha Franklin put him down in front of millions of television viewers. Days away from releasing his own soul record, *Young Americans* (1975), Bowie was chosen to present the Grammy award for best R&B singer. Looking dashing but drug-ravaged, he gave a rambling, emotional speech in which he praised John and Yoko's "language of love", and left the audience perplexed. He later admitted to having taken copious amounts of cocaine beforehand.

When he eventually declared Franklin the winner, the soul singer jumped up, grabbed the trophy and made her infamous remark about kissing David Bowie (see page 124). The comment cut him to the quick. "With not so much as a glance in my direction, she snatches the trophy out of my hands and says, 'I'm so happy, I could even kiss David Bowie,' which she didn't!" said Bowie, later. "So, I slunk off stage left." In fact, Franklin had actually gone on to say, "I mean that in a beautiful way, because we dig it."

Back at Bowie's hotel suite after the ceremony, someone mischievously put on one of the soul queen's records. Bowie jumped up and smashed it to pieces.

Nina Simone

Bowie did, however, hit it off with another soul legend.

Nina Simone was in trouble. Her career had nosedived, her protest songs had alienated key industry figures, the tax authorities were after her, the government was harassing her and the first signs of mental illness had started to emerge. Not only that, she had stopped recording and, despite having made 40-odd albums, was broke. Then, one night at a private bar in New York in 1974, someone recognized her and asked her to join him at his table. That encounter with David Bowie changed, and possibly saved, her life.

Simone was 41 at the time. Her eclectic career had spanned blues, gospel, jazz, classical and folk. She was dubbed the "High Priestess of Soul" and had been a leading voice of the civil rights movement. But those days were a long way in the past. She and Bowie talked till late, with the English singer offering a sympathetic ear. Simone went home and fell asleep, only to be woken up at 3am by a call. It was Bowie. Realizing she was at a low ebb and possibly suicidal, he told her, "The first thing I want you to know is that you're not crazy. Don't let anybody tell you you're crazy, because where you're coming from, there are very few of us out there."

Every night thereafter for the next month, according to Alan Light in the documentary film *What Happened, Miss Simone?* (2015), Bowie called the singer to reassure her that she was special and sane. One night, he turned up at her apartment in what she called a clown suit and a big black hat looking like Charlie Chaplin. "He told me that he was not a gifted singer and he knew it," Simone recalled. "He said, 'What's wrong with you is you are gifted – you have to play.'"

Simone credited her time with Bowie for not just revitalizing her love of music but also encouraging her to seek a new start in a new country, much like Bowie himself was soon to do. Within a few months, Simone, inspired by Bowie's advice, had turned her back for good on America, a place where the black revolution, she said, had been replaced by disco. She went to Liberia and eventually southern France, where she died at the age of 70.

Bowie paid what he called "my homage to Nina" by recording "Wild Is the Wind" (1976), a song she had sung in the fifties. He believed she had written the song herself and would receive some much-needed royalties. It was only when he checked the publishing details, he told his friend and Bowie historian Kevin Cann, that he realized she would not receive a penny. But the song was to have an impact on another singing icon: Sinatra was to describe the track as his favourite Bowie song.

Frank Sinatra

The friendship Bowie struck up with Frank Sinatra was one of the most unlikely relationships in music. Not just because of the age gap and musical differences, but because Sinatra had initially refused even to countenance meeting "that faggot".

In the mid-seventies, plans were under way to make a biopic about the American singer's life. Bowie's name was suggested for the lead role by no less that the singer's daughter, Nancy. With discussions underway, Bowie went to see Sinatra perform in Las Vegas, but while he was waiting backstage after the show, a minion came out to tell him that not only did Sinatra have no wish to meet him, but that "no limey faggot" was going to play the star on screen.

That would have been that, but, a year later, the two found themselves recording at the same Los Angeles studio. Sinatra's people arrived and laid down three rules: no one was to speak to the singer unless necessary; everyone was to refer to him as "Mr Sinatra"; and no one was to ask him to do a mic test. Despite the frosty orders, Sinatra bowled everyone over on arrival with his charm and sociability. Delighted to find that Cherokee Studios was run by three brothers, he spent the first hour talking with Dee, Joe and Bruce Robb about his love of families, as well as his hatred of the music business, all the while playing with their dog.

Sinatra soon found out that Bowie was recording next door. Having been initially repelled by the English singer's androgyny, the crooner was now intrigued. Both singers would sneak around corners, according to Bruce Robb, to snatch surreptitious glances of each other. "You've got this Bowie guy here in here. How is he?" Sinatra asked Robb. Bowie was even more fascinated. "Oh my

God, Sinatra's here," he told the producer. "I'd love to meet him."

When Robb suggested the two go out for dinner, Sinatra replied, "Great. Set it up." Robb arranged for them to dine at Sinatra's favourite restaurant, a small, nondescript taverna tucked away in West Hollywood that, Robb said, served the best food in the city. By the time they returned in Sinatra's limo, the two singers were chatting away on the back seat and had become fast friends.

Every day, Bowie would ask, "Is Frank in yet?" Once Sinatra arrived, he would come out of the studio and the two would chat over coffee in the large lounge, which had a 30-foot-long bar, or go out for a meal. They also sat in on each other's sessions. It was Sinatra's enthusiasm for Bowie's version of the classic "Wild Is the Wind" that ensured the song made it onto the album *Station to Station* (see page 130). Sinatra even asked Bowie to sing backing vocals on one of his records. So, somewhere on one of Sinatra's albums (Robb believes it may have been his collection of Christmas songs), buried in the chorus, is the voice of David Bowie.

Bowie was at the height of his cocaine addiction, but Robb said it was not readily apparent to the producers or Sinatra. "Everyone was high at that time but he was no more high than anyone else," said Robb. "No one had to carry him home at night. In fact, I used to find him at the end of the session tidying up all the coffee cups. I told him, 'David, you don't need to do that.' But he said, 'I like to keep the place clean.'"

Bowie had always been a fan of the 60-year-old crooner. The album notes for "Life on Mars?" state the song was "inspired by Frankie". Bowie's music publisher had given him a French hit and asked him to write English lyrics, a common practice in those days. Bowie handed in his version and the publisher called back:

"Look, Frank Sinatra wants to do it."

"That's great!"

"And he hates your lyrics."

"That's not great."

"So, we've given it to Paul Anka [the Canadian American songwriter] to do."

Anka used the melody as the basis of "My Way", but Bowie kept playing around with the chords and eventually turned it into "Life on Mars?"

By 1975, Bowie was telling journalists he wanted to be "a Frank Sinatra figure" because the American was one of the few who refused to play the music-business game. Friend and writer Rory MacLean recalled that Bowie tried to make that dream come true one night at a cabaret venue in Berlin. Acting on a whim, an incognito, dressed-down Bowie took to the small stage to perform some Sinatra songs. The crowd, unaware of his identity, were unimpressed. They asked him to step down.

Bob Dylan

- - - - - - - - - - -

Bowie's relationship with Bob Dylan also started off on the wrong foot. "I think he hates me," Bowie lamented after meeting his hero for the first time.

The young Bowie was in awe of the folk singer from early on. "Everything great about America in one album" is how he described 1963's *The Freewheelin' Bob Dylan.* "It was like this 60-year-old voice inside this young kid."

Bowie went through his own Dylan phase, writing songs with a social conscience, playing acoustic guitar on the folk circuit and perming his hair to imitate his hero's curly locks. He even wrote

"Song for Bob Dylan" (1971), which, Bowie told *Melody Maker*, outlined his own grand plan to take over Dylan's mantle. "It was at that period that I said, 'OK, if you [Dylan] don't want to do it, I will. I saw the leadership void.'" The song contains the wistful line, "I don't suppose we'll ever meet." The meeting did come to pass, but Bowie may well have wished it had not.

Bowie had gone to an after-show party after seeing his friend the singer Dana Gillespie perform in New York. Among the crowd of celebrities was Dylan. When Bowie entered the apartment, the atmosphere turned frosty. Dylan was overheard saying, "Who does this guy think he is?" and "Glam rock isn't music."

Model Winona Williams recalled Bowie buttonholing Dylan and trying to impress the folk singer by playing tracks from his upcoming album *Young Americans*. He also insisted on telling Dylan what he should be doing and where he was going wrong. But his overtures fell on deaf ears. Whatever Dylan said directly to Bowie, it so upset him that Williams felt compelled to take Bowie quietly aside to another room to console him. "He put his head on my lap, rather like a child," she said.

Bowie's recollection to Cameron Crowe was that he "talked at him for hours and hours and hours, and whether I amused him or scared him or repulsed him, I really don't know. I didn't wait for any answers." He added, "I think he hates me." He gave a similar story to the *NME*'s Michael Watts: "I had a dreadful time with Bob Dylan. Absolutely ghastly. I was fairly flipped out of my head. I didn't find him odd, that was the problem. Once, I had quite a thing about him." Seemingly unable to get over the rebuff, Bowie later said, "I think he's a prick, so I'm not that interested."

From Dylan's point of view, he was on the receiving end of a coke-fuelled harangue. It is also possible he may have harboured some resentment at being ejected from Gillespie's concert earlier that evening by Bowie's bodyguard John Bindon, a former gangster. Dylan had dated Gillespie in the mid-sixties and turned up early at the box office to say hello. Convinced the bedraggled figure in front of him was a tramp looking for a place to get warm, the bouncer barred his way. "I'm a friend of Dana's," Dylan attempted to explain. "Please tell her Bob Zimmerman would like to speak to her." "I don't care if you are Bob fucking Dylan," Bindon replied. "You can fuck off."

But the frost thawed, and both singers underwent a volte face. Incredibly, Dylan approached Bowie to produce his 1983 album, *Infidels*, because he wanted someone familiar with the latest digital technology. Although that collaboration did not happen, a photograph from 1985 shows the two of them in what appears to be a genuinely warm embrace. Bowie remained a lifelong fan. When Dylan's 1997 *Time Out of Mind* was released, Bowie was left "speechless" by its quality. "His music has such resonance that, when I first put his new album on, I thought I should just give up," Bowie said.

Outside of his lyrics, Dylan is a man of few words and, over the decades, has said next to nothing about Bowie. But in 2017 he did appear to clear up one little mystery. An interviewer asked him which was his favourite of the three best-known songs written about him (by Lennon, Bowie and Ricky Nelson, who wrote "Garden Party").

"'Garden Party'," came the gruff reply.

Then, in 2020, Dylan wrote a song called "I Contain Multitudes", its title taken from the poem "Song of Myself" by Walt Whitman. The song featured the line "all the young dudes", Dylan's first and seemingly only direct reference to Bowie (see Ian

Hunter, page 87). Perhaps Dylan thought that, alongside himself, if any artist did contain multitudes, it was Bowie.

Richard Pryor

"What's this white dude doing in my dressing room?" was comedian Richard Pryor's baffled response when a paler-than-pale Bowie appeared in the middle of a sea of black faces.

The singer had been invited by guitarist Carlos Alomar to see Pryor at the Apollo Theatre in Harlem in 1974. Bowie was not just the only white man backstage, he was the only white person in the audience. But that did not stop an unperturbed Bowie, with his orange hair and fedora, taking up his seat right at the front. After the show, Alomar took Bowie backstage. "You have to have a lot of cojones to walk into Richard Pryor's dressing room and say, 'Hi, I'm David Bowie,'" said Alomar. Despite Pryor's look of puzzlement, Bowie acted as if he were right at home. "He was fearless," said the guitarist.

Rudolf Nureyev

The after-show party was in full swing when a small group of celebrities decided to peel off and lock themselves inside the hotel suite's walk-in wardrobe. Behind the closet doors were Mick Jagger, David Bowie and entertainer Bette Midler. Giggles and strange noises could be heard by those outside who, for the most part, tried to ignore them. But one man could stand it no longer. He was ballet legend Rudolf Nureyev, one of the greatest dancers of the 20th century and a man with a renowned sexual appetite.

Striding over to the wardrobe, Nureyev banged repeatedly on the doors, demanding to be allowed to join in the fun. "I have to be in there!" he begged. What was already probably the most celebrity-packed threesome of all time almost became a mythic foursome. But as Nureyev's pleas continued, Bowie's bouncer, Mr George, who had been given orders that the inhabitants were not to be disturbed, intervened. He firmly escorted away a visibly upset and still-protesting Nureyev.

The rejection for a man possessed of a rarely denied libido must have been galling. One recent biography claimed that the dancer had affairs with three members of President Kennedy's family – two women and one man.

To add insult to injury, the party was being held in Nureyev's honour: Bowie had organized the get-together to celebrate the end of the dancer's run of New York shows.

Bette Midler

The hotel closet shenanigans became the stuff of legend. But as to what had really gone on inside, the occupants kept schtum. Angie Bowie had little doubt. "Once they all emerged, they looked terrifically stoned and seemed to have great trouble talking without sawing their molars off," she recalled.

Decades later, Bette Midler was on American TV when the interviewer asked, archly, what the three of them had "talked" about for such a long time. The answer was something of a let-down. "Ticket prices," Midler laughingly responded. "Lighting people, uh, booking...a business conversation." The singer went on, appearing to be entirely serious, to praise the two rock stars for giving her a new insight into the financial side of music.

Bowie was certainly taken by the brash Midler and even, reportedly, wrote a disco song for her called "Do the Ruby". The two were often bracketed together, being described in the papers as "mascara rock" – sex and theatre taken to the extremes. The similarities led Midler to become somewhat paranoid. "I had a nightmare that David Bowie opened up across the street from me and he had the same sets and he was wearing my costumes," she once said.

Ronnie Spector

"One look at the guy and I could see how excited he was to see me," recalled Ronnie Spector on finding a naked Bowie waiting for her in his bedroom.

The evening had begun with the Ronettes singer receiving a call from John Lennon's ex-girlfriend May Pang. "David is having a concert and wants you to come," she was told. "David who?" replied Spector.

After the show, Spector received an invitation to go back to Bowie's hotel suite. When she arrived, she found a room teeming with people and a coffee table covered in cocaine. Someone escorted her to a bedroom door. After knocking, she went in to find Bowie sitting on the floor naked, surrounded by cassettes. It was abundantly clear, said Spector in her autobiography, *Be My Baby*, that he was ready for a romantic encounter.

"Sure enough, we made love right there on the floor," she said. "We didn't even bother to kick the cassettes out of the way."

Bowie later took Spector home. They were having sex again in her bedroom when they were interrupted by a noise from the kitchen.

"It's my mom," whispered Spector.

"Your mother?!" Bowie replied incredulously. "Oh, Ronnie, that's so quaint."

David Cassidy

David Bowie implausibly once offered to write an album for wholesome teenage heartthrob David Cassidy. Even more implausibly, Cassidy rejected the songs as too boring.

Bowie had invited the clean-cut singer to his Manhattan hotel suite during his 1974 *Diamond Dogs* tour with an offer to give the Donny Osmond rival a "more adult" image. Cassidy, a fan of Ziggy Stardust, was intrigued enough to fly to New York for a meeting. On arrival at Bowie's hotel suite, he was greeted by an avant-garde carnival of transsexuals and transvestites. While Cassidy sat uncomfortably on the sofa, one of the passing troupe injected himself with a breast-growth hormone and another practised a mime routine.

Bowie ushered the singer into his room and played a couple of songs he had written for the project. Cassidy was unimpressed. One was called "I'm All Grown Up Now". "Too obvious, I thought," recalled Cassidy in his autobiography, *C'mon, Get Happy*. Getting desperate, Bowie suggested Lou Reed could also contribute, but again Cassidy rejected the offer. "I just didn't think the songs were interesting enough," said the singer, whose most challenging statement until then had been "The Puppy Song".

Cassidy's lasting memory was of a man obsessed by fame. "He really craved all of the mass adulation that I'd had enough of. Been there. Done it. Thanks."

Christopher Lee

Another implausible collaboration involved the man known to generations of moviegoers as Count Dracula. When he reached his eighties, Christopher Lee decided to make a radical career change to become perhaps the world's oldest heavy metal singer. But his chance to enter the world of rock had come several decades earlier.

In the mid-seventies, Lee received a call out of the blue from David Bowie's office to see if the actor would like to join him in a duet. Although Lee had been an opera singer in his youth, the Hammer Horror star was as surprised as anyone. "He must have heard something or knew I could sing," said Lee. It is possible that Bowie heard Lee on the soundtrack to *The Wicker Man*, one of the singer's favourite films. Sadly, the duet, which surely would have rivalled "Bing and Bowie" in the surreal stakes, never came to pass. "We couldn't find a song that we could both sing, we just couldn't find it," lamented the actor. Not that it dented Lee's musical aspirations; he released his fourth and final metal album at the age of 92.

A mystery Hollywood star

Liz Taylor once told the story of an ageing movie siren who had become besotted with Bowie after spotting a photograph of the flame-haired singer on Taylor's mantelpiece. "I want to meet him," she said. "Can you arrange it?"

Taylor agreed to hold a party but explained that it would have to wait, as Bowie was on tour. In the intervening months, according to Taylor, her friend prepared for the encounter by taking up a new exercise regime, undergoing some "nips and tucks" and getting a new hairdo. When the night arrived, Taylor said, the transformed actress confidently approached Bowie with the words, "I've gone to a lot of trouble to meet you tonight, David."

"You shouldn't have, dear," replied Bowie. "I only like black women and Asian men." The actress was left speechless.

According to a biography by Wendy Leigh, that actress may have been the Oscar-winning Loretta Young, almost as famous for her off-screen romances with Spencer Tracy, Jimmy Stewart and Clark Gable as for her on-screen performances. But Young's family have dismissed the idea as "laughable and a complete fabrication".

"I can assure you she had no designs on David Bowie," said Young's daughter-in-law, Linda Lewis. "She was not close to Elizabeth Taylor, although they knew one another. She would never have suggested meeting him. She was not a fan of rock music or rock stars. No doubt some older star might have wanted to seduce him, but it wasn't Loretta." Perhaps, suggested Lewis, the movie star in question might have been another ageing siren at the party, of which there was at least one.

Raquel Welch

Hollywood star Raquel Welch was looking for a new career move after becoming fed up with directors demanding she remove her clothes for ever-present, if redundant, shower scenes. The actress, who was regularly voted the sexiest woman in the world, decided to make a volte-face and become a cabaret singer. The person she turned to for career advice was David Bowie

Her appearance in *One Million Years B.C.* in 1966, clad only in a deer-skin bikini, had made her the world's top sex symbol.

But eight years on and fed up of being stereotyped, she arranged a meeting with Bowie and his manager, Tony Defries. Waiting to meet the singer backstage after a concert in Los Angeles in 1974, she told Angie Bowie, "You look nothing like your photos." Angie, uncertain whether this meant she was uglier in photographs or real life, took offence and stormed off. Then out came Bowie's PA, Corinne Schwab, to say, "Miss Welch, Mr Bowie will see you now." She was given 15 minutes, the bulk of which was taken up by Defries, who outlined an unusual plan for success. He suggested a convoluted money-making scheme whereby Welch would become a spokesperson for cancer research and so get funding for her cabaret act from the health industry. The actress, it seemed, was none too impressed. She rejected the offer.

Michael Jackson

Also present at one of Bowie's LA concerts was Michael Jackson, famous not just for his music but also for his dance moves, especially his trademark "moonwalk". The person he nabbed the move from was, incredibly, none other than David Bowie.

The young Jackson was a big Bowie fan, so when the English singer performed in Los Angeles in 1974, the 16-year-old went to see him, along with his parents, the rest of the Jackson 5 and Diana Ross. After the show, the Jackson family invited Bowie back for dinner, where the teenager grilled him about the revolutionary moving stage sets, the songs and, most of all, the choreography. One move he was obsessed by was something Bowie called "the backwards slide". "It didn't have a name at the time," said Bowie. "Toni [Basil] had devised it with her dance troupe and taught it to me for the *Diamond Dogs* show. It's entirely possible he copped the walk fourth-hand, so to speak." It was almost a decade later, with "Billie Jean" (1983), that Jackson was first seen performing his renamed moonwalk. The move had been revamped and become far more impressive, but the concept was the same.

"Jackson was fascinated by Bowie," confirmed Bowie historian Kevin Cann. "He went to every one of David's shows in Los Angeles. He was fascinated by his movements. Bowie wasn't a natural dancer but he had his own way of doing things." As for Bowie's memories of the taciturn Jackson, he said, "You don't get much feedback. He's not the sort of guy who sits down for a good old chat."

Jackson returned the gift to Bowie a year later at a party in California in honour of singer Al Green. A reporter for *Rock and Roll Songs* spotted this unforgettable scene: "As the guests enjoyed the cake and the champagne, both Green and Michael Jackson were seen on the dance floor teaching rock superstar David Bowie how to do 'the robot' with members of the Soul Train gang joining in. It was a truly star-studded affair that will be long remembered by all."

Luther Vandross

In 1974, Luther Vandross was a million miles away from becoming a soul legend. He was living at home with his mother and writing jingles for Kentucky Fried Chicken and Juicy Fruit chewing gum. But then the 23-year-old got a call from a bored childhood friend who wanted some company while recording nearby in Sigma Sound Studios, Philadelphia.

Vandross sat quietly at the back of the studio listening to his pal Carlos Alomar play guitar. Inspired, he started to sing, "Young

American, young American, he was a young American", before adding, with a little flourish, "All right!" Unbeknown to Vandross, Bowie had come back and overheard the ad-libbing.

"That's a great idea, put that down," Bowie said, promptly ushering the jingle writer into the studio.

Bowie was so impressed, he not only used Vandross for the whole album, he made him his opening act and recorded one of his songs, "Funky Music", which Bowie renamed "Fascination".

"Would you mind if I tweaked some of the lyrics?" Bowie asked politely.

"Of course not," replied Vandross. "You are David Bowie. I live with my mother."

Bruce Springsteen

At this time, Bowie was at his alien best: high on cocaine, skeletally thin and obsessed by UFOs. Bruce Springsteen, on the other hand, was at his most down-to-earth; an earnest rocker in jeans and leathers who travelled by Greyhound bus. That's how the young American arrived late one night at Sigma Studios when Bowie was recording there. The English singer was infatuated by the urban poet and wanted the two of them to record together.

Bowie had been an early convert to the New Jersey man. So early, in fact, that there were just eight people in the audience when he first saw Springsteen play. The time was early 1973, and the venue was a small upstairs hang-out in New York. Bowie excitedly told his companion, model-turned-musician Bebe Buell, about a new singer he was keen to see. But his initial impression was disappointment. Springsteen came out on his own and ran through a number of songs acoustically.

"I hated him as a solo," Bowie told Scott Isler of *Musician* magazine. He was on the verge of walking out when Springsteen's band came on. "It was like a different person," he said. "He was marvellous." Bowie kept leaning over to Buell, raving, "Can you believe his lyrics?!" *Greetings from Asbury Park, N.J.* rarely left Bowie's turntable afterwards. He even became the first artist to record a Springsteen song, with a version of "Growing Up".

A year later, Bowie was recording in Philadelphia when producer Tony Visconti heard on the radio that Springsteen was in town. Visconti got an invite through to the peripatetic singer via local DJ Ed Sciaky, with the hope that the New Jersey man would contribute to Bowie's cover of "It's Hard to Be a Saint in the City" ("After I heard this track, I never rode the subway again," Bowie later said of the song). But when Springsteen arrived, Bowie appeared to unnerve him.

"I was out of my wig, I just couldn't relate to him at all," Bowie told Isler. "It was a bad time for us to have met. I could see he was thinking, 'Who is this weird guy?' And I was thinking, 'What do I say to normal people?' There was a real impasse."

Writing the sleeve notes to a Springsteen album years later, Bowie said, "He was very shy. I remember sitting in the corridor with him, talking about his lifestyle, which was very Dylanesque – you know, moving from town to town with a guitar on his back, all that kind of thing. Anyway, he didn't like what we were doing, I remember that. At least, he didn't express much enthusiasm. I guess he must have thought it was all kind of odd. I was in another universe at the time. I've got this extraordinarily strange photograph of us all – I look like I'm made out of wax."

Visconti said, "David was quite taken by meeting Bruce. We played "Saint" to him and he kept a poker face the whole time.

He said nothing when it was finished." A despondent Bowie quietly shelved the version. Within the year, the breakthrough album *Born to Run* (1975) was out, and any likelihood that Bowie would release a Springsteen cover evaporated; it was one thing to champion unknown artists, another to appear to be jumping on a bandwagon.

The relationship was not all awkward. A fan hanging out in the Philadelphia studio at the time asked Bowie if there were any American artists, apart from Springsteen, whose songs he would like to cover. Bowie thought for a while and then replied, "None," which elicited a grin from his American counterpart.

The singers also shared amusing and harrowing stories of stage jumpers. Springsteen recounted a time when a large, sweaty man leapt up and gave him a bear hug, resulting in him receiving a "tremendous" electric shock. "I'm in agony and he doesn't even feel a thing!" said the singer. Bowie then mentioned the time a fan jumped onto the stage with a drug-crazed look in his eyes. Terrified, Bowie could only think to smile, which seemed to calm the man down. "Then I looked closer and saw he was holding a brick in his hand."

When Springsteen took off around 5am, the air seemed to have cleared and the two promised to meet again. Just how "out there" Bowie was at the time was recorded by local journalist Mike McGrath, who stayed behind after Springsteen left. He recalled Bowie asking if anyone had heard the reports of an alien spacecraft crashing in Akron, Ohio, leaving behind alien bodies that were "three feet tall, Caucasian, with some organic stuff: cocks and lungs and such, but different, bigger brains". When everyone confessed that they had not, Bowie said it was because of a government cover-up.

In later years, the two seemed to have been on a more similar wavelength. When Bowie died, Springsteen paid tribute in concert to "my good friend". "Not many people know," he told the audience, "but he supported our music way, way, way back at the very, very beginning. He rang me up and I visited him down in Philly. He covered some of my music. I took the Greyhound bus...that's how early it was. Anyway, we're thinking of him." Springsteen's E Street Band then launched into Bowie's ultimate rocker, "Rebel Rebel".

Gia Carangi

Bowie's hardcore Philly fans called themselves "The Sigma Kids" after the city's Sigma Sound Studios. Their leader was a girl who would soon be described as the world's first supermodel.

Gia Carangi was destined for a stellar career in fashion. Angelina Jolie would be chosen to play her in a film about her tragic life called *Gia* (1998). But in the early seventies she was just another young, rebellious Bowie obsessive. In fact, she was so obsessed, she became one of the leaders of a bunch of groupies who hung out outside the studios in Philadelphia in the hope of spotting Bowie. When it came to acts of devotion, the youngsters would try to outdo each other. Carangi usually won. At one gig, she hurdled over the barrier and jumped onto the bonnet of Bowie's moving limo, her face pressed against the windscreen. Bowie was seen to slink ever deeper into the back seat and, with the driver refusing to stop, Carangi was eventually forced to roll off. Uninjured but elated, the groupie moved on to Bowie's hotel, where she struck gold. Spotting Bowie in the elevator, she squeezed inside as the doors closed. Alone with her idol, she froze, unable to do anything more than stare at him. Bowie, perhaps recognizing his stalker, backed away "like a frightened animal", she said, and closed his eyes. Sensing her moment was about to pass, Carangi reached out and touched his arm as the elevator doors opened. "It feels really nice…he is the most beautiful person," she wrote to a friend. As he left, Bowie politely shook her hand.

Two years later, Carangi was on the catwalk. Four years later, her career was all but over. Often talked about as the model who invented "heroin chic", she appeared in one infamous magazine photograph with what appeared to be needle marks on her arm. Carangi was to die at the age of 26, one of the first female public figures to succumb to AIDS.

Cher

"Glorious", "cheesy" and "all-over-the-place". Those reviews were perhaps not what Bowie had hoped for when he went on a prime-time television show to promote *Young Americans*. But his marathon song-and-dance medley with Cher was to prove one of his most surreal appearances on TV.

The American singer was so desperate to give her image some rock chic, she agreed to pay her guest double the normal rate just to get him on. Bowie was at the height of his American cool, with "Fame" having hit number one, but his coolness was just about to fly out the window. Here, Bowie not only sings Neil Diamond's "Song Sung Blue", he dances along to it, too. The pair rattle through another 12 songs, from doo-wop to ballads, Bing to the Beatles. When some flamenco is thrown in, Bowie comically launches into a Mexican accent and shouts, "Beware the llamas." Cher, seemingly oblivious to his send-up, doggedly carries on.

Bowie performing with Cher on her TV show in 1975.

"Cher was ecstatic doing a number with someone relevant, hip and her own age," said journalist Lisa Robinson. Cher's producer, George Schlatter, agreed. "Cher was never happier than when she had legitimate rock stars on. They were what she wanted to be," he said. But Bowie remembered her as "cold and distant" and was unnerved by her eyes which, he said, "looked right through you". He later put her reserve down to his own "strange, emaciated and drugged-out" appearance.

Norman Rockwell

Bowie needed a cover for *Young Americans*. At first glance, Norman Rockwell might not appear to be David Bowie's artist of choice; his illustrations for Boy Scouts publications and calendars led "serious" critics to dismiss him as sweet and nostalgic. But Bowie loved his craftsmanship and quintessential American-ness. So much so that in 1975 he phoned the 80-year-old painter at home to ask him to do the album's artwork.

"His wife answered and I said, 'Hello, this is David Bowie,' and so on," recalled the singer. "She said in this quavering, elderly voice, 'I'm sorry, but Norman needs at least six months for portraits.' So, I had to pass, but I thought the experience was lovely. Too bad I don't have the same painstaking passion."

Kenneth Anger

In 1975, Bowie was in a very strange place indeed. He believed that witches were stealing his semen to make a "devil baby", that his swimming pool was possessed, that dead bodies were falling from the sky and that fellow rock stars were putting curses on him. Much, of course, was down to his growing cocaine psychosis. But Bowie himself blamed what he later called "his wayward spiritual search" on an encounter with one man.

"Controversial" does not do justice to cult filmmaker and occultist Kenneth Anger. His often-banned films featured bondage, gang rape and an obsession with the Devil. A committed follower of occultist Aleister Crowley, Anger had the word "Lucifer" tattooed onto his chest. One of his protégés was to join Charles Manson's sect and would eventually be convicted of murder.

The meeting in the director's New York apartment was brief and unnerving. Bowie's girlfriend Ava Cherry told Paul Trynka in his Bowie biography *Starman* that the couple could manage only 20 minutes in Anger's disturbing company before having to leave. The conversation was so repellent, she said, that she subsequently "blotted it out". But it was this meeting, she believed, that triggered something dark in Bowie. "David started getting more and more manic depressive," she said. "He saw ghosts wherever he looked."

By the end of the year, Bowie was drawing "protective" pentangles on curtains and asking a white witch to exorcise his pool. But the fascination with Anger continued. Rock writer Lisa Robinson recalled the Led Zeppelin guitarist Jimmy Page, a Crowley acolyte, and Bowie watching the same 15-minute Anger film over and over again, with a mound of cocaine in front of them. Eventually, Bowie was to flee America and flee, literally in his mind, his demons.

Jimmy Page

Satanic rumours swirled around Led Zeppelin in their heyday. Were they in league with Lucifer? Had they sold their souls to Satan? Did their albums contain incantations to the Devil if you played them backwards? It wasn't only gullible fans and America's Bible Belt who believed such things. David Bowie became so concerned about Jimmy Page's occult powers that he once felt compelled to exorcise his house after a visit from the guitarist.

The two met by chance in 1965, when Bowie was recording his first self-penned song, the less than subtly titled "Take My Tip". To give the single some gloss, the producer called up an in-demand guitarist-for-hire. Nineteen-year-old Bowie recalled seeing "the youngest session musician in the world" walk through the door. Already experimenting with new sounds, Page proudly showed Bowie a new musical device he had just received from America. The subsequent recording is believed to be the first time a fuzzbox was used on a UK record. Page complimented the band on their A-side, "I Pity the Fool", but added, "I don't think it's a hit." He was right: it sold 500 copies.

Before leaving, Page gave Bowie a gift – a riff he had been playing while warming up, and which Bowie described as "wonderful". "He was quite generous that day," Bowie told Mary Anne Hobbs on BBC radio in 1997. "He said, 'Look, I'm not using it for anything so why don't you learn it and see if you can do anything with it.' So, I had his riff and I've used it ever since!"

But the innocence of that early meeting was in stark contrast to the next time their paths crossed. Both were now superstars, both were into drugs and alcohol, and both were obsessed by the occult. Bowie had always been interested in mysticism but, come the mid-seventies, he began to become aware of its darker side. One reason was Page himself.

The guitarist was the rock world's leading expert on Aleister Crowley, a controversial and sinister occultist whose "Do what thou will" mantra was the harbinger of a liberated world to his supporters. To his opponents, including the British press, he was a Satanist and "the wickedest man in the world". Angie Bowie believed that it was to keep up with Page that David immersed himself in this new world of "Magick". Bowie, she said, found Led Zeppelin "unusually fascinating...in an awful way".

One night Page went round to Bowie's townhouse in New York. As soon as Page walked through the door, Bowie was immediately on edge, believing he sensed something unnerving about the guitarist's "aura". "Whenever the power of his aura was mentioned, Page stayed silent but smiled inscrutably," said Tony Zanetta. "It seemed that he did believe he had the power to control the universe." Bowie, who had heard that Page possessed psychic powers and was allegedly able to influence people though the power of thought, became agitated by the gnomic responses. "There was a battle of wits to prove who was the stronger," said Ava Cherry, Bowie's girlfriend at the time. "I watched their eye contact. It was very weird."

Then came a trivial domestic incident. Page accidentally spilled some wine on a silk cushion. When Bowie returned from the kitchen and saw the stain, he had a tantrum and blamed Cherry, who burst into tears and pleaded her innocence. All the while, Page remained silent. Bowie eventually realized his girlfriend was telling the truth and then vented his anger on the guitarist for allowing someone else to take the blame. "I'd like you to leave," Bowie said. When Page continued to sit there, seemingly unflappable, Bowie snapped. "Why don't you leave by the window?" he shouted. Realizing Bowie was serious, Page walked out and slammed the door behind him. Afterwards, Bowie insisted on getting the house exorcised, fearing he had been cursed. "He believed Jimmy was in league with Lucifer, and was out to get him," wrote Angie.

In his desperation to protect himself against paranormal malevolence, Bowie became obsessed with the book *Psychic Self-Defence* by the British occultist Dion Fortune. His state of mind also played a role in his escape to Los Angeles, but the paranoia only got worse. One journalist described his shock at seeing Bowie's floors and curtains daubed with magic symbols designed to ward off spiritual attacks. Bowie believed that there was a group of women trying to get impregnated by him in order to offer up the baby to the Devil. He reportedly stored his toenails and urine in the fridge, worried that they could be stolen and used to put a curse on him. Bowie even came to believe his swimming pool was possessed. Unable to separate his drug-induced fears from reality, and believing the drugs or the demons would kill him, Bowie fled to Berlin. Unwittingly, Page had played a part in Bowie's next resurrection.

Robert Plant

Bowie talked Magick with Jimmy Page, smoked his first joint with John Paul Jones and, later, would store John Bonham's much-loved sausages for him. But when he needed help, he turned to Led Zeppelin's singer, Robert Plant.

DJ Bob Harris remembered hanging out with the band one night in the mid-seventies at their home-from-home, the Regency Hyatt in Los Angeles. "I remember at 1am Robert got a call from David Bowie, who was somewhere else in town," recalled Harris in his autobiography, *Still Whispering After All These Years*. "David had some kind of problem and he'd called Robert to help him out. From one moment to the next, the mood tipped and became serious." Plant, who was widely seen as the most approachable and caring member of the band, told Harris as he left the party, "I have got to go and do stuff."

"God knows what problem David had got," added Harris. Given this was the mid-seventies, it is highly likely Bowie's plea for help was linked to his drug-induced paranoia and hallucinations.

Glenn Hughes

If Bowie's friendship with heavy rockers Led Zeppelin seems highly improbable, his best-mates relationship with Deep Purple seems downright incomprehensible. But the band's long-haired, denim-clad bassist, Glenn Hughes, was to become not just Bowie's closest friend in the summer of 1974, but his number-one drug buddy.

Hughes was at a party in an LA hotel with Keith Moon, Ronnie Wood, Harry Nilsson, Iggy Pop and Alice Cooper, when in walked Angie Bowie. Her husband had just seen a Deep Purple concert on television and wanted to meet Hughes. He was led upstairs to a darkened room, where the two men spent hours talking about music. Bowie was surprised to discover that Hughes was a "soul boy" at heart, who had somehow ended up in heavy metal.

Their close relationship over the subsequent months, during which Bowie lived with Hughes, meant the Deep Purple man became perhaps the person best able to document first-hand Bowie's descent into drug psychosis. One night, Bowie claimed that the swimming pool was possessed and had begun to bubble and foam. Hughes, himself high on coke, went out and claimed the pool was, indeed, "bubbling like a Jacuzzi". Bowie was so terrified that he asked his bassist friend to jump in to eject the evil spirit.

Hughes said he and Bowie would stay up three or four nights straight without sleep, while getting ever more paranoid. "I never saw David sleep. Ever," he said. One time, Hughes recalled, Bowie had taken so much cocaine that blood began to pour from his eye (cocaine is known to constrict blood vessels and can cause a subconjunctival haemorrhage.)

Bowie later said of this period with Hughes: "I was hallucinating 24 hours a day. I felt like I'd fallen through the bowels of the Earth." When Bowie moved to Berlin to break away from a drug culture that came close to killing him, he cut ties with almost everyone from that period. They went from being inseparable, as Hughes recalled, to having no relationship at all.

Peter Sellers

"Beware of dark stains at the bottom of swimming pools." That strangely specific warning was issued by Peter Sellers to Bowie one night at the comic actor's 50th birthday party celebrations at his Los Angeles home. Sellers had invited a host of rock star friends, some of whom formed an impromptu band. This being Hollywood, the band comprised Keith Moon, Ronnie Wood, Bill Wyman, Joe Cocker and David Bowie. "They don't have parties like that anymore," said photographer Terry O'Neill, who caught the moment on camera. "It was a one-off moment in rock and roll history."

According to biographer Hugo Wilcken in *David Bowie's Low*, during the evening Sellers and Bowie spoke about their shared fascination with the occult. The *Pink Panther* actor was so superstitious that he refused to wear green or act with anyone in that colour, and would consult Maurice Woodruff, an English clairvoyant and astrologer, before accepting any roles. Whether Sellers was joking or not about the dark stains, Bowie took the warning seriously and became so convinced his LA pool was possessed that he called a "white witch" to have it exorcised.

Sly Stone

Bowie's paranoia was a side-effect of the cocaine. His consumption had become so large that he would regularly find himself at the homes of various drug dealers in LA. During one such episode, he encountered Sly Stone.

Stone was the seventies' Prince, a multitalented musician who had a hand in the birth of soul, funk, rock, psychedelia and slap bass. He also took drugs – so many that he was rarely seen without a violin case that was allegedly packed full of the stuff. Given both his and Bowie's exorbitant cocaine habits, it is perhaps no surprise where they bumped into each other.

Bowie was going through a bizarrely normal-looking phase, wearing traditional jackets and slacks from the all-purpose Sears, Roebuck department store. So when Stone walked into the drug den, he immediately noticed "the straight" in the corner and issued the classic user's put-down: "Huh, bet he takes a lot of drugs." Bowie was deeply offended. "How dare you!" he recalled thinking. "I'm David Bowie! I do more drugs than you've fucking looked at." In reality, the singer kept quiet, bought his drugs and left.

The two musicians did meet years later, and Stone laughed when Bowie told him about the encounter. Bowie eventually managed to kick his habit. The funk singer appeared to find the struggle harder, with reports emerging of him living alone in a beat-up caravan well into his seventies.

Ozzy Osbourne

Cocaine was not the only thing Bowie was addicted to. You might imagine that when he met Ozzy Osbourne at the height of the Black Sabbath singer's notorious mid-seventies excess, it would be at an orgiastic party in front of a mountain of illicit substances. In fact, it was at an Alcoholics Anonymous meeting.

The two were regulars at the same AA get-together in Los Angeles and would sit among the less fêted addicts of the city, according to Osbourne, listening to their stories and occasionally talking about their own struggles or relapses. "The good thing about going to AA is, it's the only chance in LA you get to see fellow musicians," Moby, another Bowie friend, once said.

Bowie went on to successfully quit the booze. When he was asked by *Newsnight*'s Jeremy Paxman in 1999 if he considered having an occasional glass of wine, the singer replied, "No, I'm an alcoholic. It would kill me. I was very lucky to find my way out of that." Osborne was also to go teetotal but not till long after a legendary moment in 1979 when his own band fired him for being too drunk.

Slash

Imagine returning home from school not only to find David Bowie sitting on your sofa, but also to be told that he is your mum's new boyfriend. "It was like watching an alien land in your backyard," recalled Slash. Despite his otherworldly appearance, Bowie behaved just like a dad, babysitting the eight-year-old when his mother was working late, and reading the boy bedtime stories.

"I used to put him to bed at night, little Slash," recalled an amused Bowie. "Who'd have guessed?"

Bowie had met Slash's mother, fashion and costume designer Ola Hudson, during filming for *The Man Who Fell to Earth* (1976). He so loved her costumes that he hired her as his designer, and she went on to help create his Thin White Duke look of black pants and waistcoat. While the couple's life seemed normal to young Slash, he did recall looking on as Bowie and his mum meditated in the bedroom, where they had built a makeshift shrine. The singer would also take the eight-year-old on trips around Los Angeles, once driving him to the local psychiatric hospital to see a patient there by the name of Iggy Pop.

Bowie's relationship with Hudson survived his most tumultuous and drug-ridden period, and the couple stayed friends. So, when the Guns N' Roses guitarist became a rock legend himself, and also got addicted to drugs, it was clear whom to turn to: the father figure who had been through it all before. Bowie was only too pleased to help. He listened quietly as Slash poured out his heart, but when the guitarist mentioned that his "translucent friends" were hovering around the room as they spoke, Bowie felt compelled to interject.

"When you start hallucinating," Bowie told him, "that's when you are at your lowest point. You are exposing yourself to the darker realms of your subconscious."

Bowie stopped short of telling Slash to quit, but the guitarist said that, of all the advice he was given, it was Bowie's that hit home the hardest.

Nicolas Roeg

First, Bowie looked like an alien. Then, he became one. In what seems the most obvious casting choice in movie history, British director Nicolas Roeg picked him for *The Man Who Fell to Earth*. Bowie's cadaverous appearance, odd-coloured eyes and orange-flecked hair combined with his "curiously artificial voice", which seemed to belong to no class or place, transfixed the director. When Roeg saw the spaced-out singer on Alan Yentob's BBC documentary *Cracked Actor* (1975), he knew he had found his spaceman.

The maker of *Walkabout* and *Don't Look Now* arranged a meeting at Bowie's New York hotel. Bowie turned up at four the next morning, eight hours late. Roeg was still patiently waiting. The director outlined the idea of a lonely extra-terrestrial lost on Earth who was trying to get home. He told Bowie it would be filmed in New Mexico. "I'll be there," Bowie said. Given the size and budget of the film, Roeg pushed for more assurances but Bowie simply repeated, "I'll be there."

The film cemented Bowie's image as an otherworldly being and convinced many that he could act. The film had one other major impact. Bowie was keen to do the soundtrack and began composing a score on set. But his music was never used. Some argue it was never finished to a proper standard. Bowie himself was annoyed at being told to pitch his music alongside two other composers to see whose work was best. Either way, some of the music ended up on his next album. Six months after filming had ended, Roeg got an advance copy of *Low* through the post with an "I-told-you-so" note saying, "This is what I wanted to do for the soundtrack." "It would have been a wonderful score," admitted the director.

Bowie and Nicolas Roeg take a break from filming in New Mexico, 1975.

Christopher Isherwood

No Isherwood, no Bowie in Berlin. Christopher Isherwood's novellas and play depicting the "divinely decadent" city in the early 1930s, which inspired the Broadway musical and film *Cabaret* (1971), were a prime reason Bowie decamped there. He was entranced by the writer's depiction of debauchery and danger, sexual ambiguity and swagger, all set against the rise of Nazism, another Bowie obsession (at one point he acquired Joseph Goebbels's desk).

In 1976, Bowie invited Isherwood to an after-show party in Los Angeles. The singer promptly ignored his other guests and bombarded the 70-year-old Santa Monica resident with questions about Berlin. Isherwood soon tired of the incessant quizzing and ended up trying to discourage the singer by describing the city as "rather boring".

"Young Bowie," he said, patronizingly, "people forget that I'm a very good fiction writer."

The dismissive remark failed to dampen the ardour of Bowie, who sought out Isherwood's Berlin by choosing to live within walking distance of the writer's old apartment on Hauptstraße in Schöneberg. By then, Bowie had already adopted a slicked-back, black-and-white-suited look that recalled none other than *Cabaret*'s master of ceremonies, Herr Issyvoo.

BERLIN & SWITZERLAND
1977–81

Bowie feared that, if he stayed in America, the drugs would kill him but that, if he moved to England, the press would hound him to death. He chose West Berlin. Berlin's Nazi past, bohemian heritage and music fascinated him, but so did the promise of anonymity, something he delighted in referencing with his "*Low-profile*" album. He also got a house in Switzerland. The reason for that was much simpler: tax.

He encountered the German musicians who were quietly rewriting the rules of music, from Kraftwerk and Tangerine Dream to Neu! and Conny Plank. He attempted to work with Fassbinder, Herzog and Wenders, the three great directors of New German Cinema. And he agreed to act in a dreadful movie just to meet Germany's most legendary actress of all, Marlene Dietrich. He was to find her acting, literally, wooden.

As punk emerged, Bowie was already leaping ahead into German electronica. But he still met the stars of that angry genre, often with explosive results; his minder had Johnny Rotten kicked out of a concert, and he came close to getting beaten up while hanging out with New York Dolls. Ahead of the curve as always, he then became friends with the new faces of the New Wave.

Going to the relative backwoods of Berlin meant Bowie became the first rock star to disappear off the radar at the height of his fame. The last prominent artist to make such a dramatic move was, perhaps, Paul Gauguin, when he went to Tahiti. Yet, Bowie's decision to remove himself from the limelight kept him two steps ahead of everyone else. He became, almost impossibly, even cooler.

Kraftwerk

- - - - - - - - - - - -

Kraftwerk not only gave Bowie a new lease of musical life, they arguably saved his life, too. Bowie had overdosed several times while living in Los Angeles. In order to survive, he knew he needed to leave. When he heard "the sound of the future", he knew where to go.

Bowie was an early convert to what he called Kraftwerk's "folk music of the factories", and played "Autobahn" non-stop while driving on the endless freeways of Los Angeles in 1975. While he loved the music, it was the totality of the band's concept that captivated him. Like many German musicians, Kraftwerk were so horrified by the country's recent history that they believed a ground-zero approach was required to avoid the mistakes of the past. This would involve a new sound by new machines to convey a new message for new arenas via a new anti-image. Not since Bowie himself had someone wrapped up the whole business of music into one complete package.

"I just thought, 'Wow, I've seen the future and it sounds like this,'" he told journalist Paul Du Noyer. "And I just wanted to be in the swim, very much."

Bowie's love of Kraftwerk was most visibly on show one particular night in Paris in 1977. Iggy Pop, cabaret singer Romy Haag and friends were celebrating Bowie's 30th birthday at a private nightclub when in walked the band's two principal members, Ralf Hütter and Florian Schneider, their 1930s suits topped off with their trademark blank faces and investment-banker haircuts. Compared to the outrageous company on display, the two weirdly straight Germans were the most outlandish of all. With a mixture of admiration and affection, the crowd began spontaneously to applaud the German musicians, and then gave them a standing ovation that lasted five minutes. A transfixed Bowie kept turning to Iggy to say, "Just look at them! Just look at them!"

Bowie loved their deadpan humour. Friends remember him laughing while listening to their records. One encounter Bowie was fond of recounting was when he told Schneider that his rare, second-hand Mercedes had come onto the market only because its owner, an Iranian prince, had been assassinated. "*Ja*," Schneider nodded sagely, "car always lasts longer."

Bowie asked Kraftwerk to join his *Station to Station* tour but they declined. Bowie only had himself to blame. He had confided to Hütter that he had refused to be a support act even early on, so that people would only associate him with being top of the bill. Hütter was so taken by the idea, he rejected Bowie's offer to play second fiddle.

Band member Wolfgang Flür recalled Bowie as being keen to record with Kraftwerk. "He was so fanatical about it, wanting to do a record with us," he said. "He wanted to produce his next album with Kraftwerk. We loved him, and he loved us." It was a view echoed by Karl Bartos: "We all worshipped Iggy Pop and David Bowie." Writer Simon Reynolds believes that one reason Bowie was so fascinated by the Germans was that their own "anti-image" image offered Bowie a way out of the mirrored maze of his own stardom.

Although they did not record together, Bowie and the band did embark on a musical conversation at a distance. *Station to Station* begins with the sound of a train embarking on a journey, a homage to the car revving into life at the start of "Autobahn". Kraftwerk responded with their own train song, "Trans-Europe

Express", which mentions Bowie and Pop. Bowie replied with another namecheck in "V-2 Schneider", before recording *Low*, his most Kraftwerk/Krautrock-influenced album.

Neu!

While the Krautrock plaudits went to Kraftwerk, it was another German band that had the most profound influence on Bowie. But a plan to collaborate with Neu! was sabotaged.

The Düsseldorf band's relentlessly unchanging motorik (4/4) rhythms influenced heavy metal, punk and techno, and their ambient sounds influenced almost everyone else. As Brian Eno memorably said, "There were three great beats in the seventies: Afrobeat, James Brown's funk and Neu!"

"That Neu! sound is fantastic," said Bowie. "I was completely seduced by the setting of the aggressive guitar drone against the almost-but-not-quite robotic machine drumming." So, when it came to recording his first Berlin album, Bowie's first choice was Neu! guitarist Michael Rother. "I called Michael and asked whether he would be interested in working with myself and Brian Eno on my new album, entitled *Low*," said Bowie. "Although enthusiastic, he had to decline, and to this day I wonder how that trilogy would have been affected by his input."

Rother had, initially, accepted Bowie's offer. He had packed his bags and was preparing to head to the airport, when he received another call, this time from someone who claimed to work for Bowie. "They called to tell me, 'We don't need you anymore.' I was surprised, but this was pre-mobile phone or email, and I just thought, 'That's strange, well okay.'" Rother unpacked his bags and stayed home.

It was only 15 years later, when they two men got back in contact by chance and compared notes, that they realized they had both been duped. To this day, no one knows who made that call. But as to why someone would want to sabotage the collaboration, Rother had an idea: "You know the story of his Berlin albums at the time – they were not popular. It made sense for some people in his environment to think maybe we should not encourage David to add this crazy German experimentalist and unpopular musician, we will lose money. Maybe that was the motivation."

Edgar Froese

Michael Rother was not the only German musician whose planned collaboration with Bowie was to end in bizarre circumstances. Tangerine Dream frontman Edgar Froese had met Bowie backstage in 1976 after a concert in West Berlin, where they bonded over "a shared loved of literature, fine arts, philosophy and great intellectual debates", according to Froese's second wife, Bianca Froese-Acquaye. Froese helped the singer find an apartment and, while it was being renovated, invited Bowie and Iggy Pop to move in with him and his family.

"For Bowie, it was a horrific time," recalled Froese. "When someone goes through a withdrawal, nothing is left of the person you thought you knew."

Froese found doctors to help ween Bowie off drugs, which he said included heroin as well as cocaine. There was alcohol, too. Bowie would occasionally knock back a bottle of whisky, he said, "just to get rid of the depression". But having "recovering" addicts in the house took its toll on the hosts. "For my wife [his first wife, the artist Monika Froese] and me," said Froese, delicately, "it was not pleasant."

When word got around that Bowie was staying, the press descended. "Some particularly brash reporters paid fees to residents to watch our entrance through their curtains," said Froese. "There was no choice but to leave the house in a knitted hat and scarf after dark."

After a few weeks, Bowie moved out but Froese continued to exert a major influence. He introduced the singer to the Hansa Studios in Berlin's Kreuzberg district (where Bowie recorded *Heroes*), Romy Haag's transsexual cabaret in Schöneberg, and the Dschungel cocktail bar on Nürnberger Straße.

Although Tangerine Dream were not typical of the Krautrock bands normally associated with Bowie, he loved both their celestial soundscapes and their use of technology, and asked Froese to collaborate with him. Froese duly obliged. He flew to the studio-cum-chateau on the outskirts of Paris, where an assistant showed him to a deckchair by the side of the swimming pool. The whole day passed and no one came to check on him. Come early evening, sunburned and fed up with being ignored, Froese picked up his gear and took the first flight home. The collaboration never came to pass, and Froese never received an explanation for his treatment.

Conny Plank

Shortly after arriving in West Germany, Bowie headed to a small hilltop farm near Wolperath, a village in North Rhine-Westphalia. Here lived the man credited as the father of Krautrock.

Conny Plank was an engineering wizard whose work with

Kraftwerk, Neu!, Cluster and Harmonia went on to define electronic, ambient and dance music. When Bowie arrived at the farm-cum-studio, he was warmly welcomed by Plank's family, who would take him each morning to the village shop to buy the German cereal he had grown to love. Bowie was delighted to discover that the local supermarket had ashtrays in the aisles, so he could smoke while shopping.

Plank let Bowie stay for a few days but refused to work with him because of Bowie's heavy drug use. "My father was all right with quite a lot of drugs," Plank's son, Stephan, said, "but there was this rule that said, 'No toilet drugs.'" If drugs were to be taken, Plank declared, they had to be taken openly and could not be Class A. Given Bowie was regularly disappearing into the bathroom to take cocaine and "even harder stuff", according to Stephan, Plank told the singer to leave. The secrets of Plank's *Kosmische Musik* (cosmic music), the evocative German term for Krautrock, were not to be so easily divulged to Bowie.

Tony Visconti

It started with a kiss. Bowie had been working on one particular song for weeks. He knew it was special but he needed lyrics. Words didn't flow quite so easily these days and he tended to leave them till last. Picking up a notepad, he looked out of the studio window hoping for inspiration. All that greeted him were the same grey skies, watchtower and wall. But then something caught his eye – a couple locked in an embrace, kissing. He was floored by the juxtaposition of this small moment of love and abandonment, defiantly carried out in the giant shadow of the ultimate symbol of repression. He began writing. "Heroes" had found its heroes.

Needing some peace and quiet to write, Bowie had asked producer Tony Visconti and backing singer Antonia Maaß if they wouldn't mind leaving the studio briefly. All that existed outside were a vacant lot, a Romani encampment and the Berlin Wall. Not that the lack of amenities bothered Visconti and Maaß, as the two had recently begun an affair. When they returned, Bowie was smiling widely and told the couple that they had just made it into a song.

For years, Bowie would come up with variations on the story, unable to state the real identity of the couple because Visconti was married at the time. "David protected me all these years by not saying that he saw Antonia and me kiss by the Wall," said Visconti. When he was finally able to talk about it openly, Bowie said, "I could see Tony was very much in love with this girl, and it was that relationship which sort of motivated the song." But Visconti was far more than an inspiration for just one song. If anyone could be described as Bowie's right-hand man, it would be him.

The Brooklyn-born producer had been working with mainstream acts like Billy Fury and Manfred Mann, but the record company knew he had a propensity for the quirky, so it was suggested he work with an artist who defied categorization. Bowie and Visconti hit it off immediately. They talked about music endlessly, spent the day walking in the autumn sunshine around London and went to the cinema to watch Polanski's *Knife in the Water*.

It wasn't all smooth sailing. Visconti described the singer as musically "all over the place", and urged him to stick to one style. The first record they worked on, "Let Me Sleep Beside You", was deemed not good enough to be released by Decca Records. Eventually, when Visconti was handed Bowie's first truly great

Tony Visconti and Bowie at Trident Studios, London, May 1970.

record, "Space Oddity", he labelled it a "cheap-shot novelty song" (the record company timed its release to coincide with the moon landing), and handed it over to fellow producer Gus Dudgeon. But then Visconti and Bowie went on to collaborate on a host of albums from the sixties through to *Blackstar* that, together, read like a history of seminal moments in rock music.

In 2016, Visconti was on stage in New York with his band Holy Holy. It was 8 January, Bowie's birthday, so, on the spur of the moment, Visconti got out his mobile phone and asked the audience if they'd like to sing "Happy Birthday" to his rock star friend. He dialled the number, but the noise from the thrilled audience was so deafening that he was unable to hear his friend's reaction. That weekend, Bowie died.

Robert Fripp

Robert Fripp got off the plane from New York to West Berlin, went straight to Bowie's studio and, within minutes, had plugged in and was playing. His first notes became "Beauty and the Beast". The second thing became "Heroes". Not bad for a man who had not played guitar in three years.

Disgusted at the greed of the recording industry, the King Crimson founder had quit music in the mid-seventies and retired to America. He had no intention of returning to Britain or to music. But then he got a call from Brian Eno, an old friend, who passed the phone to the man sitting next to him.

"Do you think you could play some hairy rock and roll guitar?" David Bowie asked. Fripp explained that he had not touched the instrument in years. Bowie persisted, so Fripp told them that, if they were prepared to take a risk, he was, too. "This was Bowie, after all," said Fripp. "A magnificent live act who'd written some of my favourite songs, so yeah. Why not?"

His experimental playing defined the album *Heroes'* sound. For the song "Heroes", he had everyone fascinated when he pulled out a tape measure with musical notes written on it, and placed it in front of the amplifier. When the backing track was played, Fripp moved between the marks to get just the right feedback on the right notes. "We all just looked at each other, at how beautiful it sounded," recalled Visconti.

"Heroes" became Bowie's anthem, but the consequence for the Dorset-born recluse was even more profound. Fripp suddenly became one of the world's most sought-after guitar players. Everyone from the Talking Heads and Blondie to Peter Gabriel and Daryl Hall wanted him. "I became sucked back into a life," he said, "that I never intended to return to."

Robert Fripp, Bowie and Brian Eno at Hansa Studios, West Berlin, 1977.

Devo
- - - - - -

Devo's lead singer, Mark Mothersbaugh, was no stranger to the strange, but even he was surprised to find himself having to get naked with Bowie and Brian Eno as a way to prepare for the day.

Mothersbaugh had his girlfriend to thank for the arrangement. She had sneaked backstage after a Bowie and Iggy Pop gig in the United States to hand over a cassette of the band. Back in Berlin months later, and desperate to listen to something other than German radio, Bowie rifled through a box of old tapes and happened upon Devo. "This can't be real!" was his and Pop's reaction. So, in 1977, the quirky band from Akron, Ohio, found themselves in the old steel town of Neunkirchen in West Germany making a record with Eno and Bowie. The two Englishmen were fond of the local spa and suggested beginning each day with a visit to the sauna. After building up a sweat in the steam room, the musicians would open the doors, dash naked through the snow and leap into the ice pool.

To relax everyone further, the first day's recording began with a jam. Along with Bowie and Eno, Devo were joined by Holger Czukay, of the experimental band Can. Asked if any recording of this legendary lineup had survived, Mothersbaugh said, "You bet! But I haven't listened to it yet, because I've only just found it."

Bowie sang backing vocals, but Mothersbaugh, not wanting to be seen as Bowie's creation, furtively brought down the relevant fader when Eno was recording the final mix so Bowie could not be heard. "I'm thinking we should see what's on those tapes. I'm curious to see what the heck they did," said the Devo man.

Marlene Dietrich

Little did Bowie know that he was about to appear in the biggest turkey of his acting career, a film so bad that he later described it as "my 32 Elvis movies rolled into one". Whatever lurking doubts he may have had after reading the script, the singer believed that at least he would get to meet one of his idols – an actress whom he so revered that he had modelled his *Hunky Dory* pose on her famous heavenward gaze. But instead of being introduced to the German screen legend, Berlin bohemian and cabaret star who had defied Adolf Hitler, he was introduced to a wooden chair. This, he was told by the nervous director, David Hemmings, was "Marlene". Or rather, the chair would act as her stand-in because the actress found a return to Berlin too emotional to countenance. While Marlene Dietrich would film her scenes in Paris, Bowie was told to emote to "wooden Marlene", who would be placed to the side of the camera.

Bowie was livid at being hoodwinked. The main reason he was involved in *Just a Gigolo* (1978) was to meet the movie legend, who was the symbol of modernist androgyny. "It made an enormous impression on me that Miss D had said she would do the film if I would do it. And, likewise, I said I'd promise that if she's doing the film, I'd do it." Dietrich, who was 77 and had not made a film in 17 years, echoed that view, saying, "The only reason I did this film was that David is the only young person who has anything to say." Another reason may have been that she was paid $250,000 (worth $1 million today) for two days' work.

Despite being tricked, Bowie agreed to carry on, influenced by the fact that the crew was already on set. His main memory of the film was being asked to carry around, for unexplained reasons, a pig, which quickly grew fatter and heavier and "kept shitting" on him. It was not much better at Dietrich's end. When the director stood in for Bowie, the actress asked him, "Do they pay you extra for this shit?"

After shooting his scenes and with little time left before going back on tour, Bowie caught a flight to Paris in the hope of convincing Dietrich to pose for a publicity photograph. But when he arrived, the actress was unwilling to be further associated with the film and told him, "I did the movie, you are a great singer, but no."

An interviewer later suggested to Bowie that he must have been flattered that Dietrich had even heard of him. "Oh my God, it was incredible," said Bowie. "She said very nice things about me and, in fact, was playing side two of the *Low* album to all her friends, which I thought was just terrific."

Kim Novak

Bowie was developing a reputation for having affairs with his leading ladies. *Just a Gigolo* proved no exception. The fact that the main star, Marlene Dietrich, was 77 and stuck in Paris appeared to rule her out, so Bowie turned his attentions elsewhere. He sounded disappointed when he discovered that Kim Novak was already taken. "A splendid woman – happily married, though," he told journalists. In the end, he had a fling with his other co-star, 27-year-old American-Italian actress Sydne Rome, who would go on to launch the early eighties craze for aerobics with a series of workout videos.

Once billed as "the smart man's Marilyn Monroe", Novak shot to fame in Alfred Hitchcock's *Vertigo* and was the world's top box-office star in the late fifties. But by 1978 the 45-year-old had largely quit the movie business to focus on painting and poetry, so her decision to come out of semi-retirement for such a film is hard to explain. In the movie, she played the wife of a German general who pays Bowie, an army officer-turned-gigolo, to impregnate her. Her elderly husband insists on overseeing proceedings from his bedside chair. Facing such scrutiny, Bowie's character finds himself unable to perform and leaves.

"David Bowie and I shared a studio car from location to our hotel where we would run lines of the script for the following day," recalled Novak on her website after his death. "I remember how his breath smelled so good. Yes, sweet! Sometimes I would fall asleep with my head on his shoulder. He was good and kind, as well as lots of fun. It's been hard letting go of the life in and of David Bowie."

Bowie and his *Just a Gigolo* co-star Kim Novak, 1978.

Rainer Werner Fassbinder

Despite having taken part in *Just a Gigolo*, Bowie's cinematic aspirations remained highbrow. At the top of his wish list was a young German director who was rewriting the rules of moviemaking. Rainer Werner Fassbinder and Bowie hoped to work together on a film version of Bertolt Brecht's *The Threepenny Opera* but the project never took off. In the end, the two men only got to see each other once in passing.

Bowie was sitting in a Berlin bar in the late seventies when in walked the star of New German Cinema. "He was with a bunch of really heavy-looking guys, the kind of guys that the Hell's Angels would stay away from," said Bowie, who felt too intimidated to approach. "He hung with a heavy crowd there – a heavy dude! But he was a fascinating guy. Extraordinary use of film, and the symbolic messages in it."

Along with Wim Wenders and Werner Herzog, Fassbinder was one of the three legendary pioneers of this new direction in German cinema. Bowie was involved in discussions with all three about working together. In the end he was to work with none of them, unless you count a Nokia promotional video shot by Wenders.

Romy Haag

Transsexual cabaret star Romy Haag found Bowie leafing through her extensive collection of 4,000 LPs during a party in her Berlin flat. When she asked if the singer were looking for anything in particular, Bowie replied, "I'm looking for my records."

"I don't have any," confessed Haag.

The cabaret star had been previously invited by a friend to

a Bowie concert and had gone backstage after the show. "We saw each other, and that was it!" she said. The fact that Bowie was subsequently to discover she had never heard of him did not appear to affect their relationship adversely.

Haag was to introduce Bowie to the Berlin he had come to find. She took him to her cabaret club, notorious for its flamboyant performers, outrageous acts and extravagant clientele. "In his eyes, it was like looking in a mirror," said Haag. "The club reflected his music." Her company would lip-synch, dance and act to songs in a precursor of the video age to come.

But the two eventually fell out. Haag was particularly aggrieved when Bowie stole her signature move, which involved smearing her lipstick with the back of her hand and ripping off her wig before departing the stage. He used it in the "Boys Keep Swinging" (1979) video.

agnès B

Few people would have the gall to accuse David Bowie of having a terrible sense of fashion but French designer agnès b (whose real name is, appropriately, Agnès Troublé) had no such qualms. In the late seventies, the up-and-coming designer sent him a letter, suggesting that his brown tweed suit was not only "un-rock and roll" but, worse, "Germanic".

"Stick to black and white," she wrote, accompanying her letter with a pair of black leather trousers in case the singer failed to get the hint. Rather than being offended, Bowie was delighted. He not only kept the trousers, he wrote back and asked her to be his designer. It was a role she carried out for the next 25 years.

Bing Crosby

Where would Christmas be without music's most unlikely duet? But "Bowie and Bing" almost didn't happen.

In 1977, Bowie briefly returned to London after being invited onto Crosby's Christmas TV special. He was expecting to sing "Heroes", but on arrival he was told the 74-year-old crooner wanted them to duet on "Little Drummer Boy".

"I won't sing that song, I hate that song," Bowie said. "If I have to sing that song, I can't do the show," he added, before disappearing into his dressing room.

The producers were thrown into a panic. Too scared to mention any of this to Crosby, they gave the show's composers, Larry Grossman and Buz Kohan, an hour to find a solution. Somebody mentioned that they had seen a piano in the basement, so the two men rushed downstairs with the aim of writing a counterpoint melody to keep both singers happy. Before the hour was up, they had finished a piece they called "Peace on Earth".

When they played Bowie the new part, he was placated and even agreed to the producers' request to remove his lipstick and take out his earring for the "family show". He also agreed to act in a contrived scene in which he knocks at the door of Bing's supposed country estate, pretending to be a neighbour. He mistakes Crosby for the butler, and asks if he can use "Sir Percival's piano". It is strange, awkward and wonderful.

"David was a little nervous," recalled Bing's daughter Mary Crosby. "Dad realized David was this amazing musician, and David realized Dad was an amazing musician. You could see them both collectively relax and then magic was made."

Bowie remembered it somewhat differently when speaking

to journalist David Quantick. "He looked like a little, old orange sitting on a stool because he'd been made up very heavily and his skin was a bit pitted, and there was just nobody home at all, you know?" The only reasons he appeared, he said, were to promote his new single and because his mother loved Crosby. But, despite the jibe, Bowie did admire Crosby and was aware of his history as a ground-breaking star who moved pop music out of the big-band era into the "singer as star" future. Crosby had also done what Bowie longed to do: forge a successful, parallel career in acting.

The American crooner did not know much about Bowie but knew enough to be pleasantly surprised his guest had agreed to appear. "You may think it strange David Bowie appearing with an ancient like me to celebrate Christmas, but in this show he appears clean-shaven, and I think he's just wonderful and a very nice young man," said the American. Ever gracious, Crosby added that Bowie would make a good actor, and before they left he suggested staying in contact and asked Bowie for his phone number.

Against Bowie's wishes, the song was eventually released and got to number three. It was his biggest-selling single that year.

Charlie Chaplin

That same Christmas of 1977, Charlie Chaplin, another great of the silver screen, died. In a saga reminiscent of the darker moments of the comic's own slapstick films, his corpse was stolen. Bowie, who was his neighbour in the exclusive Swiss village of Corsier-sur-Vevey, was swept up in the ensuing events.

The grave robbers demanded $600,000, but Chaplin's widow, Oona, said her husband would have found the whole episode "ridiculous". When the body snatchers threatened not to return the corpse, she told them, "Keep it!" But then they threatened her children. Hundreds of police were drafted in to monitor the 200 public phone booths in the region. After five weeks, two men were caught making a call to the Chaplin house. The culprits confessed and led the police to a makeshift grave in a cornfield.

Bowie had been following unfolding events, not just because they were close to home but because Chaplin's son Eugene was an engineer at the Swiss studios where he was mixing "Heroes". Eugene invited Bowie to meet the family, who had gone from considering the situation faintly comic to finding themselves under police protection. When asked by a fan on BowieNet if it were true he was Chaplin's neighbour, Bowie replied, "Yeah, he lived down the road. Well, his corpse lived down the road. It was in the garden and it was nicked. A couple of terrorists demanded money from the family. It was awful."

Bowie became friends with the whole family but found himself especially drawn to Oona. Chaplin's 52-year-old widow was herself no stranger to fame: she was the daughter of playwright Eugene O'Neill, the model for Holly Golightly in Truman Capote's novella *Breakfast at Tiffany's*, and a former Hollywood actress. Bowie even spent that Christmas at the Chaplins' and fondly recalled exchanging gifts under their tree.

Oona and Bowie got on so well that rumours of an affair started, something the widow laughed off. "There have even been reports that I may marry him," she told *The Sunday People*. "It is absolutely not true, though my children were very amused by the idea." The two remained friends, with Oona describing Bowie as a "charming, intelligent and sensitive fellow who came from the same part of London as Charlie, walked in and wanted to talk".

The former actress also had a hand in Bowie taking to stage

acting. She urged him to accept the lead role in the Broadway production of *The Elephant Man*, and Bowie agreed on the condition she resurrect her movie career. Bowie lived up to his part of the deal, but Oona never did go back to acting.

As for Charlie's body, it was reburied and, this time, the coffin was encased in concrete to deter any future body snatchers.

Roger Moore

Bar the Chaplins, Bowie had few close friends nearby and often found himself alone in his Swiss chalet. But, one afternoon, a friendly neighbour knocked on the door to say hello. It was Roger Moore. According to Dylan Jones's *David Bowie: A Life*, the actor proceeded to regale Bowie with entertaining anecdotes about a host of fellow stars over dinner and drinks. The next day, at the same time, there was another knock at the door. It was Moore again. Once again, Bowie handed out the gin and tonics and listened, not quite so intently, to the same stories. The same scenario unfolded every day for the next two weeks, until one day Bowie could take no more. When the dreaded knock came, Bowie dived under a table and hid. The ploy worked, and the knocks eventually stopped.

Years later, Bowie turned down an offer to appear alongside Moore as the Bond baddie in *A View to a Kill* (1985). The reason why remains open to conjecture.

Sean Lennon

One person Bowie did try to see in Switzerland was Sean Lennon, who had been just five when his father was murdered. Bowie was always aware of the enormous impact John Lennon's brutal death must have had on Sean and did his utmost to ensure the boy had as much affection and attention as possible.

The singer would regularly pick Lennon up from his Swiss boarding school to take him to museums, all the while talking about artists and authors from Kokoschka to Asimov. "David seemed like such a parental figure," recalled Sean, who remembered Bowie not as a wild rock star but more as a "sober-minded uncle". "He would tell me to put on my seat belt, check that I wasn't running into the street or whatever."

Bowie was family, according to Sean's mother, Yoko Ono: "After John died, David was always there for Sean and me."

Yoko Ono

Even famous people had trouble telling Bowie to his face if they felt he was behaving badly. But not Yoko. As the sun began to rise on a long evening of entertainment in New York, Bowie turned to his girlfriend, Ava Cherry, and said, "I'm hungry. Cook me some food." As Cherry went to the kitchen, a shocked Yoko said, "Hold up. You don't say, 'Cook me some food.' She's not your slave." Bowie began to respond, but a furious Yoko launched into a diatribe in which she accused him of being a chauvinist. According to Tony Zanetta, Yoko was on a roll and would not be stopped. Despite that altercation, the two remained close friends. Yoko was not only invited to Bowie's and Iman's wedding, she was also one of the few he chose to tell about his cancer.

Frank Zappa

Bowie stole Frank Zappa's guitarist not just from under his nose, but from his very stage.

An early Zappa fan, Bowie could lay claim to being the first artist to cover one of the American's songs.[6] A decade later, in Berlin, he was in the wings to watch the zany Zappa himself, or rather his guitarist. During one of Zappa's extended guitar solos, his bored "lead" guitarist, Adrian Belew, spotted Bowie and, finding he had nothing to do for 20 minutes, walked over to say hello. "How would you like to be in my band?" Bowie responded. Belew was thrilled, but, fearing Zappa's response, the two decided to arrange a clandestine meeting after the gig.

"It was like a spy film," recalled Belew. The guitarist was told to go back to his hotel alone and wait in his room for ten minutes before going back outside, where a black limo would be waiting to drive him and Bowie to a restaurant. There were some 25,000 places to eat in the city. They chose the wrong one.

"We arrived, went in the front door and who should be sitting at the very first table but Frank Zappa and the rest of the band!" said Belew. Acting as if nothing untoward was happening, Bowie said, "Quite a guitar player you have here, Frank."

Zappa was not fooled. "Fuck you, Captain Tom," he replied, managing to issue both a put-down and a demotion at the same time. Further attempts by Bowie to break the ice were rebuffed with the same phrase. With little option, the newcomers eventually left. Back in the car, Bowie turned to his new guitarist and said, "I thought that went rather nicely!"

John Lydon
- - - - - - - - - - - -

Another person who became contemptuous of Bowie was John Lydon. "What a pompous prat!" was the Sex Pistol's response after Bowie's bouncers had the punk rocker thrown out of an Iggy Pop concert.

"I went backstage to say hello because I had met Iggy a year before," recalled Lydon. "Mr Bowie wanted me removed – thrown out, in fact. He wasn't touring with Iggy, he was just backstage. I've had an utter loathing for Bowie since then."

Stooges guitarist Ron Asheton remembered Lydon losing his cool with both Bowie and Pop after the two had handed out some lengthy and patronizing careers advice. "Finally, Johnny just stood up and said, 'Fuck you guys. You're full of shit," Asheton recalled. "Before that, I didn't think much of the guy. After that, I go, 'This guy's all right. He just told Iggy and Bowie to fuck off.'"

For video director Tim Pope, the relationship between Bowie and Lydon was bound to explode into acrimony as it typified the rivalry between the old and the new guard. One night, he recalled, Lydon and fellow Sex Pistol Sid Vicious were driving to a post-gig party. Bowie and Pop, who did not know the address, were following behind. Somewhere en route the two Pistols decided to lose the older rockers, and a farcical car chase through the streets of London followed.

"We were young and wanted to have fun and didn't want them trailing behind," Lydon recalled. "They weren't too pleasant to us in the first place. They were party-hoppers, really. You don't mean to cause offence so we took a few quick left turns." Bowie and Pop never did find that particular party.

Then one night in Switzerland, when Lydon was playing with

Public Image Ltd, he was told Bowie was out front and wanted to come backstage to say hello. "I said no," recalled Lydon. "But the road-crew member informed me that Mr Bowie was with his young son, at which point I immediately said yes. Maybe he used his son as a passport but it is very important not to offend the young. And then I got to know Mr Bowie at that level, as a dad, and he was all right then. When you are surrounded by a lot of celebrities, you kind of get lost in celebrity-dom. It's hard not to get conceited. I've been through that phase many a time myself."

Although Lydon's admiration for Bowie was more circumspect than that of his fellow Pistols, he did admit that the singer had been an influence, not least for his courage in admitting to being bisexual at a time when a culture of football hooliganism was rampant. "Bowie was standing up for something, saying, 'Who are you to tell me what to do?' It was a great breeding ground for punk to begin," said Lydon.

Although they were never to resurrect their initial, if cautious, friendliness, Lydon was respectful of Bowie after the singer died. He posted the Bowie track "Cygnet Committee" on his PIL website, revealing a fondness for Bowie's earlier melodic, acoustic period. "The way he planned his death, the discretion, showed a great deal of class," he told the BBC. "He didn't want no pomp and circumstance. That's how I will fondly remember him forever. I met him a few times, I always found him to be someone who was ferreting for new ideas. He was very open and honest about that."

Sid Vicious

- - - - - - - - - - - -

Sid Vicious was prepared to go to great lengths to emulate his hero, even to the point of sticking his head in the oven.

"Sid was very impressed with David Bowie," recalled John Lydon. "He loved that hairdo but he had no idea how to stick it up, so he used red paint and put himself upside down in a gas oven." The bassist even once ended up setting his hair on fire.

"How does Bowie do it?" he would ask Lydon in frustration.

"Well, just like you, Sid!" his friend would reply.

Bowie was less impressed with Vicious, describing him as a "mindless twerp". He added, "I didn't find anything romantic about him, or even interesting." After the Sex Pistol died of an overdose, Bowie took a more charitable view. "Sid was near catatonic and I felt very bad for him. He was so young and in such need of help."

Glen Matlock

- - - - - - - - - - - - - -

After being edged out of the Sex Pistols by Vicious, Glen Matlock played with various musicians before teaming up with Iggy Pop. One night, following a gig in New York, Bowie's limo turned up to drive the band down to the Mudd Club. Everyone clambered inside, leaving Matlock to sit in the only space left – on Bowie's lap Looking around the car, the bassist noticed that some small paintings were hanging where there would normally be mirrors.

"Is that Picasso?" he asked.

"Yeah," said Bowie.

"Is that Matisse?"

"Yes, it is."

"Are they real?"

"Yeah."

"You're a bit of a flash cunt, aren't you?"

"Yes," said Bowie in his poshest voice, "you could say I'm a bit of a flash cunt, Glen."

Siouxsie Sioux

Fifteen-year-old Susan Ballion was watching *Top of the Pops* in hospital while recovering from a severe bout of ulcerative colitis, when on came a singer, resplendent in rainbow colours, cuddling his guitarist and singing about aliens. It was the catalyst that changed the teenager's life. Susan changed her name to Siouxsie and then changed her wardrobe. The fact that Bowie was also from her home town of Bromley only added to the connection.

The London suburb went on to define English punk rock more than any other town. Siouxsie formed a band with Marco Pirroni, soon to join Adam and the Ants, and a "drummer" named Sid Vicious. Fellow Bromley pal Billy Idol decided to branch out on his own.

When Bowie joined Siouxsie on Jonathan Ross's radio show years later, he recalled going to see the Banshees play in the late seventies while clutching his copy of *The Scream* (1978), their debut album. He admitted that he had been influenced by that night. "What I loved was that little Apache dance you used to do on stage," he told her. "I probably nicked that for a few gigs."

Bob Geldof

Bowie was to influence the post-punk generation, too. "You remind me of me...back then," Bowie told a determined young fan, who had stolen his way backstage to grab a word with his hero. Pushing his luck, the youngster, who had hitchhiked from Dublin to Brussels, handed over a demo tape of his own band.

"What's the name?" Bowie asked.

"The Boomtown Rats," came the reply.

"Good name. Let's hear you then," said Bowie, inserting the cassette into a ghetto blaster. Out blared an early version of the Rats' first single, "Lookin' after Number 1" (1977).

"It's great!" Bowie enthused. But the young Geldof hadn't finished. He handed over the tape for Bowie to autograph.

"What? Sign your record and not mine?" laughed Bowie. "You cheeky sod."

Almost ten years later, Geldof was about to arrange the concert of the century. His plan was to get the world's biggest star on board and, by doing so, convince everyone else to follow suit, which is how Bowie ended up in a London office looking at footage of starving Ethiopian children. He cried at the harrowing scenes and agreed to take part on condition that his 20-minute set be shortened to allow time for the newsreel to be played. The screening of that footage was to become the pivotal moment of the day.

"The film ended and the world erupted," said Geldof. Phone lines crashed and the money flowed in, as the estimated total audience of 1.9 billion were reminded what the event was all about. Geldof remained forever grateful to Bowie for that compassionate act. But it was not the only generous gesture made by Bowie that day. Geldof spent much of the concert in considerable pain thanks to a bad back. Spotting the Irishman lying on a flight case groaning in agony, Bowie rolled up his sleeves and gave the prostrate figure a back massage.

Debbie Harry

"Can I fuck you?" asked the ice-cool blond.

"I don't know, can you?" replied the ice-cool Blondie.

Debbie Harry's diplomatic rejection of Bowie's blunt pass was typical of their relationship. The Ramones had been the natural choice to support Iggy Pop and Bowie on tour in 1977, but it quickly became apparent why the band with the platinum blonde had been chosen instead.

"After our sound check, both David and Jimmy [Iggy] come running up the stairs to our dressing room to say hello," said the initially flattered Blondie keyboardist, Jimmy Destri. But it soon became clear that the singers were not interested in chatting to the musicians. "They were both rakishly misogynistic guys looking for Debbie," said Destri. But it wasn't only Bowie who was trying to prise Harry, then 31, away from Chris Stein, her guitarist boyfriend. "Bowie and I both tried to hit on her backstage," admitted Iggy. "We didn't get anywhere, but she was always very smooth about it. It was always, 'Hey, well, maybe another time when Chris isn't around.'"

"The whole thing was mind-blowing to be on tour with them in the first place," said Harry. "And to have flirtations with guys like that was just the icing on the cake." Sometimes it went beyond flirtation. After Harry had once found cocaine for Bowie, he pulled down his trousers as a "reward", "as if I were the official cock-checker". Although Harry added that she was flattered by the attempt to impress her. "I'm sure he wanted to put the moves on Debbie," said Stein. "But the time wasn't right, apparently."

As for Bowie's initial support of Blondie, Harry believes that it was crucial to their eventual chart domination. "Without this visionary and his friend Iggy Pop, where would Blondie be today?" she said.

The Ramones

Iggy Pop is often referred to as the "godfather of punk", but Bowie was just as significant a figure for the movement. For instance, singer Joey Ramone's first stage name was Jeff Starship, in homage to Ziggy Stardust, and his first band a glam rock outfit

Joey Ramone, Linda Stein, Bowie, Dee Dee and Vera Ramone, 1978.

called Sniper. Joey and Bowie would hang out together in New York in the seventies at Club 82 and go to see concerts, like The Clash, together. For Blondie's Chris Stein, it made sense that the Ramones wanted to be seen with Bowie, as their whole sound was indebted, he believed, to one particular Bowie song, 'Hang On to Yourself'. The Ramones themselves confessed to ripping it off.

"His voice is so incredible," Joey said of Bowie, according to Ramones biographer Jari-Pekka Laitio-Ramone. "The way he sings a ballad is like...I think he's my favourite singer."

David Byrne

Before he was the uber-hip New York new-wave geek, David Byrne was a shaggy-haired, bearded folk singer who played the ukulele on street corners. One day, in the early seventies, he walked into the ultra-cool Max's Kansas City hoping to catch a glimpse of the legendary Warhol crowd. Instead, he spotted Bowie dressed in the full glam regalia of a space suit and platforms topped off with towering orange hair. "I don't fit in here," thought Byrne and promptly left. As a result, the ukulele was dropped and the Talking Heads were formed.

Byrne's first brief encounter with Bowie came after choreographer Toni Basil invited him to see the singer on stage in *The Elephant Man*. After the show, Bowie gave Byrne a copy of *Collected Speeches of Fidel Castro*, saying, "You might enjoy this." Castro was, infamously, one of the most long-winded orators of the century, with speeches lasting up to seven hours. It is tempting to think that the gift was a Bowie joke. Either way, Byrne ploughed through the book, admitting afterwards, "Castro could really ramble on. *Really* ramble on."

The two met properly a few years later when the Talking Heads were playing in Montreux, Switzerland, and Bowie dropped in from his nearby home. Dressed in a brown anorak and a tweed cap, Bowie seemed shy but perked up when he saw the snacks provided by the promoter.

"Are you going to be eating that cheese?" he asked the band.

"No," they replied. Bowie then carefully wrapped up the food in a napkin and put it in his pocket.

"Are you going to be eating those nuts?" he asked.

"No," they said. He did exactly the same with the nuts, this time giggling as he did so.

Strangely, according to Byrne, these two intellectuals of modern music never had any deep conversations, though they did become friends. Byrne was delighted to discover he had influenced Bowie, who copied Byrne's manic preacher style on "DJ" (1979). He was even more thrilled to be on stage one night and spot Bowie dancing in the wings. Bowie gave the Talking Heads vocalist a pelvic thrust and a thumbs-up. "This made me so happy that I glided through the rest of the show as if on a cloud," said Byrne.

Jim Kerr

"I don't know why, but I didn't think David Bowie would be a cheese-eating guy," said Jim Kerr, recalling a time when Simple Minds, Iggy Pop and Bowie had a night of excess. For the band and Pop, the substances on offer were of the illicit sort; for Bowie, they were of the dairy sort.

Kerr became familiar with Bowie, or rather Bowie's bottom, as a 14-year-old. The teenager had just seen a matinee performance of Ziggy Stardust in Glasgow and, wishing to avoid the crush as the evening crowd piled in, decided to leave by the rear exit. As he made his way out by the stage door, the band were already switching back into their opening outfits for the next audience.

"Bowie was trying to change into this Japanese thing while smoking a cigarette at the same time," recalled Kerr. "His skinny ass was hanging out. It was amazing!"

The second time Kerr encountered Bowie was in 1979 when, to the Simple Minds singer's amazement, he discovered Bowie and Iggy Pop were recording in the same small studio in rural South Wales. The young band were still a couple of years away from having their first hit single but were confident enough to ask Bowie to play sax on one of their songs. Bowie declined but asked if, instead, they would like to sing backing vocals on an Iggy Pop track called "Play It Safe" (1980). After a few failed takes, Bowie told the Glaswegians to adopt a cockney accent and try to "sound like me". According to their manager, Bruce Findlay, the result was hilarious. It was also out of tune, even for the supposed terrace-chant effect Bowie was after. Kerr remembered Bowie politely getting around the problem by saying, "Why don't those who sing professionally step nearer the microphone, and those who don't, step back."

"That's how I came to find myself sandwiched between David Bowie and Iggy Pop," said Kerr. While singing, Pop even managed to shoehorn in a lyrical dig at his new backing band for being "too simple-minded".

When it came to the evening, there was usually a party with various substances on offer. One of the reasons Bowie and Iggy had picked the secluded Welsh farm was to keep the latter away from illicit substances, but the ploy didn't work. Iggy soon worked out where the action was and, come evening, would hook up with Simple Minds before "taking our goodies and all our women and heading off into the night", recalled Kerr. The image that stayed with Kerr, though, was that Bowie also arrived one night armed with a can of Heineken in one hand and a large block of cheese in the other. The Glasgow singer still shakes his head and laughs in disbelief when recalling the incongruous image.

John Bonham

For Led Zeppelin's drummer, it wasn't cheese, it was sausages. Bonzo loved them so much that he refused to go on tour without a frying pan, a grill and a large supply of Wall's pork bangers.

Every morning, the band's roadie, Gully, would set up a barbecue on the balcony of whatever five-star hotel they were in and cook Bonham his fried breakfast. But one day in 1977 at the Montreux Palace Hotel in Switzerland, there was a problem. The band's equipment had arrived but the big question was: where to store the sausages? The room's fridge was not big enough, and Gully, believing Wall's bangers were the height of British cuisine, feared they would be stolen if he stashed them in the hotel kitchen. Gully turned to the only people he felt could help: the Bowies.

If Bonzo does not get his bangers, the fretful roadie said, there would be hell to pay. Aware of the hard-drinking drummer's temper, Angie took the sausages back home to the couple's nearby chalet, put them in the fridge and gave Gully a door key. Disaster had been averted.

Tom Verlaine

Intrigued by the influential pre-punk, post-punk sounds of Tom Verlaine and Television, Bowie asked the New York guitarist to play on his *Scary Monsters* album. When Verlaine showed up, he proceeded to try out all of the studio's 30 amps. As the hours drifted by, and with Verlaine no closer to finding his sound, Bowie and Tony Visconti decided to go out for lunch. When they returned, Verlaine was still experimenting, so the two men switched on the TV and whiled away a few more hours. By evening, and with Verlaine seemingly no closer to recording, Bowie went home.

Eventually, the guitarist found a suitable amp and managed to record his track. But despite all the effort, Bowie did not rate the final product and brought in a replacement guitarist. The irony was that the song in question was "Kingdom Come", a song Verlaine himself had written and already recorded.

G E Smith

Bowie's ambiguous and often wilfully obscure lyrics have been pored over for meaning for decades. But one line in particular from his *Scary Monsters* period has provoked more than its fair share of theorizing. In "Ashes to Ashes" Bowie sings about "little green wheels" following him. One theory suggests the phrase is from a Dadaist poem by the German artist Kurt Schwitters called "To Anna Blume", which contains the line "Red is the colour of her green wheels". Another idea maintains that it is from an alleged incident when a paranoid Bowie kept seeing a boy on a green-wheeled bicycle outside his LA home and became convinced the youngster was out to steal his urine for a nefarious ritual. Yet another speculation is that the wheels referred to his drug dealer's car, a vehicle which Bowie deliberately once rammed in fury. But it seems the real inspiration came from a more prosaic source.

G E Smith, the guitarist for the *Saturday Night Live* TV studio band and Hall & Oates, became friends with Bowie and one day asked his new pal for the real meaning behind those words. "If you are performing at the BBC," Bowie told him, "a woman comes along pushing a tea trolley and it has these little green wheels on." Maybe Bowie was right in leaving the meaning up to the listener.

Human League

Bowie bounded into the Human League's dressing room to issue what would become a famous proclamation: "You", he said, "are the future of rock 'n' roll."

"It was like Jesus stepping out of a medieval painting and walking into your front room," said keyboardist Martyn Ware. Singer Phil Oakey was more phlegmatic. "People forget that the other band Bowie said was the future was 'Legend'," he observed.

Amusingly, Bowie and Iggy Pop were turned away by doormen when they first tried to see the Sheffield band. "That could have been that," said Ware. But two weeks later, Bowie tried his luck again and arrived at their concert in Fulham.

"We were just four lads from Sheffield, and there was Bowie and his entourage, something like eight people, turning up out of the blue in this tiny dressing room about twice the size of your average toilet cubicle, with no door on it," recalled Ware. Oakley was pleasantly surprised by Bowie's chattiness. "I thought he'd come in and be moody and hum sections of *Low* and try to depress you," he said. "But he's a very enjoyable bloke to talk to." The two even swapped phone numbers.

When the show started, Bowie turned to the band's "visuals director" and said, "Oh, bugger, I was going to do something like that." And he did. Bowie's friend Jayne County even claimed Bowie's sound changed overnight after hearing the band.

Giorgio Moroder

"I've heard the sound of the future," Brian Eno announced to Bowie upon hearing Donna Summer's "I Feel Love". He went on to declare that the track, penned by Giorgio Moroder and Pete Bellotte, would change club music for the next 15 years. "He was more or less right," agreed Bowie.

So, when Moroder approached the singer to collaborate on a song for the film *Cat People*, Bowie readily agreed. Knowing most artists got up late and liked to record even later, Moroder asked, "What time should we start – five, six in the evening?"

"Let's have breakfast and then we go," replied Bowie. The producer described the session as his fastest ever. Everything was wrapped up in a matter of minutes, with Bowie first-take perfect. Director Paul Schrader, who was sitting in on the recording, rushed out as Bowie was putting on his coat. "Wait! Wait! Wait!" he said. "You can't possibly be done yet!" Bowie shrugged and offered to do another take but, as far as he was concerned, it was job done.

But while Bowie's time with Moroder was to be a musical success, it was to bring about the demise of one of the singer's long-held dreams. Bowie had been profoundly affected by Fritz Lang's 1927 sci-fi film *Metropolis*, one of the key influences behind his dystopian set design for the *Diamond Dogs* stage show. For years, he had dreamed of writing a soundtrack to the silent movie but had never enquired into buying the rights because, he believed, no one else would ever consider such a "harebrained" idea. But right after the recording, Moroder confided to Bowie that he had been thinking of putting music to an old movie and had finally found the right one.

"No one has ever heard of it!" gushed Moroder. "It's called *Metropolis*, and I've bought the rights!"

Bowie inwardly groaned. "I didn't even tell him," Bowie told *Movieline* magazine. "It ruined my week."

COMMERCIAL HIGH TO CRITICAL LOW
1981–89

In 1983, Bowie was 36 years old and 14 albums into his career. In rock terms, he was ancient. Fed up with being regarded as a fringe genius and wanting finally to be wealthy, he decided to explore the one area he had ignored – making hits. Not only did he succeed in his ambition, he became the most famous rock star on the planet. But success bored him, and his records got worse. Things got so bad that, at one point, Mickey Rourke rapped on one of Bowie's songs – and it was the best thing on the track.

It was in this period, too, that he turned more determinedly to acting, giving one of his best performances in *Merry Christmas, Mr Lawrence*, although the most memorable moments tended to happen off-screen, such as the time he ran over a member of Monty Python. He had a three-year-long affair with a Hollywood actress, which, incredibly, they managed to keep quiet. And he got another punch in the face from another rock singer.

Bowie seemed to become increasingly lost and lonely. He was also regularly seen with a suntan. It all felt wrong. But this was the era when he was to give his most emotional concert in a performance that unified a divided city and helped change history. Even at his worst, Bowie was still making profound changes.

Jon Bon Jovi

As a tea boy in a New York studio, Jon Bon Jovi was present at what he called "one of the most unbelievable moments in rock history". Despite his lowly status, the wannabe rocker was able to sneak into the control room and witness first-hand Bowie and Freddie Mercury putting the finishing touches to "Under Pressure" (1981).

Like any fan, Bon Jovi was grateful for the smallest amount of attention. "I remember Bowie let me open a beer for him," he said. "There was no bottle opener and I was the gopher, so I ran down three flights of stairs, back up, opened the bottle of Heineken and gave it to him." Bowie was, he recalled, extremely grateful. "Bowie was my childhood hero, so you remember when somebody like that was nice to you."

Bon Jovi would have been delighted to know that, years later, he would be mistaken for Bowie, although the circumstances were not to be as he would have hoped. When Bowie died, a Thai newspaper scrambled to get the news on its online front page. In its haste, the *Thai Rath* confused the names Bowie and Bon Jovi, and declared that the big-haired rocker had passed away with the headline, "Much loved singer of 'It's My Life' dies". The song had been a monster hit across Asia for the American rockers and could always be heard being played somewhere on a Thai beach. Jon Bon Jovi fans in Thailand went into meltdown, and the paper's website was bombarded with thousands of grief-stricken messages. It was to be several hours before the paper realized its mistake and took the story down.

Joan Jett

- - - - - - - - - -

As for Bowie and Mercury, they were never to sing together live on stage – although that potentially legendary moment did come close to happening.

It was June 1982 and Queen were performing outdoors at the Milton Keynes Bowl. The previous year "Under Pressure" had hit the top spot, and rumours were rife that Bowie was about to fly in by helicopter to reprise his role on the record.

Joan Jett, who was the support act that night as well as a big Bowie fan, was one of those living in hope. That hope turned towards expectation halfway through her set when she happened to glance to the side of the stage. There was Bowie together with Mercury, both of them watching her perform. "If that doesn't put pressure on you, what does?" said the former Runaways singer.

The news that Bowie had been sighted spread throughout the crowd so, when the opening bass riff to "Under Pressure" began, there was an added electricity in the air. But Bowie did not appear. For reasons never publicly explained, he had decided not to take part. He was only ever to perform the song once with Queen, and that was ten years later at a concert to honour the now-dead Mercury.

Gary Numan

- - - - - - - - - - - - - -

Bowie was rarely offended by his many imitators, but he found one singer such a plagiarist that he had him kicked out of a television studio. Bowie had been booked for *The Kenny Everett Video Show*, a comedy and music TV programme, in 1979. Video director David Mallet thought it would be a nice idea to invite along Gary

Numan, who had had a number one with "Are 'Friends' Electric?" that year. Bob Geldof, his then girlfriend Paula Yates and some other well-known figures were present, but when Bowie realized Numan was also watching, he called a halt to proceedings and asked the security guards to have him removed. "I was gutted. I mean, what was I to him?" said Numan. "Just some little upstart who'd popped up with a quirky record. Fucking wanker."

"Before then," Numan said, "I thought he was a god. I used to get into fights at school protecting his name. Then, all of a sudden, this bloke I'd adored for years was throwing me out of a building because he hated me so much. It really upset me. I can only imagine he was going through an insecure patch." Numan gleefully pointed out that, at the time, he was outselling Bowie four to one.

Bowie was clearly annoyed by Numan telling Yates, then a columnist for the music weekly *Record Mirror*, "He's not only copied me, he's got all my influences in there too. I never meant for cloning to be a part of the eighties."

In 2000, Bowie offered a more conciliatory view. "If he were asked not to come on to the set, it would have been during rehearsals. I do remember having told the studio people that he was welcome to come to the actual shoot." Bowie even went so far as to say of the "Cars" singer, "He's written a couple of the finest things in British pop." It was enough to appease Numan who said, "Later, he said some nice things about me, so that made the whole thing better!"

Numan added, "As I've grown older and seen my own career ebb and flow I understand far more how he would have felt, even though I've never had the same fears or the need to try to harm someone else's career."

Princess Margaret

That was not the only time Bowie had someone removed. No respecter of royalty, he allegedly once kicked a drunken Princess Margaret out of a party.

In the eighties, Bowie bought a house in Mustique, an island noted for its famous residents. Neighbours included Mick Jagger, Bryan Ferry and the Queen's younger sister, whose alleged drinking and affairs often appeared in the tabloids. Once a year, usually on New Year's Eve, Bowie would hold a party and invite all the locals. According to artist Edward Bell, who provided the illustration of Bowie for the cover of *Scary Monsters*, Bowie told him he had once felt obliged to eject the whisky-loving Princess from one of his own parties because she was so drunk.

"She was so fucking pissed and so out of order, I had to kick her out," Bowie said.

"Not unlike your typical rock star behaviour, then," Bell responded. Bowie did not appreciate the comment and walked off.

There was another link between Bowie and Princess Margaret. Newspapers at the time were fond of suggesting a liaison between the Princess and Bowie's one-time minder, the notorious John Bindon, an ex-gangster, who was regularly seen on Mustique and whose famous party trick involved hanging five half-pint tankards from his lengthy appendage.

Edward Bell

Up-and-coming artist Edward Bell was holding his first solo exhibition in London when the gallery owner pointed out a nondescript man in the corner who wanted to talk about the artwork. At first glance, Bell was none too impressed. The man was wearing an insipid yellow, short-sleeved shirt, bright red trousers and shades. "I thought it was strange to be wearing dark glasses in a gallery if you wanted to see paintings," recalled Bell. "I thought he must be an American tourist."

Bell politely went over but paid scant attention until the man started to talk intelligently about the paintings. "Then it dawned on me: Jesus Christ, it's David Bowie!"

Bowie asked Bell to design the cover for *Scary Monsters* and within the week, according to Bell writing in *Unmade Up: Recollections of a Friendship with David Bowie*, the project was completed. Bowie would continue to wear the shades when the pair went off drinking together in dingy pubs off London's Earl's Court Road, with no one ever recognizing the person underneath.

Steve Strange

Steve Strange was famously to turn away Mick Jagger from his uber-hip Blitz club in Covent Garden, despite the Rolling Stone protesting, "Don't you know who I am?" But things were very different a week later when David Bowie appeared at the door.

It was 1980, and the Blitz was the home of a flamboyant scene soon to be called New Romanticism. Strange was the movement's leader, but Bowie was the honorary godfather. So, when the singer turned up in a black limo wanting to be let in, Strange's first thought was how to keep the news quiet and stop a riot breaking out. Arrangements were made for the star guest to be ushered in clandestinely via a fire exit and taken upstairs to a sealed-off area. Even so, word got out and extra security had to be dispatched to the foot of the stairs.

Bowie sent a message to Strange inviting him to join him at his table, but the Blitz man was on door duty and, a stickler for the rules, said he could only come after his shift finished. When Strange finally did sit down, Bowie told him, "I've been watching you and love what you've been doing, and I'd like you to be in my next video." Strange was delighted and gathered some of his more outlandish friends, although surprisingly not fellow Blitz worker Boy George, who was deeply upset at not being asked, and they set off early the next morning.

The colourful collection of hungover New Romantics presumed they would be flown to some fabulously exotic location. Instead, a coach arrived and they were driven to the East Sussex coast where they spent the day in freezing temperatures on a beach shooting the video for "Ashes to Ashes". Despite the weather, the video itself was a marvel and would set the tone for the early eighties.

Bowie's fondest memory of that day came from an unexpected quarter. "I start singing but as soon as I do, this old geezer with an old dog walks right between me and the camera," Bowie recalled. "Knowing this is going take a while, I sat in my full costume, waiting for him to pass." As the old man ambled by, the frustrated director pointed at Bowie and said, "Don't you know who this is?"

"Of course I do," replied the man. "It's some cunt in a clown suit."

"That was a huge moment for me," said Bowie. "It put me back in my place and made me realize, 'Yes, I'm just a cunt in a clown suit.' I think about that old guy all the time."

Hazel O'Connor
- - - - - - - - - - - - - - - - - -

Hazel O'Connor remembers being asked to cut Bowie's hair armed only with a pair of kitchen scissors and a dirty dishcloth. She was completing her breakthrough album, the soundtrack to the film *Breaking Glass*, when her producer suggested meeting a friend. The producer was Tony Visconti, the friend was David Bowie, and O'Connor was duly thrilled: her spiky androgyny and punky theatricality owed plenty to the singer she most admired.

The conversation started a little tetchily when Bowie asked the 25-year-old if *Breaking Glass* was named after his song of the same name.

"No, we actually thought of that title ourselves," replied O'Connor.

"I could write some songs for you for the film," suggested Bowie.

"No," said O'Connor, "We've already recorded them, thank you!"

Bowie then changed tack. "You cut Tony's hair, don't you?" O'Connor nodded.

"Would you give me a haircut?"

O'Connor was delighted to oblige. "I didn't have my hairdressing scissors but I went and found some old shears that were just in the office. We didn't have anything to put around his shoulders so I just used dirty tea towels and chop chop, I cut his hair! All I could think was, 'Oh, my God, I'm touching David Bowie's skull!'"

"He was so nice," she recalled. "You imagine putting dirty tea towels round the neck of your hero and then chopping their hair!" After the cut, Bowie said he would like to go to see her in concert. "I was like, 'Yeeeesssss!'"

John Cleese

Bowie was all set to join his favourite comedy troupe, Monty Python, on stage. But then the Minister of Funny Walks stepped in.

The Secret Policeman's Ball was the biggest comic event of the year, an annual benefit for Amnesty International which attracted the most famous names in entertainment. In 1981, co-creator Martin Lewis had gone to great lengths to get Bowie to make an appearance. The singer agreed on one condition: that he be allowed a walk-on role in a Python sketch. His close friend Eric Idle was in favour, but Cleese vetoed the idea.

"He's a pop singer," Cleese said. "I'm not having him in a sketch. Tell him he can bring his banjo and do a song." In the end, Bowie did neither.

Graham Chapman

A drunk Graham Chapman once tried to hurl himself into the back of a fast-moving jeep in a bid to emulate a stunt he had seen in an action movie. But, unlike the film's hero, the Monty Python comedian painfully bounced off the side and ended up in hospital. As for the unwitting driver, his name was David Bowie.

The two had come together, less literally, a few years before. Bowie and wife Angie had turned up at a gay club in London in the early seventies only to find a male couple already seated at their reserved table. The men, Chapman and his partner David Sherlock, refused to budge.

"Do you know who we are?" shouted an exasperated Angie.

"Do you know who I am?" responded Chapman.

"I was kicking him under the table saying, 'It's David Bowie and Angie,'" said Sherlock. "But he'd no idea who they were."

Bowie and Angie retired defeated, but the singer could claim revenge a few years later. By then, Bowie had become friends with another Python, Eric Idle, who asked him to appear in the pirate comedy *Yellowbeard* (1983), which Chapman co-wrote. The movie was being filmed on a beach in Mexico.

"One mad night at a party," recalled Idle, Chapman spotted a jeep speeding along a dirt path through the palm trees. He drunkenly convinced himself he could re-enact a scene from a movie and launch himself into the back of the moving vehicle. He shot up from his seat and raced through the trees on a direct collision course. He almost made it.

Doctors at the hospital later said his injuries were so severe that he would not be able to go back to work for weeks. The future of the film was thrown into jeopardy. But, dismissing the medics' concerns, a patched-up and hobbling Chapman was back on set within a couple of days.[7] As for Bowie, when he was told of the carnage left in his wake following his late-night ride, he was, according to Idle, "mortified".

Eric Idle

Despite the run-ins with Cleese and Chapman, Bowie was to become great friends with at least one Python. In fact, he was to become so close to Eric Idle that he asked the comedian to be godfather to his son, Duncan Jones.

The Tyne and Wear-born comedian was "the musical one" in the comedy troupe and composed most of their songs, including "Always Look on the Bright Side of Life". In turn, Bowie was also known for his sense of humour and once gave his friend an idea.

The Pythons had been desperate to follow up *Life of Brian*, their crowning achievement, with a sequel. But the sketches never gelled. Then, when Bowie and Idle were on holiday together in the singer's home on the island of Mustique, Bowie suggested a prequel instead, which focused on the Old Testament. Idle was so excited, he immediately called Palin, who was just as thrilled. "We've done the hard bit of the Bible," Palin wrote in his diary, "now we can do the fun bit – special effects, loopy characters, invasion, sacrifice, empire-building – the usual Python territory, in fact." Sadly, the project never got off the ground.

Bowie and Idle had first met in the seventies when the singer asked the comedian to collaborate on a Ziggy musical and handed over a tape of *Diamond Dogs*. After listening to the music, Idle, who admitted to not being a particular fan of the singer, was unsure how to respond. "It's very loud," he said. Bowie burst out laughing.

Richard Curtis

Comedy writer Richard Curtis once harboured hopes of becoming one of the great stand-ups. David Bowie was to ruin that dream.

Curtis had been on the comedy circuit for four years but was becoming increasingly frustrated by the fact that all the laughs seemed to go to his sidekick. Refusing to be cowed, Curtis kept plugging away. Then, one night, Bowie came backstage to congratulate the double act. The singer heaped praise on Curtis's partner, a comedian by the name of Rowan Atkinson, but when he spotted Curtis, he congratulated the comic not for his performance but for the efficiency of the scene changes. He had assumed Curtis was the stage manager.

"He had been watching me for nearly an hour but my face didn't ring any bells at all," said Curtis. It was the moment the comic decided to quit stand-up and focus on writing.

Kate Bush

Imagine this scenario. It is 1981, and Kate Bush and David Bowie have secretly rented a secluded mansion in a remote part of England to make an album together. The music is incredible, but the two eventually decide never to tell the world about their clandestine collaboration. That is the conceit underpinning a play, *Kate Bowie* (2014), by the Canadian Theatre Replacement Company, and its global popularity reflects the public desire to imagine two of the great British eccentrics working together.

In real life, the two did meet, although their first encounter was brief. Bush was recording at Abbey Road Studios and popped into another studio to say hello to a fellow musician.

"I was stopped in my tracks," she recalled. "Standing, elegantly poised, behind the console was David Bowie. He was lit from above and was smoking a cigarette." Bowie issued a friendly, "Hello, Kate." But Bush was so shocked that all she could say was, "Er...hello," before leaving the room to catch her breath. "I didn't dare go back in again," she said.

Her studio fright was explained by the fact that she had been obsessed by Bowie since adolescence. In fact, she had been so bowled over by seeing a Ziggy Stardust concert that she even booked Bowie's mime teacher, Lindsay Kemp, for lessons.

"We've met many times since then," she said of Bowie, "and I don't have to leave the room anymore."

Prince

Prince and Bowie met just once. But it was an evening that was to have an impact on musical history. It was 1987, and Bowie was playing in Minneapolis, Prince's home town. The local singer, who was in the audience, invited Bowie back to his sprawling Paisley Park residence for a party.

What happened that evening was to enter fan folklore. Asked on his now defunct dawn.com website if the two had played together that night, Prince replied, "You should have been there." Bowie added to the rumours later when he laughingly said on *Video Soul*, hosted by DJ Donnie Simpson, that the two musicians had "jammed until the wee hours". Sadly, the rumours of the two jamming together appear to be just that. Simpson believes both musicians were simply tantalizing their fans. He should know, as he was there that night. But what really happened was perhaps more significant.

Prince put on an album he had recently written. It was the follow-up to *Sign o' the Times* (1987) and was intended to herald a new, funkier direction. Everyone danced to the record, including Bowie and his band, recalled Simpson, before the small gathering left in the early hours.

But Prince allegedly became convinced his record was evil. As the LP was being readied to be sent to the stores, he ordered the copies to be destroyed. *The Black Album* quickly became the stuff of legend and the most bootlegged LP of all time. A surviving copy entered the record books as the most expensive piece of vinyl sold online. But there was at least one other reason Prince changed his mind, and it occurred the night he was with Bowie.

Years later, Prince told Simpson: "Remember that night?

You're the reason I didn't release *The Black Album*. You said, 'This has such a groove,' and the record was so much more than that." Simpson was crestfallen that his praise for the album had been seemingly misinterpreted.

As for the jam that never took place, Bowie would certainly have wanted to play with the Minnesota star. "He's probably the most eclectic artist I've seen since...me!" Bowie said. "I'm always floored every time I see him live."

The two were often compared, with Prince called the eighties Bowie. Did Bowie agree? "In terms of the more exhibitionist forms of theatricality and musicianship, yeah, absolutely," he said. "I don't think anybody else could handle the job better." The similarity sometimes sparked jealousy, especially when Prince went into acting. Video director Julien Temple recalled Bowie and Mick Jagger emerging from the cinema having seen *Purple Rain* (1984), with both singers irritated that the movie was so good.

"I only met him once," Prince told an audience after Bowie's death. "He was nice to me. He seemed like he was nice to everybody. Just wanted to say that." Prince then played "Heroes" on piano.

Three months after Bowie died, Prince was dead, too. His last concert was a small show on a Monday night involving just him and a piano, and "Heroes" was, once again, on the set list.

Abbie Hoffman

The sixties counterculture hero had been on the run for six years. Accused of selling drugs to undercover cops, US political activist Abbie Hoffman had decided that he, too, needed to go undercover. Abandoning his wife and children, Hoffman changed his name, underwent plastic surgery and started to dress as an Orthodox Jew. Despite being one of the most wanted fugitives in the United States, he disappeared off the radar. Then, one day, out of the blue, he got in contact with the world again – and the person he reached out to was David Bowie.

Hoffman managed to get a note to Bowie's office to request a meeting in a run-down restaurant he frequented in New York City. "For some reason, he was fixated on talking to me," Bowie said. "He liked my material, although some of this seemed to be about pulling rank and meeting 'David Bowie'," laughed the singer. "I was gaga. This was the leader of the Yippies [the Youth International Party]. This was someone who knew Huey Newton and Bobby Seal and Eldridge Cleaver. This was real American history."

Hoffman had lost none of his political zeal, but he told Bowie that he was beginning to tire of the deceit. Six months later, he would hand himself in and serve four months in jail (Hoffman always maintained he was framed).

Two decades later, Bowie introduced a song called "Seven" to the audience with these words: "I do recall the revolutionary Abbie Hoffman saying to me over a drink, 'Tomorrow isn't promised,' reminding us that if we move one grain of sand, the earth is no longer exactly the same. Which brings us to this song of now-ness."

Catherine Deneuve

A steamy, naked shower scene between two icons of cool kicked off the 1983 cult vampire film, *The Hunger*. Bowie and Deneuve shared a kiss, then more, as the camera panned over two wet bodies. When the French movie siren was asked why she had chosen this particular role, she replied, "It allowed me to meet David Bowie." She certainly got her wish.

Bowie had a track record of having affairs with his leading ladies, and this time was no exception. But despite their obvious similarities (pale, cool and glamorous with a penchant for Gitanes), it was not Deneuve who attracted Bowie, but his other co-star, the fiery Susan Sarandon.

Bowie and Deneuve did become friends, though, and were often spotted together in between shots, leaning casually against a railing or wall, elegantly smoking their cigarettes – an image as cool as anything in the film. "He's actually rather shy," said the French star, who bonded with Bowie over a shared love of paintings and antiques.

After the film's release, Deneuve finally snapped in response to a never-ending tirade of questions not about the movie but about her co-star. "I did not do it for Bowie," she said, poutily. "I'm not a *midinette* [starry-eyed young girl]."

Susan Sarandon

Bowie may have shared a shower scene with Deneuve, but it was his other co-star, Susan Sarandon, who knocked him off his feet.

Their meeting on the 1983 set kick-started a three-year love affair, with Bowie describing the 37-year-old American actress as "pure dynamite". "She is one of the brightest, wittiest, bestest [*sic*] actors I've ever worked with," he later said. "She's delightful and intelligent. She's fantastic!" Bowie even composed what he called "a paean to Susan Sarandon", although he later changed the lyrics and turned it into the less romantic-sounding "Dead Man Walking".

Bowie, Susan Sarandon and Catherine Deneuve, New York, 1982.

The singer had often spoken about his lack of interest in marijuana, but the actress appeared to have won him over to her drug of choice. When asked if the two of them often shared a joint, she enthusiastically replied, "Yeah!"

Doctors had told Sarandon – wrongly as it turned out – that she was infertile. That, she said, influenced her decision to choose a roving rock star like Bowie, who appeared to have little interest in starting another family. Sarandon was heavily into politics and her impassioned monologues could make Bowie's eyes "glaze over", according to biographer Chris Sandford, but he became a keen supporter of many of her social causes, including a therapy unit for people living with schizophrenia.

Despite their celebrity status, the two incredibly managed to keep their lengthy affair out of the media and even stay on good terms after the split. "He's worth idolizing, he's extraordinary," she said of him 30 years later. After his death, she commented, "I was very fortunate to have our paths cross again toward the very end, so I got to say and hear everything you'd want to say and hear."

Pete Murphy

Goth was born on the day Bauhaus released "Bela Lugosi's Dead". Its doom-laden intonations about the undead made the song a natural choice for *The Hunger*. And it was on set that singer Pete Murphy was to meet his inspiration, the man whose ghostly pallor and dark lyrics had so influenced not just punk but also its introverted, black-clad cousin. Murphy, however, was to be so overwhelmed by the encounter that he ran off and got drunk.

For the film's opening scene, Bauhaus had been asked to mime to their Gothic anthem in a dark, empty club. Empty, that is, except for the crew and one spectator. "There was this balcony above us," recalled Murphy, "and during the third take, I just kind of felt that Bowie was there. It was tangible when he arrived." A previously lacklustre performance suddenly took on new life, as the band sensed there was someone worth impressing. Murphy eventually got the courage to look up and there, indeed, was Bowie, looking down on him as if from the heavens. "He gave me this kind of approving nod," said Murphy. But even this small acknowledgement proved too much for the elfin-like singer, who stopped the performance and ran off stage. "I had to leave," said Murphy. "I was like, 'Stop looking at me, Bowie!'"

Grabbing a brandy from his dressing-room bar, Murphy gulped

it down, feeling he had made a fool of himself in front of his hero. After some minutes, there was a knock at the door. Hanging onto his half-empty bottle, Murphy opened it and found Bowie standing there. The only thing the Bauhaus frontman could think of doing was to thrust the bottle in Bowie's face and say, "Want some?"

"I must have looked like a complete drunk," said the singer. Murphy had recently performed his own version of Ziggy Stardust on *Top of the Pops* and, as Bowie got up to leave, he whispered in Murphy's ear, "I wish we had done Ziggy like you did it." It was a comment Murphy would forever treasure. "He was awesome," said the Bauhaus frontman.

Pete Burns

Not everyone attempting to cover Bowie's songs met with his approval. The androgynous Liverpudlian singer Pete Burns once asked Bowie if he could cover "Rebel Rebel" but alter the lyrics. "I'd rather you didn't record it at all," Bowie replied, "dead or alive."

Burns loved the pun so much, he told his friend Boy George, who refused to believe that such a perfect anecdote could be real. Years later, when the Culture Club singer got the chance to ask Bowie himself, the singer confirmed the quote was accurate. "I love it when gossip comes true," said George.

John McEnroe

One night in 1982, "Rebel Rebel" was being played loudly, and badly, on guitar by someone in the rented apartment above and it was keeping Bowie awake. The singer had a TV appearance early the next morning and, eventually, could take no more.

"So, I went upstairs to show the person how to play the thing," Bowie told Bill DeMain in *Performing Songwriter* magazine. "I bang on the door. The door opens and I say, 'Listen, if you're going to play...' and it was John McEnroe. I kid you not!" Bowie invited the tennis champion downstairs for a drink. "Just don't bring your guitar," he added.

Nile Rodgers

The King of Disco became a fan of Bowie while naked and high on LSD on a beach in Miami. His girlfriend had brought along her ghetto blaster and played *Ziggy Stardust* all night long. By the time the sun came up, Nile Rodgers was a convert.

He got to meet Bowie in the early eighties when he walked into a New York nightclub with his friend Billy Idol. "It's David Bo-weeeee," said the Generation X singer, vomiting on the floor as he finished the sentence. Without even breaking stride, the unflustered Idol walked straight up to Bowie, who was sipping orange juice in a corner on his own, introduced his two friends and then fell into a catatonic state.

Rodgers and Bowie talked into the early hours about jazz. "It was like we were the only two people in the room," said Rodgers. They got on so well that they decided to work together. Rodgers was delighted. This was the opportunity he had been looking for – a chance to gain credibility after years spent churning out "mere" disco songs. But it was not to be quite as he hoped.

"Nile, darling, I want you to make me a hit album," Bowie told him. The former Chic frontman was crestfallen.

"David, my career is plummeting because I make hits. I want to make a creative flop with you!"

Bowie was not to be dissuaded. He had just come to the end of a ruinous management contract which had siphoned off most of his profits. One reason he had been so experimental and uncommercial in Berlin was to get his own back. Now, not only would he be paid well for what he wrote, he could also show his old manager that he could have been making serious money all along. As an example, he played Rodgers a simple folky song on guitar. "I think this could be a hit," he said. Rodgers accepted the brief, rearranged the song and wrote new chords. "Let's Dance" (1983) went on to become Bowie's biggest hit.

Stevie Ray Vaughan

Playing guitar on "Let's Dance" was to catapult Stevie Ray Vaughan to international fame. Life had been very different just a few months earlier. The man soon to be fêted as "the second coming of the blues" was touring in a beat-up, old milk truck that leaked oil and regularly broke down. Life on stage was grinding to a halt, too.

In July 1982, Vaughan and his band were playing their first major international concert. Their hopes had been high, but the Montreux Jazz Festival crowd, perhaps expecting something more sedate, had begun booing. After the show, a despondent Vaughan was to be found sitting on his guitar case with his head in his hands. His first shot at the big time appeared to have come and gone. But then, failure turned to success.

"David Bowie would like to meet you at the bar," a festival organizer told the band. It transpired that the one member of the audience who truly loved them was the one who mattered most. "They completely floored me," Bowie said. "I probably hadn't been so gung-ho about a guitar player since seeing Jeff Beck."

Bowie, Stevie Ray Vaughan and Nile Rodgers, 1983.

Surprisingly, it was Bowie who was the more nervous of the two, saying he had to take his courage in his hands to ask the hard-core blues man to play on a pop record and join him on tour. "Hell, yeah," replied Vaughan, "I tour real good."

"To tell you the truth, I wasn't very familiar with David's music," the guitarist admitted, "but David and I talked for hours and hours about our music, about funky Texas blues and its roots. I was amazed at how interested he was."

The success of "Let's Dance" helped launch Vaughan's career internationally. But the relationship turned sour and was to end in the memorable image of Vaughan standing alone by the side of the street, guitar in hand, as the tour coach pulled off without him. Vaughan blamed Bowie, accusing him of reneging on a promise to let his band Double Trouble open the shows: "It was just a line of bullshit. He wanted just me. So I didn't go."

But that was not the only area of disagreement. Vaughan was unhappy with Bowie's ban on drink and drugs. "Stevie was shouting at David, 'What the fuck do you mean no dope? What the fuck are you on?'" recalled a friend of the guitarist. "'Look. I've bloody well got to put on a show,' Bowie responded. 'If you don't like it, perhaps you should leave.'" Vaughan also took time off because Muddy Waters had died. "Did you know him?" he was asked. "Not really," replied Vaughan, "but you do not tell a bluesman to just keep on walking when Muddy Waters has died."

On the morning of the tour, as the coach waited outside the hotel in Brussels and as Vaughan and his management still debated the contract, Bowie decided he had had enough. His tour manager took Vaughan's gear out of the trunk and dumped it on the pavement. With the rest of the band already on board, the bus drove off, leaving Vaughan standing alone outside the hotel, clutching his guitar case. Bowie called up his old guitarist, Earl Slick, and said he had three days to learn 28 songs.

But Vaughan and Bowie's relationship was to end on a happier note. Just months before Vaughan died, the two made up. "We started going to each other's gigs, he'd come to see mine, and I went to his, and we really started to buddy up," said Bowie. "He had changed an awful lot – he'd got a lot of problems that he had had earlier in his life out of his life. He just seemed to be so buoyant and enthusiastic, full of life."

Vaughan was killed in a helicopter crash in 1991, but not before he had returned to Montreux and exorcised some ghosts. This time, there were no boos, only cheers.

Keith Richards, Tina Turner and Bowie, New York, 1983.

Tina Turner

When Bowie's 15th album *Let's Dance* (1983) was about to be released, he was asked by record executives to attend the launch party in New York. "I'm sorry," he told them, "but I'm going to the Ritz to see my favourite singer perform." It was a decision that Tina Turner, then out of contract and out of fashion, credits with saving her flagging career.

"Well, that started a stampede," said the Nutbush singer. "Suddenly, my manager was being bombarded by calls from music executives who were desperate to get tickets." She added, "Luckily it was a great show. Seeing it, and the crowd's reaction, turned round how Capitol [Records] viewed me." She was signed up, and her album *Private Dancer* (1984) shot her back into the limelight. As for that night, Turner, Bowie, Keith Richards and Ron Wood headed back to a hotel suite to jam. "It was a rock 'n' roll dream," said Turner

The soul singer was one of the few stars who turned Bowie into an awe-struck child. Carlos Alomar recalled Bowie being so nervous about going to dinner with Turner that he asked his guitarist to tag along. "Get some balls, man," Alomar replied. "She's Tina Turner. She's not going to bite you."

Interestingly, it was Turner's mother who gave one of the best critiques of Bowie's "lost years" after seeing Tin Machine perform. "I liked it better when David was singing songs," she told her daughter.

Nagisa Ōshima

Robert Redford's hefty wage demands had forced Japanese director Nagisa Ōshima into a desperate, last-minute rethink. With just weeks to go before shooting was due to begin on his next film, and with not enough money to land his first choice, the director was a lead actor short. But where does one find another Robert Redford?

Having hit a dead end, Ōshima happened to be watching TV in Japan when on came a Pepsi advert featuring Tina Turner and a blond-haired scientist trying to make the perfect woman by using a photocopier (he succeeds and celebrates by dancing with his creation to "Modern Love"). The director could not believe his luck; he had found his man. "I don't like acting," Ōshima explained. "What I'm looking for is a person's *jinkaku* ('true personality')."[8]

"The last thing I wanted to do was make another movie," said Bowie, who had just finished *The Hunger*. But the chance of working with the director of *In the Realm of the Senses*, initially widely banned for featuring real sex scenes, was too great to miss. The project was renamed *Merry Christmas, Mr Lawrence* (1983), and within weeks, Bowie was on the Cook Islands in the South Pacific for the prisoner-of-war film.

Often bored on set, Bowie adored Ōshima's speed. "I've spent more time making movies just sitting on my arse," he said. "Ōshima cancelled that out for me. Two takes and it was done, then he'd take the film out of the camera and send it, literally in a brown paper bag, back to Japan." He also admired Ōshima's kimono-clad sartorial style: "He is the very best-dressed director I have worked with."

As for the director, he loved Bowie's playful off-screen mimes so much, he included one where Bowie mimes having a luxurious shave. Bowie was to say his performance was his most credible, and that working with Ōshima was "one of the highlights of my artistic life".

Ryuichi Sakamoto

From *Gone with the Wind* to *Titanic*, there have been many famous screen kisses. Among them is the one between Ryuichi Sakamoto and David Bowie. Although better known as musicians, the two met as actors on the island of Rarotonga, where they were shooting *Merry Christmas, Mr Lawrence*. They were introduced to each other on an empty, pristine beach. Sakamoto was so nervous at meeting Bowie that, even after they shook hands, he remained stock-still and speechless.

But the Japanese musician soon put any awkwardness behind him. After filming, the two would head to the small beach bar and entertain the locals by playing rock and roll songs on guitar and drums. "I was struggling to keep up with him," said the Yellow Magic Orchestra man, "but people seemed to like it and would cheer every song."

In the film, Bowie plays a British prisoner of war, Jack Celliers, and Sakamoto his camp commander, Captain Yonoi. When a fellow inmate is about to be executed, Celliers steps forward to bestow a Christ-like kiss on Yanoi's cheek. It is the pivotal moment of the movie. But, as they finished the scene, the cameraman shouted for a retake as his film had briefly jammed. Director Nagisa Ōshima, well known for hating second takes, went over to review the footage. He was so disarmed by the stutteringly surreal effect, he kept it in. It may have been a fluke but it left the critics lavishing praise on the emotional power of the unusual "technique".

Bowie would later visit Sakamoto and his family in Tokyo, carrying Sakamoto's young daughter, Miu, around on his shoulders while shopping. "Great musician. Great guy. Great makeup," he said of his Japanese co-star.

Merry Christmas, Mr Lawrence kick-started an Oscar-winning career as a soundtrack composer for Sakamoto, who wrote the song "Forbidden Colours" for the film. He wanted Bowie to sing the track, but Bowie declined, saying he needed to focus all his attention on his role. In his place, Sakamoto turned to the next closest thing: David Sylvian.

David Sylvian

Almost every new artist of the seventies and early eighties took something from Bowie. But if there was one genuine doppelgänger, it was David Sylvian. The sound, the haircut, the voice, the look, the androgyny, even his group's name, Japan, were a nod to Bowie.

Japan were on the cusp of being the biggest act of the whole New Romantic movement but then they broke up. Sylvian went on to work with Bowie's closest collaborators, including Visconti, Fripp and Sakamoto, but never got to meet his hero. The 18-year-old did once see Bowie and Marc Bolan together in a largely empty private nightclub in Manchester on the day the two glam stars performed for Bolan's TV show, *Marc*. But the shy teenager didn't approach either of them.

Sylvian came even closer to meeting his hero at the height of Japan's fame, when their manager, Simon Napier-Bell, invited Bowie to meet the band after one of their concerts. Bowie's limo drove up to the back of London's Hammersmith Odeon, where it was stopped by a suspicious security guard. Bowie was told to roll down his window.

"Who do you think you are?"

"I'm David Bowie."

"Well, I'm President Reagan, so you can piss off."

"Which he did," said Napier-Bell. "Which left Japan quite upset."

Takeshi Kitano

Takeshi Kitano was known as "the Benny Hill of Japan" for his slapstick comedy, so there was widespread surprise when he appeared as a prison-camp guard opposite Bowie in *Merry Christmas, Mr Lawrence*. When the movie came out in Japan, Kitano snuck into a cinema to gauge reaction to his new role. "The moment I appeared on screen, every single person in the theatre burst out laughing," he said. "I was devastated and humiliated."

Rather than quit, Kitano swore that he would play only dark, serious characters from then on. By the end of the nineties, he was not only Japan's most famous "hardman" actor, but also one of its most celebrated directors.

When Kitano met Bowie again on a Japanese chat show, he made a point of saying how impressed he was at the singer being able to switch from being a musician to being an actor. He himself remembered, he said, how difficult it was to convince the public that you could be more than just one thing.

Masayoshi Sukita

Bowie belongs to England, the country of his birth, the United States of America, where he chose to live, and Germany, where he wrote such influential albums. But he also belongs to Japan. The country not only influenced his look (see page 78) and provided his most fanatical fanbase, it was also home to his unofficial portrait photographer. Masayoshi Sukita was visiting London in the early seventies when he came across a poster of Bowie. The singer looked so unusual that Sukita bought a ticket for the concert. He was so bowled over that, afterwards, he sought out

Bowie's manager and asked to photograph the singer. It was the beginning of a lifelong relationship.

When Bowie was next in Japan, he asked Sukita to take more photographs but, given just a few hours' notice, the photographer found himself in a tight spot. All Tokyo's studios had been booked weeks in advance. With few options, Sukita asked a friend if he could use his flat, which had a small room with one table where his friend took commercial photographs of shampoo products. Sukita also realized that he had no option but to shoot Bowie as he was, without any makeup or costumes. "Instead of giving directions, I just captured the nature of Bowie," said Sukita, who cleared away the shampoo bottles and began snapping as the singer went through an array of playful poses. Bowie liked the result so much he asked if he could use one of the shots for his new album. The black-and-white of Bowie in his leather jacket was to become the cover for *Heroes* and remains Sukita's most famous portrait. In fact, it is the only photograph to make it onto the cover of two Bowie albums; the singer used the photograph, with a little twist, for *The Next Day* (2013).

Rupert Everett

As a teenage runaway, Rupert Everett fled to London where he led a dual life: by day a member of the jet set, by night a rent boy.

Ever a charmer, Everett quickly made friends with people like Bianca Jagger and Andy Warhol, and one night found himself seated opposite David Bowie at The Embassy, a flamboyant Mayfair club for celebrities. Everett remembered being "lectured" by Bowie on theories such as "the mystical potential of the number seven" and how "the inside of an isosceles triangle is the perfect combination of the spiritual". Despite the occult beliefs, the two got on well, so much so that when in London Bowie would often take Everett out for dinner or to a film.

As to why Bowie was interested in the young actor, Everett had a simple answer: "Because I listened," he said. "The frustrating thing was that I was quite a funny character, but I was dumbstruck by these people."

Icehouse

Bowie was to build up a good relationship with almost all his support bands. With "Let's Dance" riding high in the charts, Bowie asked Australian band Icehouse, who recorded the Bowiesque global hit "Hey Little Girl" (1982), to join him on tour. Singer Iva Davies was delighted to accept, partly because he was a Bowie fan but partly to see how someone dealt with fame on such a scale. One night in the grimy Dutch port city of Rotterdam, he was to find out. The band and Bowie had gone out for a post-gig drink when news quickly spread that Bowie was in the bar.

"Within minutes," recalled Davies, "the place became so packed it became incredibly dangerous. We only managed to get out by being passed over the heads of the crowd." Davies was used to crowd-surfing at gigs, but this was the first time he had crowd-surfed just to get out of a pub. "I remember thinking, 'Wow, that's a life,'" he said.

Thompson Twins

Thompson Twins would normally leave the venue after finishing their support set, but this was different. This was David Bowie. Bang on time, a black limousine drove up to edge of the stage and out climbed the main act.

"He just kind of nodded, walked right up to the microphone and started singing," said lead vocalist Tom Bailey, who watched the whole show, transfixed. When the concert finished, the same thing happened in reverse. Bowie walked straight off the stage, into the limo and was driven away.

"That's a way of making a gig exciting," said an impressed Bailey. "Not being there for the build-up but arriving seconds before, you have got to be brilliant." The limo routine was not Bowie's idea; it was a showbiz trick Elvis used to create the illusion that he was untouchable.

Suggs

Not only was there no limo for Suggs, but he was stuck in LA traffic and running late for Madness's slot as Bowie's support act. By the time he arrived, his band were already on stage and had begun playing "One Step Beyond". In his haste, Suggs dashed straight out, forgetting that it had been raining. Unable to stop on the slippery surface, he sailed past the microphone and found himself rapidly sliding towards the edge of the stage. And then he found himself not just one step but several steps beyond. Suggs bounced painfully through the scaffolding to the ground 20 feet below. The American audience went wild, assuming it was all part of "the English nutty boys" act. Bruised, Suggs slowly clambered back up and took his place behind the mic. As he looked across to the wings, he saw Bowie doubled over with laughter.

That's not the only embarrassing moment Suggs experienced in front of his hero. Bowie had invited the singer and his family to stay with him in Switzerland. As the guests drove up to the chalet with suitcases piled high on the car roof, Bowie came outside and pressed a button to raise the garage door. But it turned out that the luggage was higher than the garage roof, a fact Suggs was to learn only after he had parked the car.

"All my dirty underwear is blowing around Bowie's driveway and there he is picking up my socks and vests," said Suggs. "It wasn't the impression I was hoping to make."

Come breakfast, Bowie turned to the writer of "Our House" and "Baggy Trousers" and said, "I like your lyrics – how do you do it?"

"David Bowie, asking me about lyrics!" Suggs laughingly recalled.

The Beat

David Bowie popped into The Beat's caravan backstage to check on his opening act. The only member inside was their elderly Jamaican saxophonist, Saxa, a legendary figure who had played with Desmond Dekker and Prince Buster.

"Do you have everything you need?" Bowie asked.

Saxa mistook Bowie in his white tuxedo and black trousers for a waiter.

"Come with me, sonny bwoy," said Saxa, putting an arm around the singer. "Look in this fridge, you see any Red Stripe beer?"

"No, I don't," admitted Bowie.

"You're learning tricks, silly boy. Yes, no Red Stripe for me."

"I'll go see what I can do immediately," said Bowie.

According to Louis 'Sir Lou' Khan at englishbeat.net, a quarter of an hour later, Bowie returned and dropped off a couple of six packs of the Jamaican lager. A satisfied Saxa turned to singer Dave Wakeling and said, "Nice young man dat, who him to come into our dressing room asking like dat?"

"That's David Bowie," replied Wakeling.

"Bloodclaaat! A-me-a thought he was a waiter!"

Kevin Rowland

A man who liked to reinvent himself while donning the occasional dress would revel, you might imagine, in the opportunity to be Bowie's support act. Not, apparently, Kevin Rowland. In 1983, his band, Dexys Midnight Runners, were on the bill with Bowie for a concert in Paris. Not shy of provoking a reaction, Rowland loudly proclaimed in between songs, "David Bowie is full of shit!" For good measure, he added, "And a bad copy of Bryan Ferry." The crowd began booing, whistling and then hurling missiles, forcing Dexys off stage. Rowland later "explained" his outburst by saying, "We only agreed to the show because France is an important market for us – not because I have any respect for Bowie."

The probability is that Rowland was simply baiting the audience, preferring some reaction to none at all. He was, after all, enough of a Bowie fan to be at the opening of the *David Bowie Is* exhibition years later at the Victoria and Albert Museum.

The Psychedelic Furs

The Psychedelic Furs were one of Bowie's favourite bands, so when their promotions manager heard Bowie was in Sydney, he invited him to their gig. Backstage, Bowie was in a playful mood, accusing dapper singer Richard Butler of stealing his famous "Life on Mars?" blue suit. When the band's cellist walked in, Bowie asked to borrow the instrument and impressed those present with his dexterity, having just learned the cello for his role in *The Hunger*. On a roll, Bowie then picked up an empty beer can, balanced on top of it with one foot and bent down to tap the sides, collapsing it like a pancake, to a round of applause.

The circus-like antics went on into the wee hours but ended on a serious note when Bowie spoke about a new disease that had recently claimed the life of his friend, the countertenor Klaus Nomi. It was 1983, and the illness had yet to be called AIDS. As sunrise approached, Bowie said he and his girlfriend, Geeling Ng, had to go because they were scheduled to begin shooting a video on a beach for a song called "China Girl".

Over the years, there was talk of Bowie and the band working together. After one Furs gig in New York, Bowie and David Byrne went into the band's dressing room to say, "We were just arguing about who was going to produce your next album." But, according to Butler, the get-together never happened because when the band was ready, Bowie was busy, and when Bowie was free, the band did not have any new songs.

Rosie O'Donnell

Actress and chat show host Rosie O'Donnell became friends with Bowie's wife Iman after they appeared together in the 1994 comedy thriller *Exit to Eden*. But such was her obsession with one particular Bowie song that even Iman became wary of inviting her friend out. "I want to go to dinner with you," said Iman, "but please don't bring up 'China Girl', Rosie, no, no, no!"

Every time O'Donnell met Bowie she would beg him to play her favourite tune. Bowie eventually became so exasperated that he replied, "I hate that song! Bloody shut up about it."

When Bowie appeared on O'Donnell's chat show, he walked out with a guitar in hand and told her he had an early Christmas present. He sang "China Girl", switching the lyrics to "My little Rosie girl", before handing her a quickly shot video of the moment in the hope it would finally end her requests.

John Foxx

In the mid-eighties, John Foxx, the original lead singer of Ultravox, was invited to a typical Aussie barbecue, except for the fact that among the burgers and beer were David Bowie and his bodyguards. Cameras were banned, and guests were ordered not to approach the star. However, a record executive offered Foxx the chance to meet his hero. "They had a great rave together," said Virgin's Bruce Butler. Watching that meeting unfold was another singer, James Freud of the Models, Bowie's support act. Freud tugged on Butler's sleeve and also asked to be introduced.

"You're touring with him. Haven't you met him yet?" Butler asked.

"No, not Bowie!" replied Freud. "John Foxx!"

"Bowie thought it was hysterical," Butler said later, "that someone was more interested in meeting John Foxx than him."

As to what Bowie and Foxx talked about, the Ultravox singer may have mentioned his small role in the making of *Low*. Back in 1976, the band were recording their debut album when the studio phone rang for their producer, Brian Eno. It was Bowie, who wanted him to come to Berlin. Eno rejected the offer, saying he felt a responsibility to help the young band, but Foxx was adamant: "Don't be stupid! Go on, do it!" Eno was eventually persuaded. "Of course, he really wanted to do it, all along," Foxx added.

Noel Edmonds

Knowing Bowie was scared of flying, TV presenter and licensed helicopter pilot Noel Edmonds went to every effort to ensure his celebrity passenger was comfortable on the short flight to Wembley for Live Aid in 1985. Having been told the singer would only fly in a blue chopper, Edmonds went to considerable lengths to acquire one in that colour. When Bowie arrived at the pad, Edmonds proudly pointed out the paintwork.

"He looked at me as if I were mad," said Edmonds. "He didn't give a shit what colour the helicopter was."

Princess Diana

Inside the stadium, the biggest cluster of stars ever seen was soon to gather on stage for the grand finale. Getting up to join Paul McCartney, Bono, Sting and the rest was Bowie, who paused to ask Princess Diana, seated in front of him, if she cared to join him.

Bowie seated behind Princess Diana at Live Aid, July 1985.

"I might be able to sing a bit of 'God Save the Queen' but that's as far as my vocal talents go," she quipped, diplomatically declining the offer.

Diana was a big fan of Bowie's, but, sadly, it was her appearance at one of his concerts in 1987 that kicked off the deadly game of cat and mouse that was to end in her death. She had gone to the gig with David Waterhouse, a major in the Household Cavalry. The press assumed he was her lover. The next day, a photograph of Diana resting her head on his shoulder while watching the concert was splashed across the front pages "I was in tears," she said. "I was hysterical." But while she was angry with herself for being caught like that, Waterhouse appeared to enjoy the publicity, so much so that Diana ended their relationship. By then, the media obsession with her had gone into overdrive and was never to abate.

Sting

Sting and his heavily pregnant wife, Trudie Styler, were watching Bowie from the wings when the singer bounded over to the couple during a break between songs to kiss the mother-to-be's bump.

"When's it due?" he asked.

"January," replied the startled Styler.

"Ah, a Capricorn like me," replied Bowie. Then, with a winning smile and an apologetic "I've got to get back", he ran back onto the stage, just in time to sing the opening lines to "Let's Dance".

"We were totally captivated by his energetic charm," said Sting. "We felt as though he'd actually blessed our baby!"

Bowie was once asked what he would have chosen as an alternative career. "I would like to have been Sting," he said with a cheeky smile.

Mel Giedroyc

Comedian Mel Giedroyc fondly remembers the time she exchanged bodily fluids with David Bowie.

Before forming a comedy duo with Sue Perkins, the struggling stand-up worked in the kitchen of a trendy London café. One day, in the late eighties, in walked Bowie followed by his entourage. The owners immediately ushered the staff into the back and warned them not to approach the star.

Sensing her chance to meet her hero was about to vanish, Mel thought to herself, "I'm not going to get to say hello, so what can I do to feel I have 'entered' him?" Her answer was to lick the slice of cake he had just ordered. "Only a little polite lick," she clarified. "Just to be close to him."

Keith Haring

- - - - - - - - - - - - - -

At one point in the eighties, Keith Haring's colourful jelly-bean characters were everywhere, appearing on mugs, T-shirts and students' walls. Among his many admirers was Bowie, who commissioned the American Pop artist to design the cover of his 1983 single "Without You". Haring was to die at just 31 from AIDS-related complications, but in the early eighties, he was in the thick of the ultra-cool party set. Here is his throwaway description of what may well have been the coolest party of the decade. "I brought Madonna and the artist Martin Burgoyne. Andy [Warhol] was already there. Bob Dylan. David Bowie and Iggy Pop…just sort of in the kitchen." He added, "You can't believe you're there."

Tim Pope

- - - - - - - - - - -

At another party, it was Lou Reed who was in the kitchen with Bowie. Who could resist eavesdropping? And that is exactly what video director Tim Pope did.

Pope, whose quirky work with The Cure helped define the eighties, had spotted that the two intellectual icons of rock had peeled off from the crowd and were now in deep discussion on their own. Were they talking about philosophy, art, the next stage for music? Pope had to know. He edged closer.

"I bought a bowl," he heard Bowie say. "By the time I got home, it had cracked."

They were talking about shopping on their holidays. "It was the least esoteric conversation I could imagine," said Pope.

Keith Richards

What did two of rock's wildest men do when they met up at night? Images of rock and roll excess flood the mind, but the reality was more mundane: they played Trivial Pursuit. According to Bowie, Keith Richards was an ace at the general-knowledge board game. His uncanny recall convinced Bowie that Richards's "out-of-it" image was just a publicity ploy.

But while Bowie adored the Stones' music, Richards was less flattering about his pal's. "It's all pose," he said of Bowie's changing image. "It's nothing to do with the music. He knows it too." Once pushed to name his favourite Bowie track, he eventually came up with "Changes", before adding, "Maybe...that's about it. Not a big fan." Richards did not rate Bowie's acting either, saying, "I'm not an actor. Nor is David Bowie."

Werner Herzog

Not that such disparaging remarks about his acting dissuaded Bowie from pursuing a career in film, especially when it came to experimental or art-house movies. He made attempts to contact each of the holy triumvirate of directors who defined New German Cinema. Bowie worked with Wim Wenders, discussed collaborating with Rainer Werner Fassbinder and was rejected by Werner Herzog, who dismissed the singer as having the depth of a light bulb.

Herzog and Bowie had both fallen in love with a book by British author Bruce Chatwin called *The Viceroy of Ouidah* (1980), which depicted the life of a slave trader in West Africa. Herzog wanted to turn the novel into a film but lacked the money and, above all, the energy. Previous films had ended with him and his lead actor, notorious wild man Klaus Kinski, trying to kill each other on location – Herzog by attempting to set fire to the actor's house, Kinski by using a gun.

When the director heard Bowie also wanted to make the Chatwin film, he was delighted and suggested they collaborate. But Herzog became frustrated as negotiations for the film rights dragged on. He appealed to Bowie directly to cut out the Hollywood money men who, he believed, wanted to turn the movie into a franchise. Eventually, an exasperated Herzog turned against Bowie himself, who had been keen on playing the lead role, and the German decided to make the project alone.

"Bowie has star quality, forever glowing, but with an artificial quality," said Herzog, explaining his reasoning to Paul Cronin in *Werner Herzog: A Guide for the Perplexed*. "The man is a neon light bulb. There is no real depth to him. He lacks the dark, dangerous, brooding intensity that the character demands."

Incredibly, the director replaced Bowie with his muse-cum-nemesis, Kinski, and, again, the pair almost murdered each other. A notorious photograph from the 1987 filming of *Cobra Verde* shows an enraged Kinski seemingly ready to saw Herzog's head off with a machete. Herzog later joked about the incident, but the photographer who took the notorious shot remained convinced that the actor, who had to be physically pulled off Herzog, was genuinely intent on trying to behead his director.

Carl Perkins

The idea of Bowie rocking and rolling with Carl "Blue Suede Shoes" Perkins is an image to savour for any music fan. But this rocking and rolling was done not on stage but on a carpet, as the two fought to the death in the comic caper *Into the Night*. At the climax of the 1985 film, the celebrity wattage goes off the scale: Perkins pulls a knife out of his chest to attack Bowie, who is holding Michelle Pfeiffer hostage, as Jeff Goldblum looks on. Locked in a deadly embrace, Perkins and Bowie tumble out of a window to their deaths. The film sank just as quickly. Off-screen, Bowie did jam with one of his co-stars, but strangely it was not Perkins and it wasn't rock and roll – it was Goldblum, a keen piano player, and it was jazz. As for director John Landis, his greatest challenge was trying to make Bowie look like a grubby gangster. "We put grease in his hair, kept him unshaven and put a Band-Aid on his forehead, and still David managed to look stylish," he said.

Martin Scorsese

Behind all Bowie's attempts to be recognized as a decent actor was a long-held ambition to get behind the camera itself and be a director. No less a figure than Martin Scorsese was to give him the opportunity to fulfil that dream. "I had seen his rock videos, and I thought they were very interesting," said Scorsese. "I remember calling him and suggesting that he direct one." *Thirteen Ways to Kill a Poet* was to be a series of short films by unusual directors about the deaths of artists. The first three filmmakers had been picked and they were at the very top of the tree: Francis Ford Coppola, Michael Powell and Scorsese himself. The fourth one was to be Bowie. Scorsese discussed the project with the singer over several dinners in his New York loft apartment but it proved too complicated and never took off.

Although Bowie never did find the right project to direct, he and Scorsese worked together on *The Last Temptation of Christ* (1988), with Bowie playing the part of Pontius Pilate. Scorsese raved about Bowie's performance, saying it was like looking into the face of the ancient world. Bowie was also a huge fan of the director. "With somebody like that, you don't even question the role. You say, 'Scorsese? Yeah, I'm doing it.'"

It is tempting to speculate that Bowie's thwarted ambition to direct may have inspired his son, Duncan Jones, to take that path.

Steven Spielberg

Spielberg was also a fan of Bowie's acting. So much so that in the mid-eighties, when the director decided to make a musical about Peter Pan, his first choice was the English singer. Bowie was open to the idea of a musical fantasy and, around this time, agreed to star in *Labyrinth* (1986), directed by Jim Henson. That may be the reason why he turned down Spielberg's offer. Either way, having failed to get his man, Spielberg decided to put the project on ice and took the opportunity to change tack to pursue a more "serious" direction based on a book he had read called *Schindler's Ark*. Years later, Spielberg came back to Peter Pan but, without Bowie's involvement, he jettisoned the idea of a musical and asked Dustin Hoffman to play Captain Hook, the role originally conceived for the singer.

Jim Henson
- - - - - - - - - - - - -

Bowie wanted to be remembered for his part in Jim Henson's *Labyrinth*, and he certainly was. The size of his appendage, as revealed by the ballet tights he wore as Jareth the Goblin King, resulted in numerous column inches. The codpiece controversy centred on whether the singer had been given extra padding, and whether such revealing underwear was appropriate in a children's movie.

The other contender for the part was Michael Jackson. But when Henson met Bowie, he was left in no doubt as to why the English singer had the edge. "David embodies a certain maturity with his sexuality, his 'disturbing' aspect, that characterizes the adult world," said the director cryptically. Costume designer Brian Froud was more direct when he described the tights as "Bowie's perv pants", although Froud refused to divulge whether he had inserted a codpiece or not.

Derek Jarman
- - - - - - - - - - - - - - - -

David Bowie had gone around to meet the English director with a view to making a film but ended up running out of the door, fearing he was in the presence of a Satanist. At least that's the way Derek Jarman saw the encounter.

The maverick filmmaker had invited Bowie round to his apartment to discuss working on a post-nuclear apocalypse movie called *Neutron*. The conversation started well, but then Jarman noticed his guest chain-smoking nervously and casting furtive glances towards the bookshelves and drawings on the wall. In the middle of the conversation, Bowie made an excuse and left.

Minutes later, his bodyguard came back and retrieved Bowie's cigarette stubs from the ashtray.

The director later came to believe that Bowie must have noticed his collection of works by Dr John Dee, the Elizabethan astrologer whose magical system had influenced the occultist and alleged Satanist Aleister Crowley. Bowie, Jarman presumed, was seemingly scared that the cigarette stubs could be used in a curse. In fact, the director had originally acquired the material on Dee as research for his film *Jubilee* (1978).

Bowie had certainly been freaked out by talk of Crowley in the seventies when he was going through his cocaine psychosis (see page 151). But when he was asked if such fears had stopped the project with Jarman, he replied, "No, absolutely not. I would've given my arm to work with Jarman. My remembrance of the thing was that, as usual, he couldn't get the funds to actually make the movie."

Also present at that meeting was artist Edward Bell, a friend of Bowie's (see page 210). Although Bell did not recall any minder returning to Jarman's flat, he did remember Bowie getting upset and leaving in a huff. At some point during the conversation, Bell recalled, Bowie noticed an empty, crumpled packet of the singer's Marlboro cigarettes on Jarman's mantelpiece. Whether the director had put them there as a sacred object to brag to friends, "You'll never guess whose cigarette packet that is", or whether he had other nefarious purposes, Bell had no idea, but Bowie, he said, was not pleased. "Oh, don't be silly, Derek," Bowie said, getting up, taking the packet and walking out.

The film never got made. And although Jarman died in 1994, Bowie held onto the script and set drawings, and continued to talk about wanting to approach the director's family to make the movie posthumously.

Raymond Briggs

Bowie had just finished narrating the opening to the 1984 US version of what would become a Christmas staple, the animated TV film *The Snowman* (1982). Outside the recording booth, the whole production team had assembled to meet the star.

"I remember us all lining up to shake his hand like he was the Queen," said the graphic author Sir Raymond Briggs. On reaching the writer, Bowie said, "I admire your work." The 48-year-old, not known for his love of rock music, responded, "God! I wish I could say the same." Unperturbed, Bowie smiled and soon won the author over as he talked about his love of the book.

"It was fun meeting him," recalled Briggs. "He was wearing these wonderful, glittering pink shoes. Never seen pink shoes on a man."

Alan Bennett

A dinner party with Alan Bennett and David Bowie as guests would normally be a guarantee of an entertaining conversation, but not so, according to the Yorkshire playwright. "It's not to disparage David Bowie," wrote Bennett in his diary, before proceeding to do just that. Looking back at their meeting at the home of director John Schlesinger in the mid-eighties, Bennett described the singer as making no impression at all: "I remember him as a slight, almost colourless figure, who was somehow Scots." It was hard to believe, he added, that even half the posthumous tributes to the singer could be true.

Warming to his theme, Bennett then recounted a story given to him by an anonymous friend on the day Bowie died. "M. recalls how someone he knew picked up Bowie when he was still David Jones," Bennett wrote. "Jones offered to come round, bringing his guitar as he wanted to try out some songs. They had sex and then he wanted to play more, only his host pleaded another appointment and sent him away."

Michael Caine

Bowie and Michael Caine came close to meeting in the mid-seventies when Bowie was the first choice to act alongside Caine in the war film classic *The Eagle Has Landed* (1976). Studio politics resulted in a last-minute change, and Bowie's role ended up going to Robert Duvall. However, the two Londoners soon got to know each other.

Caine and his wife were holidaying in the south of France and had been hobnobbing with the super-rich and famous. The previous week they had dined on a boat with Frank Sinatra, Roger Moore and Barbara Harris, the widow of Cary Grant. This particular day, the couple were due to dine on Bowie's new vessel in the Bay of Cannes but were running late. Worried that Bowie might set sail without them, Caine asked his driver to use the car phone to say they were just a few minutes away.

"If you make a call from here," his chauffeur said, "it'll go 30,000 miles to a satellite, bounce off to a station outside New York and then to the ship. Why don't you wave this at them?" he added, producing a handkerchief. "This I did; they saw me, waved back and the situation was saved," said Caine. On the jetty, the actor bumped into Eric Idle and, as the two looked up at the huge vessel, Caine said, "Fuck me, Eric. We're in the wrong business."

According to the actor, Bowie was still in the first "euphoric" stage of ownership. "There are a mass of sayings about buying yachts," said Caine. "One of them is that there are two great days in owning it – the day you buy it and the day you sell it."

Caine added, "David had a tremendously exotic aura and a sort of mystery as an artist. But he comes from exactly the same place as I do and started out as a small-part actor a few years after I did, so when I talk to him the conversation is on a less ethereal plane." The yacht, said the actor, matched the owner's character: "It was sleek and unfussy with no luxurious trimmings."

Beyond being working-class south Londoners who kept their accents, Caine and David had something else in common: both had brothers who had been incarcerated in the local psychiatric hospital, Cane Hill, in Coulsdon.

Caine's mother had an illegitimate child who, given the times, was sent to the institution. The boy suffered from epilepsy and was often locked in a cellar with a stone floor. By the time Caine discovered the family secret, his mother was dead and David, his brother, was a deeply traumatized 66-year-old. From time to time Caine went to see him, but his brother's words had to be interpreted by a nurse because of the difficulty he had in speaking. "He was bouncing about on that stone floor and bashed himself into a bloody brain abnormality," said Caine. His brother died within 18 months of their meeting. As for Bowie's brother, Terry, he had died seven years earlier after lying down on train tracks to kill himself.

Patsy Kensit

Patsy Kensit was just 16 when she landed her breakthrough role in *Absolute Beginners* (1986). The teenager was doubly thrilled because her adolescent crush, David Bowie, was in the cast. For years, she had dreamed of how she would make the singer fall in love with her.

Bowie was distant and otherwise occupied during the first days of filming, but then one day, when Kensit was sitting alone in the makeup room, he walked in. He said hello, picked up a brush and started combing her hair. "He probably only did about three strokes," said Kensit. Bowie then put down the brush and, without saying another word, left. "It felt like the most erotic thing I'd ever had in my entire life," recalled the young actress.

Mickey Rourke

As well as an actor, Mickey Rourke has been a boxer, screenwriter, animal-rights activist and enfant terrible. He has also been, ever so briefly, a rapper. In 1986, Rourke asked his new pal David Bowie if he could appear on one of his records. "Shining Star (Makin' My Love)" is, as the title suggests, a cheesy eighties pop song, written at the lowest point of Bowie's career. Rourke appears halfway through, uttering meaning-laden lines like "Blew heads outta shape for the name of Trotsky, Sinn Féin, Hitler". Bowie amusingly described Rourke's performance as "method rapping".

Bowie had befriended the actor earlier that year in London when the American was filming *A Prayer for the Dying* (1987). The year 1987 was a bad one for both of them: Rourke quickly disowned the critically panned movie, and Bowie described his

LP released that year, *Never Let Me Down*, as "the nadir" of his career. "I really shouldn't have even bothered going into the studio to record it," he said. "In fact, when I play it, I wonder if I did."

But their friendship did provide Bowie with what he called "my biggest up" when Rourke told him that, as a teenager, he had dyed his hair green and worn stack-heeled boots and leather trousers in a bid to look like Ziggy Stardust. All this in 1973 humdrum Florida, where, Rourke told him, no one was aware of, let alone into, glam rock. "I was so encouraged by that," Bowie later told *Q* magazine. "A guy like that, and it was a major part of his life."

Axl Rose

Bowie has the dubious honour of having been hit by three different rock stars. As well as the infamous battering from Lou Reed and a swing by a drunk rock star (yet to come), there was the time that Axl Rose punched him for ogling his girlfriend.

Bowie had got to know a very young Slash, having dated his mother in the seventies (see page 159). So, catching up with old acquaintances, he showed up at a Hollywood nightclub in 1989 where Guns N' Roses were making a video for "It's So Easy". While the band were performing, Bowie began chatting to Rose's 23-year-old partner, Erin Everly, the inspiration for Guns N' Roses' single "Sweet Child o' Mine" (1988). Believing Bowie was being overtly flirtatious, an enraged Rose jumped off the stage, swung a punch at his 42-year-old peer and then had him kicked off the set. A security guard claimed he saw Rose chasing Bowie down the alleyway shouting, "I'm going to kill you."

Sometime later, Bowie returned, apologized for overstepping any line and the two made up. A photograph that night shows them smiling with arms around each other after having shared a meal at a Chinese restaurant. "Bowie and I had our differences," said Rose. "Then we talked and went out for dinner. I was like, 'I want to thank you for being the first person that's ever come up to me in person and said how sorry they were about the situation and stuff.' I never met anybody so cool."

Months later, the Guns N' Roses singer was approached backstage by Mick Jagger and Eric Clapton, who had heard the story about the punch-up and wanted all the lurid details. "Jagger doesn't really talk a lot, right?" recalled Rose. "All of a sudden he's like, 'So you got in a fight with Bowie, didja?' So, I told him the story real quick and him and Clapton are going off about Bowie, saying things like when Bowie gets drunk he turns into the Devil from Bromley. I'm just sitting there listening to them bitch like crazy about Bowie. It was funny."

Grace Jones

The Jamaican singer was flying to the United States to appear in a Christmas TV special when she bumped into Bowie on the plane. He laughingly recounted his own appearance on a festive show with Bing Crosby a decade earlier, when he was almost forced to sing a song he loathed (see page 183). That gave Bowie an idea. Why not, he suggested, sing the same song? Jones, who once described herself as "half disco diva, half David Bowie", loved the in-joke.

Come the day, Jones, never one to disappoint sartorially, burst out of a wooden crate wearing an armoured breastplate and blue oven gloves. She then launched into "Little Drummer Boy". She later recounted the story to host Pee-wee Herman to explain why she had chosen that song. According to Herman, Bowie even had a hand in composing the eighties electro backing, which, given how bad it was, seems highly fanciful.

The Berlin Wall

Not many pop stars can claim to have helped bring down a dictatorial empire and freed millions of people from tyranny. David Bowie can. No less than German Chancellor Angela Merkel and her government thanked the singer for helping bring about the end of communism. It all started with an encounter at the Wall.

In 1987, Bowie arranged an outdoor concert which backed onto the East German watchtowers. As he sang "Heroes", he began to hear a sound from behind the stage. It was East Berlin singing along. Thousands had gathered on the other side but so too had armed soldiers, who began beating and arresting people. Refusing to be cowed, the crowd sat down and started chanting, "The Wall must fall." As the chant reached those on the West, tens of thousands more voices joined in. It was the first time that people from both sides of the divide had communicated so directly since the Berlin Wall was erected in 1961. Bowie was so overwhelmed that he began to cry on stage.

"God, even now I get choked up," he said in 2003. "It was breaking my heart. I'd never done anything like that in my life and I guess I never will again." Singing "Heroes" that night, he said, felt more like a prayer than a song.

The state violence was seen as a new low by East Berliners, and, as news filtered across the communist city, disgust at the regime grew. One song had sparked a combination of hope and anger which was to prove a turning point in the history of Soviet-occupied Eastern Europe. Bowie would say, ever after, that no matter how many times he sang "Heroes", it could never match that night.

ARTISTIC REINVENTION
1991–2004

This is the decade Bowie discovered love, drum and bass and yet another version of himself. He also became a hero to the latest generation of bands about to change the musical landscape. Stephen King and he planned to make a horror concept album, while Tony Blair stopped a debt-relief meeting to pose an urgent question: "When is Bowie's new album out?" From prime ministers to painters, it appeared that there was no one who was not influenced by him.

Bowie expanded his horizons, not only renewing his love of painting but also becoming an art journalist. So keen was he to show that he was not out of his depth, his questions were often more intellectual than the answers.

The rock and roll lifestyle was gradually being left behind. Pomegranate juice replaced alcohol. When he went on tour, he sometimes asked to go on first to beat the traffic home. When his final tour started, he was 56. He had never sounded nor looked healthier. The cigarettes, booze and drugs had gone. He was happy playing the crowd favourites and happy writing new stuff. Unlike just about all his contemporaries, he was still cool. Then, he had a heart attack and everything went quiet.

Jeremy Irons

Although Jeremy Irons met Bowie, it was the singer's future wife who bowled him over. Irons was so taken with Iman after meeting her at a photoshoot in New York that he asked the Somali model out for dinner.

"Oh no, I can't," Iman replied. "I'm going to Los Angeles."

When Irons asked why, Iman said, "I'm going to look for a husband."

She found him.

Iman

Like so much in Bowie's life, it all came down to a haircut. Teddy Antolin, Bowie's hair stylist in Los Angeles, was aware that his client was lonely. "It was so sad, all this hard work each day and then he was alone," said Antolin. Killing two birds with one stone, the hairdresser decided to fix up Bowie with another of his single customers.

"Hi, David, what are you doing tonight?"

"Not very much as I recently split up with my fiancée [Melissa Hurley]."

"Oh, well, come and have dinner, it's my birthday. I know this girl called Iman."

"A man? You know a girl that's a man?"

It was a conversation Bowie loved to repeat in later years. Once the gender was cleared up, he accepted the invitation and was an early arrival at the party. Then, Iman arrived. "The minute she walked in, it was love at first sight," recalled Antolin. "She and David looked at each other – you could feel the electricity."

Iman and Bowie, 1992.

Bowie told *Hello* magazine in 2000 that he knew immediately he had met his future wife. "I had never gone after anything with such passion in all my life," he said.

The next day, Bowie took Iman out for afternoon tea. "He told me he was so nervous he just said 'tea'. He never drinks tea," said Iman. "He had a coffee."

Iman told Bowie about having once seen her "ideal" engagement ring in a small jewellers in Florence. Unknown to her, Bowie tracked down the store only to discover that the ring had long since been sold. Not to be deterred, Bowie asked for the address of the buyer and wrote a letter explaining that the engagement to the love of his life hung on this small piece of jewellery. The owner was swayed, Bowie got his ring and the couple were married within the year.

Piers Morgan

While performing on stage in London, Bowie had been hit in the eye by a packet of cigarettes thrown from the audience. *The Sun* newspaper wanted a comment so sent their cub showbiz reporter, Piers Morgan, to Bowie's hotel, where he waited patiently outside, pen and notebook in hand, hoping to catch the rock star. After an hour, Bowie, wearing an eyepatch, came out and walked right up to the journalist.

"You don't want to interview me about being hit in the head," Bowie told him.

"Don't I?" replied the confused reporter.

"No. You want to ask me whether I'm getting engaged."

"Do I?"

"Yes."

Unsure if he was having his leg pulled, the journalist took the plunge and asked, "David, are you getting engaged?"

"Yes," replied Bowie, laying out in detail his plans to marry Iman.

"He gave me the scoop in the street," said an astonished Piers Morgan. "I'll never forget that. He gave me an hour-long interview standing on the pavement."

Christie Brinkley

"It took two blondes to get me pregnant – David Bowie and Christie Brinkley," Iman once said.

American supermodel Brinkley was a long-standing friend of the couple and had witnessed their emotional upset as they tried unsuccessfully to have a baby. One day, Iman mentioned to her friend a Somali tradition that advised women who were having trouble conceiving to cradle an infant for a day. Brinkley got the message and returned with her one-year-old daughter, Sailor, whom she promptly handed over.

"Sure enough, it worked!" said Brinkley. "After seven years of trying, Iman got pregnant."

David Lee Roth

In the nineties Bowie was to become so friendly with David Lee Roth that he would call up the Van Halen frontman for advice on married life. But the relationship had not started off well.

Roth was rarely short of confidence. One night, in 1982, still two years shy of mega-hit "Jump" (1984), he swaggered into New York's hip Peppermint Lounge club. "All flowing blond hair and leather chaps and a shirt opened down to the waist, he flaunted masculine confidence and a king of the jungle persona," recalled the rock writer Lisa Robinson. That is until he walked over to Bowie and Paul Simonon, of The Clash, to tell them how much he admired them.

Roth embarked on a rambling monologue that petered out as it dawned on him no one at the table (Debbie Harry was also there) had the faintest idea who he was. "Everyone just stared at him and said nothing," recalled Robinson. "Embarrassed, he eventually skulked away."

Given that encounter, it is perhaps surprising that Bowie and Roth became friends. Roth recalled Bowie once calling him for a heart-to-heart shortly after meeting Iman. "I'm in a quandary and I'm being serious," Bowie nervously confided. "Tell me what you think...I bought furniture."

Roth believed that this act of buying such a symbol of domesticity represented a life-changing moment for Bowie. "He had never put down an anchor, not romantically, not spiritually, not morally or musically, anywhere," said the American singer. "David had put out to sea as a very young man. When he finally came to shore in New York City and got married, everything he knew ended." Buying his first piece of furniture was, Roth believed, the moment Bowie's rock-and-roll lifestyle finally came to an end.

Pixies

Each member of Pixies has their own personal recollection of the man who believed they were "the great forgotten American band". Kim Deal remembered being invited back to Bowie's hotel in 1991 to listen to his new album after the band had supported him on tour in Germany. The excited bassist went to the bathroom to get ready but spent so long there that, by the time she reappeared, everyone had left. Deal was devastated at missing the chance to hang out with Bowie. But perhaps she could take solace from the fact that the new LP Bowie was to play that night was by Tin Machine (*Tin Machine II*), his much-maligned band.

Guitarist Joey Santiago remembered going out for a curry with Bowie and sneaking a look at the singer's credit card as he paid for everyone. Just as he hoped, the name written on the plastic was "David Jones".

And singer Frank Black remembered his delight when Bowie invited him on stage for the rock star's star-studded 50th-birthday celebrations at Madison Square Garden. What song did the mischievous Bowie ask the bald, rotund Pixie, known as "the least fashionable man in indie rock", to sing? "Fashion".

Robert Smith

Also invited to Bowie's birthday concert was the singer of The Cure. Frontman Robert Smith may have been somewhat surprised to have been asked because, the first time he met Bowie, he had drunkenly insulted him.

A nervous Smith had hit the booze early that day in 1995, ahead of his planned interview of Bowie for Xfm radio. "I think my opening gambit was, 'We can both agree you've never done anything good since 1982,'" Smith said. Even today, Smith winces in embarrassed disbelief at the memory.

During the interview, Smith went from garrulously drunk (talking over Bowie), to emotionally drunk ("Good grief! This is all too much for me!") to angrily drunk. What made him so "enraged" was Bowie's suggestion that it was the consumer, not the artist, who defined the meaning of art.

Despite this, Bowie harboured no ill feelings. In fact, he continued to speak glowingly of The Cure as one of Britain's most eccentric bands. A couple of years later, Bowie called Smith at home to invite him to his 50th-birthday party at Madison Square Garden. Was there a particular song from Bowie's own back catalogue that Smith would like to sing? As a lengthy list of favourites flashed through Smith's mind, Bowie jumped in and said, "How about 'Quicksand'?" "You bastard!" Smith recalled thinking, having not even considered that song. But when it came to the night in question, the pair's version of that melancholic numnber was the emotional highlight of the evening.

"I got my dream come true," Smith said. "He invited me to sing with him. Unreal, actually, for something like that to happen." The Cure singer also gave Bowie the most apposite birthday present of all: a fossilized chameleon.

Scott Walker

But it was another present that was to bring Bowie to tears. BBC Radio 1 had invited him on to celebrate his 50th birthday with a special programme. Well-wishing messages poured in from stars such as Bono, Robert Smith and Brett Anderson. But then the station played a brief, crackly recording from someone across the Atlantic who was far less well-known. For the next 30 seconds, there was silence. Tears sprang into the speechless Bowie's eyes. For seasoned presenter Mary Anne Hobbes, it was "the most emotional moment of my career".

She waited for Bowie to compose himself. The 30 seconds felt like an eternity, she recalled. Finally, Bowie said, chokingly, "Wow. That's...that's amazing." After another pause, he added, "I see God in the window. You really got me there." It was the most emotionally raw moment of Bowie ever captured on tape. When the recording was later broadcast, the BBC producers were forced to cut the silence down to just a few seconds as the emergency dead-air tapes would otherwise have automatically kicked in.

The man responsible for causing such a heartfelt reaction was Scott Walker, an eccentric American singer who had briefly been as popular as the Beatles in the mid-sixties before rejecting fame to write a series of uniquely odd and influential albums. He had also been Bowie's idol since his late teens.

"I would like to thank you, especially for your generosity of spirit when it comes to other artists," Walker told Bowie on the tape. "I've been the beneficiary on more than one occasion, let me tell you. So, have a wonderful birthday. By the way, mine is the day after yours, so I'll have a drink to you on the other side of midnight. How's that?"

Speaking about the show, Bowie said, "The one that killed me was Scott Walker. He came on and just said some really lovely things and I was just so knocked out. That really got me, that did. The man has got such great integrity and doesn't deviate from his particular vision. He's as selfish as I am, in that he pays no notice to the audience, and just does what he wants to do. And he's always someone that I've looked at when I think what should I be doing."

Bowie was once asked, "If you could pick someone to sing with, who would it be?" "Scott Walker," he replied without hesitation.

Harvey Keitel

What 50-year-old wouldn't want to be a cowboy? Even so, Bowie's choice to mark his half-century by appearing in a low-budget Italian Western surprised not just his fans but Bowie himself.

Director Giovanni Veronesi said he courted the singer "as a plain man might court a beautiful, unobtainable woman". To the director's amazement, Bowie was successfully wooed. "Bowie told me I was crazy to offer him that film, but then said that he was even crazier because he accepted!"

Bowie had just one stipulation: no barking dogs within earshot. Given the plethora of strays in Tuscany, this was no easy task. Veronesi hired a van and rounded up as many canine waifs as possible. Not knowing what to do with them all, he kept them, even after filming ended. "I still have some of them!" he said years later.

While Bowie's relationship with the director of *Gunslinger's Revenge* was good, his relationship with his American co-star was fraught. Harvey Keitel enjoyed spoofing around on set, but his jokes aimed at Bowie were more like ferocious barbs, said Veronesi. "They acted like friends but I thought they were pretending," said the director.

Bowie's best scene happened off-camera. His Italian co-star Leonardo Pieraccioni told this story: "The first day Bowie arrived on set, he came up to me, and everyone went off, leaving us alone. He began this very long story in English. I wanted to stop him to say I couldn't speak English but didn't because I was too ashamed. So, I let him carry on talking. Then, at the end of this long speech, he smiled at me. I looked back at him. I didn't know what to do. So, I said, as meaningfully as I could, '...Yes.' He looked crushed. Evidently, he expected something more appropriate."

The Legendary Stardust Cowboy

There was one cowboy for whom Bowie had a particular soft spot. The Legendary Stardust Cowboy was a genuine oddball outsider who lived up to his self-proclaimed billing not so much because of his records, which sold in the dozens, but because it was from him that Bowie got part of the name for Ziggy Stardust. On a trip to America, Bowie was asked by a record executive if he liked "weird shit". When Bowie replied yes, the exec handed him over a single and said, "Well, this is the weirdest shit we've got."

"I immediately fell in love with his music," said Bowie. "Well actually, the idea of his music, as the music itself wasn't too recognizable as being such."

Years later, Bowie was trawling the net and came across a letter by "the Ledge", aka Norman Odam, which read, "I've reached the point where I need help going further. It sure would be nice if David Bowie would pay me something for using part of my name in Ziggie [*sic*] Stardust." Feeling guilty, Bowie recorded one of his songs. Odam was delighted when he realized this would mean receiving a couple of hundred dollars every time it got played. Bowie then went further and asked Odam to appear at an event he was curating, London's Meltdown festival in 2002. The Ledge lived up to his billing as the outsider's outsider. "An idiot-savant of screaming, yelling and bugles," recalled one spectator. Odam's encore involved walking on stage, dropping his trousers and walking off.

"What a professional!" Bowie joked when he followed.

Amusingly, the Ledge did not rate Bowie's music. "I just don't care for dobro [a resonator guitar], banjo and violin," he said. Quite what era of Bowie he was referring to, he did not say.

Coldplay

Also chosen by Bowie to appear at Meltdown was Coldplay. The singer came in for some flak for that decision, with some in the press criticizing their inclusion as proof that Bowie had become mainstream and unadventurous. The criticism stung Bowie into action; he penned a letter to *The Times* to defend his lineup, writing, "My choice reflects both my populist and my fringe tastes in music."

Given the public praise, Coldplay frontman Chris Martin must have thought he was in with a chance when he asked Bowie to sing on a track he had written. No such luck.

"Not one of your best," Bowie replied briefly in a text, and that was that.

"He was very discerning," drummer Will Champion commented with a laugh, and confessed that, in hindsight, they should have offered him a better song than "Lhuna".

The Smashing Pumpkins

Billy Corgan remains both puzzled and a little hurt that he and Bowie never got to make a record. Mutual friends like Trent Reznor, Moby and Arcade Fire had all got to record with Bowie but, despite countless hints, Bowie never took the bait to team up with the Chicago frontman.

"I don't understand why, because I kept throwing it out there through the back channels," said Corgan. But the Smashing Pumpkins singer was completely overlooked. Bowie, though, loved the Smashing Pumpkins and asked the singer to join him on stage for his star-packed 50th birthday celebrations at Madison Square Garden. Bowie suggested they duet on "All the Young Dudes". When Corgan asked why he had picked that song, Bowie replied, "Oh, because there's that line in the song, 'Billy's pulling stars off his face' and I thought of you."

"I mean, hello! I'm good!" an emotional Corgan told an online show when recounting the story. "I wish that was the end of the podcast, right there!"

The Prodigy

Usually, when it came to rejection, it was Bowie doing the rejecting. But, occasionally, it was the other way around.

Bowie adored The Prodigy. "Phew, I've got to measure myself against this!" was his response after seeing them on the festival circuit. "There is no other band, stage-wise. They're The Clash meets house, punk-dance."

He was so impressed that he even embarked upon his own drum-and-bass period. So, who better than The Prodigy founder, Liam Howlett, to produce his next record? Howlett, however, had other ideas. "Bowie is a wicked guy but through my youth I wasn't listening to that, so it didn't mean anything," he said, and declined the offer.

Unruffled, Bowie said the effort to keep up with the high-energy electro ravers helped him rediscover his confidence on stage. "We started doing festivals in the mid-nineties, working with top-rate bands like Prodigy. You know what? That did such a lot for my confidence as a performer."

As for the main topic of conversation backstage? "We had some great chats about drugs," said Howlett.

Goldie

Two men natter away over their knitting in a caravan on the Isle of Man like a couple of old ladies. It's a homely image, and not one that immediately comes to mind when thinking of Bowie and the gold-toothed drum-and-bass pioneer.

One of the more unlikely musical friendships of the nineties happened in the fittingly improbable surroundings of Fortnum

& Mason. DJ Pete Tong, who knew that Bowie loved drum and bass, suggested he meet Goldie over cream tea in the formal Piccadilly institution. They got on so well that they ended up not just recording a song together, called "Truth", but also appearing in a film, after Goldie convinced his new pal to join him in a gangland movie.

"I remember us sitting in this caravan on the Isle of Man," recalled Goldie. "There's some pretty serious Moss Side gangsters on that set but I looked over at the Duke and he was knitting. He said it chilled him out."

Goldie was at the height of his drug use at the time, "doing three to four benders a day", and believed he was living on borrowed time. Bowie's gentle encouragement, he said, gave him faith in music and ultimately saved his life.

Björk

Bowie was also to meet Goldie's Icelandic partner. "I always wondered what you would look like as a bird laying eggs," he told her. Most people might take that as an intriguing, if somewhat odd, comment and leave it there. But not Björk.

In 2001, she was nominated for an Oscar for Best Original Song ("I've Seen It All" in *Dancer in the Dark*). Thinking about what to wear for the Academy Awards, she recalled Bowie's words and decided to become a bird for a day by donning a white feathered dress designed to resemble a swan, with the bird's long neck draped around her own.

When she hit the red carpet, Björk took the image a step further. She lifted up her dress, squatted down and started to "lay" eggs, real eggs (ostrich eggs, in fact, which were the largest she could find). The cameras started clicking away like crazy. The perplexed security guards followed her around the carpet picking up the eggs as fast as Björk could lay them, saying, "Scuse me, ma'am. You dropped this." It became the most talked-about event of the evening.

The press ridiculed the singer, describing her as looking like a refugee and as "Alice in Blunderland". Comedian Joan Rivers said Björk belonged "in an asylum". But Björk and Bowie had the last laugh. The dress is now described as "the gown which changed red carpet fashion" and is on display at New York's Museum of Modern Art.

Madonna

Bowie wrote two songs about Madonna. Neither was flattering.

With lines like "Who died and made you material girl?", "Lucy Can't Dance" seemed to imply Madonna was a plagiarist who followed cautiously in his wake. It was, according to writer Chris O'Leary, "a vicious put-down of an artist that many considered to be his successor".

But that song was as nothing compared to "Pretty Thing", which seemed to poke fun at an alleged domestic incident. "Tie you down, pretend you're Madonna," sang Bowie in apparent reference to her being tied to a chair, an incident later denied by both Madonna and then husband Sean Penn. But Bowie stoked the fire when he jokingly said, "I've been hanging out with Sean. He told us a few things. Know what I mean?"

Bowie described Madonna as "conventional in the extreme", but she seemed to rise above it all. Just a few years later, she was chosen to induct Bowie into the Rock and Roll Hall of

Fame. Madonna spoke about how her father grounded her for the summer after she had sneaked out to a Bowie concert as a teenager. Bowie did not make an appearance, but when he saw her flattering remarks, he appeared to realize that he might have overstepped the mark in the past. "I saw what Madonna said and I thought it was incredibly generous of her, frankly. She really went up in my estimation because of that."

As the years passed, Bowie became more effusive in his praise of the one artist who matched him for image changes. "She's quite miraculously gathered all these elements that were mere seedlings in seventies performers. She's a top-drawer plate-spinner. And I think she's looking really lovely at the moment."

There is a record of them meeting only once, backstage after a Bowie concert in 1987. After Bowie died, Madonna posted a photograph of the encounter with the caption: "So lucky to have met you!!! Hot Tramp, I love you so!" Also in the shot were American comedian Sam Kinison and Billy Idol. The snap of the four stars was Kinison's favourite and he would "casually" leave it on his coffee table whenever he had guests. He also had a more functional use for the photograph. "That was my coke picture," he said.

Annie Lennox

With her spiky orange-haired androgyny, Annie Lennox was even more overtly influenced by Bowie than Madonna. So much so that, when she was asked for her favourite concert of all time, she did not refer to anything with Eurythmics, but the time she got to sing with Bowie. "It was less a gig, more an out-of-body experience," said Lennox.

It was 1992, and she had been asked to join the surviving members of Queen for a Freddie Mercury tribute concert. Joining Bowie on "Under Pressure", she found the rehearsals hard work. "It's not an easy song to sing by any means," said Lennox. "It's like jumping out of a plane not knowing if your parachute is going to open." So, when Bowie lent over to speak to her, she was expecting some polite advice. Instead, he asked, "What are you going to wear? I think you should wear a frock." He then recommended his favourite designer at the time. Lennox took the advice and requested something black with the idea to make her look "like a fatal virus trying to seduce David". When she recounted the anecdote to a book-launch audience, she was asked if her ruse to seduce Bowie had worked. "You don't need to know," she laughingly responded.

The two were certainly close. When Eurythmics did a live request show on television, one of the "surprise" callers was Bowie. Before he could even make his request, Lennox interrupted to check if he had taken his echinacea after a recent bout of flu. Bowie tactfully tried to carry on but was eventually forced by the mother hen-like Lennox to admit that, yes, he had followed her advice. Only after eliciting explicit confirmation did she allow Bowie to make his request (his choice was "There Must Be an Angel").

Her fellow Eurythmic, Dave Stewart, also became good friends with Bowie, although such a relationship could come with strings attached. Stewart once had the unenviable task of giving his opinion on a new LP by the much-derided Tin Machine to Bowie himself. It was a like being asked by a woman to guess her age, recalled Stewart. Sounding more enthusiastic than he felt, he praised the record, knowing that his friend would be devastated if he was truthful. "He only listened to the criticism," said Stewart.

Annie Lennox and Bowie at the Freddie Mercury tribute concert, 1992.

Françoise Hardy

Courted by Salvador Dalí, idolized by Bob Dylan and lusted after by Mick Jagger, actress and singer Françoise Hardy was the essence of sixties new-wave chic. Among those besotted by her soulful looks and melancholic songs was a young David Bowie. "I was, for a long time, very passionately in love with Françoise," he said. "Every male and a number of females also were, and we still are."

When the two met in 2003, Hardy was also captivated by the "charismatic" Bowie. But she said she found his intense gaze so "troubling" that she avoided going back to his dressing room later. Their encounter on a French TV show came at Bowie's request. She immediately enthused about his album *Outside* (1995). The fact that she had focused on one of his more recent and overlooked LPs delighted Bowie. They exchanged compliments, and he invited her to his concert in Paris that night.

Hardy turned up early and opened the door to her concert box to find Bowie standing there on his own. "I fell directly onto him!" she said. "He was waiting for me, and told me all sorts of kind things. Nobody has done me that honour, not Jacques [her partner], or even Thomas [her son]. He treated me as if I were his youthful fantasy."

"The word 'charisma' is used a lot today, often wrongly," she added. "He had that look that pierces you. He impressed me a lot. He troubled me too. That's why, apart from this unique meeting, I avoided going to greet him in his dressing room every time I went to see him in concert."

David Lynch

Few things embarrassed David Bowie, but one was his attempt at a Louisiana accent for David Lynch's 1992 film *Twin Peaks: Fire Walk with Me*. Bowie appeared as an FBI agent, and Lynch asked him back for the *Twin Peaks* TV series filmed just before his death. Bowie was too ill to appear but gave his permission for the old footage of him to be reused on one condition – his voice be dubbed over by a genuine Louisianan.

"Someone must have made him feel bad about his Louisiana accent," said Lynch. "But the Louisiana actor we got sounded exactly like David Bowie!"

Bowie had always admired Lynch's films, sensing a fellow outsider, and was delighted when Lynch enthused about one of his more recent songs, "I'm Deranged". "It was one of my favourite tracks," said Bowie, "but nobody ever mentioned it until David called up one day and said, 'Heck! I really adore "I'm Deranged". By golly, that's a great piece of work!'" Lynch used the song for his movie *Lost Highway* (1997). Bowie loved the result: "The film has a wonderful incomprehensibility and open-endedness, but that will outrage most people because they want their myths to be complete. There has to be a moral base, and a good person and a bad person, but that doesn't relate anymore. It's not a mirror of what we are living through."

Ben Stiller and Owen Wilson

Bowie was to be much happier with his cameo role in *Zoolander* (2001), the spoof film on the fashion industry. The film pits two dim-witted male models, Ben Stiller and Owen Wilson, against each other, and they eventually square up in a fashion show "walk-off".

"Who's going to call this sucker?" Wilson asks the crowd.

"If nobody has any objections, I believe I may be of service," says David Bowie, rising from the audience, as if out of nowhere.

Stiller had pictured Bowie when creating the part but had never seriously considered the singer might get involved. "He turned down a lot of stuff. How did we slip through the cracks?" puzzled Wilson. "It's a mystery we will never know," agreed Stiller. "We were all in shock. He really legitimized our movie by being in it." Bowie even came up with some of his own material. "He did a bit of improv," said Stiller. "He was a great actor, as well as a musical genius."

Alongside several other cameos in the film, one other truly stands out. The surprising result is that David Bowie's name appears alongside that of Donald Trump in the movie's credits.

Russell Crowe

Russell Crowe recalled once talking with a friend about Bowie when his pal said, "You know, I did two albums with Bowie."

"Like backing vocals?" Crowe asked.

"No, no, no," replied the man. "I was his coke dealer."

Crowe laughed, convinced his mate was pulling his leg. But years later he got the chance to put the story to the test when both men went to see Bowie in concert.

"Good to see you, David!" shouted Crowe, backstage. Convinced he was going to embarrass his mate, the actor added, "Hey, David, can I just introduce you to a friend of mine? Apparently, he knew you quite a long time ago?"

"Bowie's face went white, white as a sheet, like a ghost," Crowe told Angela Pulvirenti for *The Truth about Us* on the Bio channel. "He is shaking. He's like, 'Michael, I don't do drugs anymore,' and Michael's like, 'David, David, neither do I! You know, I'm 15 years clean!'"

Tony Parsons

David Bowie by David Bowie. It was the book that every Bowie fan longed for: the definitive statement on the man, by the man. But not one of the many dozens of books about Bowie is an autobiography. The official "big book" will now remain forever unwritten. But Bowie not only knew who he wanted to co-author his autobiography, he asked him. Tony Parsons declined.

Bowie felt he did not have sufficient time to devote to a book about his life so, in the nineties, was on the lookout for the perfect biographer. Then, he did an interview for *Arena* magazine. Bowie got on so well with the interviewer, former *NME* reporter and author Tony Parsons, that the singer offered him the Holy Grail of music journalism; a chance to write Bowie's biography with full access to everyone he knew. Parsons, who wanted to focus on his own career as an author, responded by saying that he could not spare the time.

Parsons did admit to being flattered. He described Bowie's life as music's greatest story, greater than that of either Elvis or Lennon. But he said that, given he took three years to write a novel, he did not have the necessary time for such a large undertaking.

Bowie never did find another writer whom he felt he could trust with the task. It was a literary tragedy for fans. Parsons would not only have been able to ask Bowie himself anything he wanted, he would also have been able to give the illuminating insights of a friend: "He was the only musician I've ever met," Parsons once said, "who helped me into my coat."

Sean Combs

Puff Daddy, P Diddy, Diddy, Puff, Brother Love and Sean Combs – the American rapper has had his fair share of stage names. The credit for those aliases he gives to David Bowie. "A lot of people don't know this, but he gave me the courage to change my name so many times," said Combs.

The two collaborated on a remix of Bowie's "This Is Not

Bowie and Sean Combs in the studio, 2001.

America" for the 2001 thriller *Training Day*. The rapper was impressed by the firmness of Bowie's handshake. "Man," said Combs, "I want to know what exercise machine you use."

"It's called holding onto your money," replied Bowie, quick as a flash.

Lenny Kravitz

Lenny Kravitz also changed his name in homage to Bowie. More significantly, perhaps, when the New York singer was torn between a career in acting or in music, it was a Bowie song that helped him make his choice.

In the late eighties, Kravitz auditioned for a role in Spike Lee's musical comedy, *School Daze*. All the other hopefuls chose to sing hits of the day, with Whitney Houston's "The Greatest Love of All" proving the most popular. Kravitz decided to go his own way. Just before going on, he jettisoned the tape deck and launched into an a cappella version of "Life on Mars?" When he finished, he was greeted with a deathly silence from the panel.

"They were looking at me like, 'Who the hell is this kid, and what is this song?'" Kravitz recalled.

After a brief pause, he heard someone on the panel shout, "Next," and that was that. Kravitz took the rejection as a sign to quit acting and focus solely on music. Within two years, he was a superstar.

The choice of Bowie for his audition was no coincidence. As a teenager, Kravitz had adopted his own Bowie-inspired alter ego: a party-mad dude by the name of "Romeo Blue". So he was delighted when, now established as a musician himself, Bowie not only asked him to be the support act on his tour but also to play guitar on the original music Bowie wrote for the 1993 TV serialization of Hanif Kureishi's novel *The Buddha of Suburbia*.

"This man changed my life," wrote Kravitz after Bowie died. "I'd have to write a book to describe what he meant to me."

Hanif Kureishi

Teachers at Bromley Tech used to issue a threat to unruly boys by invoking the name of a former "disgraced" pupil. "Behave," they'd warn, "or you'll end up like that David Bowie." Hanif Kureishi remembers the warning well since, as a former Tech student himself, he was often on the receiving end. It was some time before the teachers cottoned onto the fact that Bowie was exactly the sort of rebel hero the unruly boys dreamed of becoming.

Seven years older, Bowie had left the school by the time Kureishi arrived, but the two became good friends in adulthood. Hoping to use some of Bowie's songs for a TV version of his book *The Buddha of Suburbia* (1990), Kureishi arranged a dinner date. The singer loved the idea and offered to write original music for the project. Working at full tilt, he finished the score within days, but an awkward Kureishi felt compelled to ask for alterations and confessed to "shitting himself" when he had to ask the rock god to make changes. Without a word of complaint, Bowie redid the whole thing. The subsequent "soundtrack" album (1993) inspired by the series is now widely regarded as one of his best.

From then on, the author became Bowie's trusted sounding board. When he had a new record coming out, he would ask Kureishi around, put the record on and, armed with pen and paper, sit opposite the writer ready to take notes on whatever his friend said. It was, admitted Kureishi, a terrifying experience.

Stephen King

When Bowie was casting about for collaborators to write a concept horror album, there was only one contender, the master of horror himself. "He called me up and we talked about a concept album, kind of a scary thing," said King. "Nothing else came of it, the schedules didn't fit, but I did have that conversation with him." If the project had come off, surely horror legend Christopher Lee would have been able to find a suitable song this time around.

Just a few years earlier, King had named his sci-fi TV series after one of his favourite Bowie tracks. *Golden Years* was intended as an original novel for television, said the author, who felt its mysteriousness made it a perfect fit.

King was such a fan that he felt Bowie's songs had been underrated. "There was such an emphasis in the press on how damn good-looking he was and how he was a trendsetter in terms of style," said the writer. "I thought they ignored his music a bit. He made such interesting music."

William Boyd

Bowie's career took a wholly unexpected turn in 1994 when he entered the world of journalism and high-art criticism. He was appointed to the board of the magazine *Modern Painters*, alongside aged Oxbridge professors who had spent their lives immersed in the world of art history. Bowie was so nervous about his first board meeting at The Ivy that he asked to bring along a friend "for protection". In the end, he went alone and ended up sitting next to author William Boyd. The novelist recalled Bowie sounding anxious and ill at ease when speaking, while the attendant professors, many of whom appeared never to have heard of the singer, seemed to be thinking, "Why is he here?" "It was pretty much Daniel in the lions' den," recalled Boyd.

But when the board reconvened at The Ivy the next month, all the dons turned up in their most flamboyant outfits and snazziest ties, in a bid to impress their new member. One later admitted that they knew all along who Bowie was; they were just so in awe of him that they had tried to act as if he were no one special.

Bowie injected new life into the magazine, providing scoops about the world's top artists from Roy Lichtenstein and Balthus to Damien Hirst and Jeff Koons, all of whom were delighted to be interviewed by a fellow artist.

Boyd and Bowie stayed in touch, and when the author came up with an idea to fool the art world with a biography of a "dead" fictional artist, Bowie gave a public address to commemorate the "rediscovery" of Nat Tate. Boyd's abiding memory of that event was of Bowie turning up on his own in a New York cab. Wasn't he concerned about being hassled by the public or the driver? Boyd asked.

"Not at all, I just carry one of these," said Bowie, holding up a Greek newspaper.

Balthus
- - - - - - - - -

Bowie's jump into journalism began when he offered the art world the unobtainable: an interview with 'the least known great painter of the 20th century'. Balthus was the last survivor of the School of Paris, a group of diverse, innovative artists, including Picasso, Matisse, Chagall, Mondrian and Modigliani, who rejected established artistic practices. Bowie's scoop was down to the fact that he happened to live near Balthus in Switzerland and had bumped into the reclusive artist's wife at an exhibition. "I gave him a call and proposed a meeting," said Bowie, who suggested bringing along a "proper" journalist. "Good heavens, no," replied Balthus. "I can't stand art journalists. They are always so intellectual. I'd prefer you to do it, dear boy."

Bowie almost did not make it to the 86-year-old's Swiss chalet. "I was so petrified, I nearly turned back three times," he said. Not only would this be his first "serious" article in a "serious" publication, it would also define whether he would sink or swim in the new world of high art and intellectualism. "I wanted to show my mettle," Bowie said, who had just joined the board of *Modern Painters*. "Being a rock singer – Rock GOD – it's quite hard to convince people that your interests extend outside the parameters of purely being up on stage wearing funny trousers."

The two men hit it off from the start. They talked for four hours, and the resulting 20 pages was the longest interview the magazine ever printed. "That was a joy to do because he was such a gentleman and so mysterious and knew he was pulling you into his myth," recalled Bowie. Balthus spoke about lunching with Marlon Brando. Picasso, he said, had defended him when he was accused of being a fascist for painting figurative art. Balthus also mentioned how the German poet Rainer Maria Rilke, his mother's lover, had helped him as a young boy publish his first book at the age of 11.

Balthus himself was unaware of the extent of Bowie's fame. "Are you used to photographers?" he asked innocently, as a cameraman took snaps of the two. "Unfortunately, yes," replied Bowie.

"There were so many secrets about him," said Bowie, although the most notable "secret" – the allegations of paedophilia –

was scarcely touched upon. Paintings of pre-pubescent girls in provocative poses, allied with allegations of affairs with his young "models", had swirled around the painter since the 1930s. Museums had banned his work, and Tracey Emin was not alone in labelling him "a pervert". But then Balthus brought up the issue himself with one of his most controversial paintings, "The Guitar Lesson". This features a young girl, skirt pulled up and naked from the waist down, lying on the lap of a female music teacher whose pulled-down blouse reveals an aroused nipple. "I was in bad shape and I wanted to make a name for myself," Balthus told Bowie. "You know, David, in these days, the only way to make a name for oneself was to scandalize."

Rather than point out that Balthus had carried on painting explicit images of pre-pubescent girls, Bowie replied, "Provocation has paved the way and fostered the careers of many." Unprompted, Balthus went on, "I am simply attracted to the immature forms of a teenager, that is all." Again, Bowie declined to take up the offer to delve into that most talked-about aspect of the artist's career, as any trained journalist would have, and instead asked about the artist's symbolic use of books and mirrors. Maybe Bowie thought the allegations of paedophilia were spurious, or that "the work" was more important than the life, or that a challenge from a rock star might feel hypocritical.

Bowie concluded that he and Balthus were both prepared to shock to pursue their beliefs or, as the singer termed their philosophy, "Put it out and be damned." Emotionally, there was a connection, too. "As with any aged gentleman that I come into contact with, my immediate need is to treat him as the grandfather I never knew or the father I needed more of," Bowie told *The Independent*'s David Lister. "We are time and worlds apart, which has made for a rather lovely friendship." The singer was delighted by the article's impact: "I see it now quoted in academic things saying, 'From the Bowie interview'. Whoa, that's me!"

Damien Hirst

Bowie was to become friends with several artists he interviewed, including the most celebrated, and certainly the most notorious, of the Young British Artists. His friendship with Damien Hirst led to plans for some grand collaborations. One such idea involved an attempt to create

Bowie with Damien Hirst and Julian Schnabel, New York, 1996.

a real-life version of a mythical monster, the Minotaur. Bowie was obsessed by the half-man, half-bull creature, convinced that it represented one of our earliest and most primal fears, and resided deep in our unconscious mind. One day, he and Hirst decided they would attach the head of a bull onto the body of a decapitated person and place it in the middle of a purpose-built labyrinth on a Greek island. They did end up working together but on a less ambitious project: making spinning tops, an idea Hirst had first seen on the children's TV show *Blue Peter*.

Bowie was a big fan of the younger man, describing Hirst as having made art accessible to people in a way that had "never happened before". The two met in the mid-nineties when Bowie interviewed the artist for *Modern Painters*. They got on so well that Hirst invited Bowie to his studio to take part in a "spin painting". He told him to come in old clothes but the singer tuned up in an expensive, brand-new outfit, not caring that it was about to be splattered in paint. "I loved that," said Hirst, who described Bowie as possessing a childlike enthusiasm.

Hirst encouraged Bowie to dress as a Martian, stand on a ladder and throw paint at a spinning canvas. At one point, a carefree Bowie stuck his expensive watch on one of the spinning machines – it got smashed against a wall. "We had a ball," said Bowie. "I felt like I was three years old again."

The singer went as far as to liken Hirst to Picasso. "He also set parameters in the studio that produced a kind of playfulness out of which came a very pure thing," said Bowie. Their joint effort ended up selling at Sotheby's for £775,000.

As for their plan to create a real Minotaur, a modern art lover bequeathed his body to the project. As far as is known, he hasn't lost his head, yet.

Tracey Emin

At 15, Tracey Emin left home for good, carrying a rucksack containing all the essentials she needed to confront the outside world: a few clothes, some underwear and two David Bowie LPs.

The singer had been the biggest artistic influence on her adolescence in the provincial seaside town of Margate. The first time she heard of Andy Warhol was on Bowie's eponymous song. And her introduction to Egon Schiele, one of her major influences, was when she discovered that Bowie's pose on the cover of *Heroes* was taken from a painting by the Austrian Expressionist.

"Once being told this stunning piece of information," she said, "I rushed to Cliftonville's [a district of Margate] one and only bookshop and looked up the name." She found the one book on Expressionism and, inside, a tiny drawing by Schiele. "Seeing this image," she said, "was going to determine the rest of my life." Bowie was not only influencing the next generation of musicians, he was also shaping the tastes of the next generation of artists.

The two met in 1996, when the 23-year-old Emin was dining with some friends at a Lebanese restaurant in west London. A man at the next table leaned over and said, "I'm so sorry to interrupt you. My name is David Bowie and can I just say I really like your work."

"I looked up," Emin told the BBC, "and it really was David Bowie."

"'Likewise,' I said. 'Can I just say, I really like your work, too.'"

The two hit it off immediately or, as Bowie put it in *Modern Painters*, "Within 30 minutes of meeting her, I have a full rundown on her newest intimate relationships, her hopes and dreams for her personal life as well as proffered opinions on Balthus ('a dirty old man, a pervert'), and my interviews with Damien Hirst ('You're obsessed by him')."

Emin never got to grips with email, Bowie's preferred medium of communication, so Bowie would telephone and lengthy conversations would ensue. Bowie said her "fractured energy" made her great to listen to for hours on end, while her "elastic lips, broken teeth and half-closed eyes" made her "extraordinarily sexy". Their conversations were often frank. Bowie spoke openly of Emin's "solipsistic overdrive", said her tastes were those of "any 18-year-old art student" and that booze was her 24-hour-a-day companion. For Emin's part, she described Bowie's paintings as "naive" in comparison to his music.

Bowie confided in Emin that he would have chosen to be a visual artist given a choice. Meeting Andy Warhol and other artists, he told her, had left him "feeling stupid" in their company.

Bowie undoubtedly adored Emin's work. While seeing a show of hers in Toronto, he noticed two young women sitting in front of one of Emin's video monologues with tears running down their cheeks. "Now, that's art," said Bowie.

Willem de Kooning

When Bowie visited painter Willem de Kooning, he was given the brush-off. He arrived at the home of the Abstract Expressionist to find him leaning over his canvas, brush in hand, immobile and seemingly lost in concentration. Minutes passed as the painter appeared to have forgotten he had company. Eventually, de Kooning stopped, walked over to his guests and plonked himself down in a rocking chair. "Oh, fuck visitors," sighed the elderly painter. They were to be the only words he uttered all afternoon.

After several minutes of refusing to answer Bowie's questions, de Kooning wearily got up and returned to his canvas, leaving his guests to make their own way out. Bowie believed the artist was deliberately making them feel uncomfortable, and described de Kooning as being in a "fake catatonic" state. "He wanted us to realize we'd disrupted his day," Bowie told *Movieline* magazine. But it's probable that the painter was suffering from the early stages of Alzheimer's, a disease which was to kill him.

The frosty reception, however, did not dampen Bowie's view of the artist. "Now, there's a man who is aware of the existence of life and death at the same time," he said.

Roy Lichtenstein

Pop artist Roy Lichtenstein gave his final interview in the winter of 1997, aged 73. The interviewer was David Bowie.

"I did the last interview with him about two weeks before he died," recalled Bowie. "That was an extraordinary experience. I enjoyed the heck out of it, knocking on some famous painters' doors and saying, 'Hello, I'm your interviewer!'"

While Bowie's questions are serious-minded, Lichtenstein's answers are often light and self-deprecating. "Most people think painters are kind of ridiculous," he says at one point, then adding, "I've just been saying the same thing again and again for 35 years."

Why had he chosen to paint Mickey Mouse? asked Bowie. "It's what people really see," replied the painter. "It's McDonald's, not Le Corbusier."

Jeff Koons

Jeff Koons needed "a look". He was about to have his first portrait taken by a professional photographer and was nervous. By chance, he had recently come across a photograph of Bowie in a glossy magazine, resplendent in a shiny gold suit. The artist was smitten with the reflective sheen of the image, sensing it mirrored his own work. "The photograph looked like it was glass, and if you touched it, it would just shatter," he said admiringly. Koons called up the photographer. "Can you do the same for me?" he asked.

Ten years later, Koons appeared in a magazine, this time alongside Bowie, who was the interviewer. "He is so ultimately American, a dream," said Bowie. "Very sweet, simplistic, almost a naive presence. Terrific company."

Koons was the Warhol of his era, said Bowie, who felt the kitschy absurdity of the American's work meant people failed to take him seriously. "There's a naivety about both of them but you can't help suspecting there's something else going on," he said.

Jean-Michel Basquiat

Jean-Michel Basquiat was to become famous for his street art, but the painter was, initially, just as interested in becoming a musician. Not that his bandmates in noise group Test Pattern saw it that way. "He was on this ego trip, schmoozing with Eno and Bowie instead of taking care of band business," complained keyboardist Vincent Gallo, who quit the group as a result.

The "schmoozing" took place at New York's Mudd Club around 1980. Their encounters delighted the painter, as Basquiat would "play and play" *Low* and *Heroes* all day, as his girlfriend Alexis

Adler recalled. For his part, Bowie saw a kindred spirit, and described the "burning immediacy" of Basquiat's frenetic style as rock music on a canvas. "His work relates to rock in a way that very few other artists get near," said Bowie.

Basquiat died at the age of just 27 from a heroin overdose, but his older friend continued to think about him. Bowie appeared as Warhol in the film *Basquiat*, about the artist's short life. He was also delighted to discover, while on a trip to South Africa, that many of Africa's artists looked upon the Haitian-American artist as "their Picasso".

Photographer David Bailey recalled that Bowie was so "obsessed" by the dead painter around this time that Basquiat was "all he could talk about". When Bowie's art collection was sold, one of the most talked about paintings was Basquiat's *Air Power* (1984), a piece Bowie bought for $100,000 but which sold for $9 million. Not that the money was an issue for Bowie. "I should have liked to have seen [him] all grown up," he wrote wistfully, at the end of a long homage to the dead painter.

Laurie Anderson

Another artist Bowie was to befriend was Laurie Anderson, the wife of Lou Reed. Bowie loved her multimedia projects and her one hit, the unique "O Superman", from the early eighties. But the two were to bond following a meeting of minds.

"I'm pretty sure you can read minds," Bowie said to Anderson. "I'm pretty sure I can't," she replied. Refusing to be dissuaded, Bowie devised a paranormal test. For the next three weeks, he would call Anderson every day at a set time. On receiving the call, and without exchanging a word, both would put their receivers down and draw whatever came into their minds. They would then fax each other the results. On the first day, Anderson drew a bush, a house and a pole coming out of the second storey, from which a man was hanging. Bowie, according to a stunned Anderson, drew exactly the same thing.

"What are the chances of two people both drawing that?" she said, flabbergasted. "The chances are zero. They're zero."

She was so won over by the experiment that she and Bowie planned to release their drawings as a book on mind reading.

REM

REM were facing personal and career disaster. On tour for the first time in six years, they were nearing the end of their concert in Switzerland when drummer Bill Berry collapsed on stage. He had suffered a brain haemorrhage. Fortunately for Berry, Lausanne was home to one of the world's best brain surgeons, who saved his life. The band cancelled all their concerts and spent a month in the country, smuggling in doughnuts to their friend, as they waited for him to recover.

"We were stuck in Switzerland waiting for him to live or die," Michael Stipe told the BBC's Matt Everett. "He lived and everything's great but it was a really tense moment."

While in limbo, the band were invited to dinner by Claude Nobs, the man behind the Montreux Jazz Festival. Nobs never did things by halves. "He had flown in a band to perform from somewhere and a chef from somewhere else to cook," said Stipe. "Upon arriving at his beautiful home, he said, 'A few people are going to be joining us tonight, including David Bowie.'"

Stipe was emotionally and physically drained by what had

happened to his bandmate and the first thing he did upon arrival was to take a nap. "At whatever point, someone came in and woke me up and said, 'Mr Bowie has arrived and dinner is served,'" said Stipe. "It took me three espressos to walk down the stairs, look David Bowie in the eye and say, 'How do you do? It's nice to meet you, finally.'"

According to the REM singer, Bowie did not stop talking for the next three hours. "It was unbelievable – he was so engaging, so funny and so smart," he recalled. Bowie had brought a book which contained some of his own paintings and drawings, as well as some miniature sculptures he had made. He also showed them a photograph he owned of the actor James Dean perched high up in a tree, completely naked, with a radiant smile on his face while proudly showing off an erection.

One subject that fascinated Bowie that night was the growing trend for tattoos. "He was really convinced that people were getting tattoos and piercings because of the upcoming century change," said bassist Mike Mills. Bowie believed people were suffering from millennial anxiety and were getting pagan images tattooed onto their body as a subconscious appeasement to the gods. David Bowie could not have been more "David Bowie" had he tried, said Stipe.

Glenn Branca

When no-wave guitar experimentalist Glenn Branca met David Bowie, he thought a stand-up comedian had walked into the apartment. "For the first ten minutes, he does this comedy act, impressions, everything," said Branca. "It was unreal. It was surreal. It was tremendous." Bowie, he believed, felt a crushing expectation to be extraordinary, to be "Bowie". "I can understand that, I mean he's one of the most famous rock stars in the world and you don't expect him to just come in and say (slurring), 'Does anyone have something to drink, I'm completely spaced.' No, he played the role of the major rock star that he was."

Bowie suggested to Branca, whose *Ascension* was one of his favourite all-time records, that they work together. He sang over one of Branca's existing pieces but the music was never released because of a record-label dispute. "It's still sitting on my shelf," said Branca. "But I wouldn't release it without David's permission."

Branca died in 2018, two years after Bowie, so any release could be a long way off.

Denis Leary

Denis Leary confessed to having always been "a little gay for David Bowie". So, when the singer agreed to perform a song on Leary's TV chat show, the comedian was thrilled. But he was also nervous that he might miss his hero, as the bands tended to play early, pack up quickly and then leave. "I was like, 'I don't give a fuck what happens, I gotta meet David Bowie,'" recalled Leary.

In the end, it was the singer who came to him. A chain-smoker, Leary was having an early puff in the alley outside the TV station, when someone came up behind him and asked for a smoke. It was Bowie. "I couldn't even talk, so I gave him a cigarette," said Leary. Without pausing to inhale, Bowie launched into a rapid-fire interrogation about Leary's fellow comedians:

"What's Bobcat Goldthwait like? Is he weird? Is he weird?"

"Yeah, he's weird but not as weird as the guy he plays on stage," replied Leary.

"What's Steven Wright like? Is he weird?"

"Yeah, he actually is weird. He really is weird."

Leary began to get excited that he was on the verge of having a real conversation with his hero. But the quizzing was relentless.

"So, Bobcat," Bowie continued. "Does he really wear those clothes in real life?"

"No," replied Leary.

At that point Bowie was called back into the studio for the sound check and the interrogation ended. "And I never see him again," said the rueful Leary.

Michael Parkinson
- -

Michael Parkinson conducted over 2,000 interviews, so it is understandable he would forget the odd guest. Maybe less understandable is that one of those he forgot was David Bowie.

"When he died, a friend told me that an interview I did with him was trending on Twitter," said the chat-show host. "Honestly, I had no idea what he was talking about. I know it might sound strange but you do forget."

Despite Bowie not impinging deeply on Parkinson's memory, the TV interview is one of the most illuminating of the singer's career. Bowie talks candidly about his mother, and how she would sing along to the radio, telling her son she could have been a singer. That, he said, inspired him to think that he too could become a singer.

In rehearsals, the studio audience were treated to a rare delight when Bowie sat down unaccompanied at the piano to sing "Life on Mars?" "It's those genuine musical moments that make it all worthwhile," said the show's producer, Danny Dignan, one of those present who did remember.

Terry Wogan

The other great stalwart of the British chat show, Terry Wogan, was once asked who was his most difficult interviewee in 50 years of broadcasting. David Bowie, he answered. In fact, the Irishman found the singer so infuriating, he said, "I thought a solid slap would have helped the situation."

Bowie's band Tin Machine had been asked to appear on the prime-time TV show. "Was this a deliberate attempt by you to go in a different direction?" Wogan asked. "Hi, Ron!" replied Bowie, evasively, perhaps hoping to be treated as just another member of the band. But there were some genuinely funny moments. "How are you all getting on?" Wogan asked the group, each of whom was dressed in a clashingly garish suit. "We have colour problems," replied Bowie.

"I didn't hit him, of course," said Wogan. "But it came close."

Liam Gallagher

The lead singer of Oasis also came close to hitting Bowie. The altercation with Liam Gallagher came during rehearsals for the music TV show *Later... with Jools Holland*. Backstage, the apparently drunk Mancunian reportedly confronted Bowie and called him "a washed-up old fart" before, according to Bowie biographer Nicholas Pegg, swinging a vague punch in his general direction. As a result, the Oasis man was escorted off BBC premises, leaving brother Noel to take over singing duties. Keen perhaps to keep the incident under wraps, Holland told the audience, "I must have coughed in Liam's tea because he now has my throat and is unable to sing."

As for the music, Bowie described the Oasis version of "Heroes" as sounding like it had been recorded "at the end of the night in the pub". More flatteringly, Noel expressed surprise that he had never been sued by Bowie. "I got three different songs out of 'All the Young Dudes' alone," he said.

Damon Albarn

It would have been the ultimate Britpop artefact, an album made by the genre's Holy Trinity. "For about 24 hours, I was making a record with David Bowie and Ray Davies," revealed Damon Albarn. The project between the three English songwriters got as far as the studio but, because of other commitments, no further.

Albarn and Bowie, though, did get a chance to sing together, when appearing on a French TV chat show in 2003. Bowie was effusive in his praise of Blur, describing their latest album as "superior to anything out there for Britain, including the last album by Radiohead. It's never been out of my CD player." In fact, Bowie loved "Song 2" so much that he would get his band to play the popular riff in between songs when on stage.

The French host suggested there were similarities between the two singers. But Albarn demurred. "This goes for everything tonight," said the Whitechapel-born singer, "he does it better than me. But we both have a certain soulfulness in the voice, and we both love Anthony Newley and Jacques Brel."

Bowie then teasingly hinted at their failed collaboration, saying, "Hey, Damon, whatever happened to that track we never recorded?" What did happen was that the two sung together for the TV audience, choosing to duet on "Fashion".

Jarvis Cocker

When Jarvis went to jail, Bowie bailed him out. It all happened one February night in 1996 at the Brit Awards. Michael Jackson was on stage singing "Earth Song". Bathed in white light and surrounded by waif-like children who appeared to be miraculously cured by touching his hem, Jackson stepped onto a crane and ascended heavenwards. One member of the audience could take no more of the messianic pretensions.

"I was just sat there watching it, feeling a bit ill because he's doing his Jesus act," said Cocker. "It seemed to me there was quite a lot of other people who found it quite distasteful as well, and I just thought, 'The stage is there, I'm here and you can do something about it, and say this is a load of rubbish.'"

Pulp's keyboard player, Candida Doyle, may have given her bandmate the final push. "Yeah," she told him. "But you would never dare do it!" All of a sudden, the cameras spotted a stick-thin man running around the stage, lifting up his shirt and bending over while performing wafting motions near his bottom. "I knew I had to move fast," said Cocker. "Once I was there, it was really more what to do."

One of the male dancers tried to grab Cocker, but the Pulp singer skilfully managed to evade his clutches. Jarvis then ran up the stage ramp and, silhouetted against a giant, luminous moon, gave a birdlike goodbye flap before flying off yet again, closely pursued by an ever-increasing number of Jackson's team.

Jackson's aides called the police, alleging Cocker had punched and knocked some of the children off stage. After two hours of questioning, he was arrested and taken to the police station. Jackson's team of lawyers were insisting charges be brought, when in walked comedian Bob Mortimer. Formerly a solicitor at the local town council, Mortimer offered to defend Cocker.

Despite the comical elements, Cocker was deeply worried. The story was on the front pages, with some of the country demonizing him and others calling for him to be knighted. Footage of the night failed to clear the matter up, and a court date was set. But then, Bowie came to the rescue. His own camera team had been present that night to record him receiving an award. When Bowie heard about possible charges, he happily passed his tapes onto the police. That footage exonerated the Pulp frontman.

"Among many other things I'm grateful to David Bowie for, that was amazing," said Cocker.

When the Pulp singer was asked if he ever felt resentful towards Jackson, Cocker replied, "Anyone who invents the moonwalk is all right by me." It seems he may have Bowie to thank for that, too (see page 142).

Brett Anderson

"Of all the tapes you've ever sent me, this is the only one I knew instantly that was great." That was Bowie's reaction to *NME* journalist Steve Sutherland, who mailed him a cassette of early Suede.

Sutherland decided to bring Bowie and Brett Anderson together but kept the younger singer in the dark, fearing Anderson, who was already being dubbed "the new Bowie", would be crestfallen if his hero failed to show.

Bowie did turn up, and the meeting was to provide one of rock music's most open conversations. Topics ranged from fame to fascism, LSD to ecstasy. Anderson described taking E the first time as giving him "the most amount of happiness that anyone's ever had since Julius Caesar". Bowie said one unexpected benefit of cocaine was that it made him so forgetful that he had to live in the present, which helped him focus on his work. But he also spoke about having overdosed several times in the seventies. They talked about the death of Jim Morrison from alcohol, with Bowie saying there needed to be fewer photographs of him looking mean and moody and more of "the stupid fat berk lying in his bath tub". And they talked about Morrissey. Anderson lambasted his politics on race, but Bowie was more circumspect, wary of condemning someone without knowing the exact quote and the context.

But from all their freewheeling talk, the one thing that was to stick in Anderson's mind was not Bowie's words but his smell: "He came in and he smelt beautiful, that was the most important thing. He smelt like Chanel."

Morrissey

"You know," Bowie told Morrissey during their brief friendship, "I've had so much sex and drugs that I can't believe I'm still alive."

"You know," replied the Smiths singer, "I've had so little, I can't believe that I'm still alive."

Their first encounter had been decades earlier, when Morrissey was just 13. The teenager was waiting outside a Ziggy Stardust concert in Manchester when Bowie's black limo started to make its way slowly through the crowd. Sensing his moment was at hand, Morrissey pushed a scrunched-up note through the rolled-down window and into his hero's hand. "Smiling keenly, he accepts the note of a dull schoolboy whose overblown soul is more ablaze than the school blazer he wears, and thus I touch the hand of this inexplicably liberating reformer," wrote Morrissey in his autobiography. On the piece of paper, he had written his home phone number. Even at that age, Morrissey did not want for self-confidence.

Amazingly, Bowie was to make that call, albeit 20 years later. The two had briefly met when Morrissey went backstage after a concert, again in Manchester, to express his adulation in person. Soon after, Bowie suggested they sing together. So, one night, with Morrissey on stage in Los Angeles singing T. Rex's "Cosmic Dancer", out walked Bowie. "The 12-year-old within me – unable to leave for school unless I'd soothed my sickness with at least one spin of 'Starman' – bathes in the moment in disbelief," wrote Morrissey.

When the two bumped into each other at the hotel buffet for breakfast, the outspoken vegan saw Bowie eyeing the ham and salami slices. "David, you are not actually going to eat that stuff, are you?" asked an appalled Morrissey. "Oh," Bowie sighed, leaving the buffet with an empty plate, "you must be hell to live with."

Bowie was intrigued by the man he called "a sexual Alan Bennett". According to biographer David Buckley, Bowie saw him as "his son and heir, a charismatic anti-star and classic commentator on suburban boredom and angst". Bowie even covered one of his songs, "I Know It's Going to Happen", although whether this was a tribute or a riposte is not clear.

"It occurred to me that he was spoofing one of my earlier songs," said Bowie, "and I thought, 'I'm not going to let him get away with that.'" But, if there was a jibe, Morrissey missed it. Bowie invited him to the studio to listen to the final version, and an overcome Morrissey began to cry. "Oooh, it's so grand!" he said. "I cried for a week."

Things turned sour when Bowie asked Morrissey to join him on tour, with the latter walking out without explanation after just a few dates. "I left that tour because he put me under a lot of pressure, and I found it too exhausting," Morrissey later said. But he was also upset at Bowie's suggestion that the Smiths singer end his set with a Bowie song, as his own band were replaced, one by one, by Bowie's band. "It effectively deprives people of saying goodbye to me, so I thought it was very, very cagey," said Morrissey. "So, I eventually left the tour, and received enormous bad press for it. He never spoke to me again. You have to worship at the temple of David when you become involved. He was a fascinating artist but not now."

When asked directly what had led to the falling-out, Bowie was more discreet. "I'll tell you what happened. After about four gigs, he did his sound check, got in a car and that's the last we ever heard or saw of him."

The defection must have rankled Bowie because, in 2006, he declined an offer from his great friend Tony Visconti to sing "You've Lost That Lovin' Feeling" as a duet with Morrissey. "I loved this idea, but David wouldn't budge," said the Smiths singer. "I know I've criticized David in the past, but it's all been snot-nosed junior high ribbing on my part. I think he knows that."

However critical Morrissey was of Bowie in the press ("I wish David Bowie was killed in a car accident right after he finished making *Low*" was one such alleged comment), he remained in thrall to his hero. "Put it this way, Mozzer," he wrote. "You have a card from Dirk Bogarde here. You have Alan Bennett sitting in your kitchen having tea. You have David Bowie having sung one of your songs quite beautifully. What more could there be?"

Neil Young

- - - - - - - - - - - -

Neil Young was present at one of the most significant moments in Bowie's life – the birth of his son, Duncan Zowie Haywood Jones. Angie had gone to hospital, but, as was common then, her husband was told to go home to await news. So, as his wife went through a long and difficult labour, Bowie spent the fretful hours listening to one album, and one album only – Young's *After the Goldrush* (1970).

When the call finally came through, the elated father immediately wrote a love song to his new son. "Kooks" was a whimsical, folky tune, written in the style of the singer who had helped him through those worrisome hours. For Bowie, the connection between Young and his son forged a deep attachment to the Canadian-American singer, and it was a bond which was reinforced by their like-minded attitude.

Like Bowie, Young would continually reinvent himself, even at the risk of career suicide; Young's own record company once sued him for making records that, they said, were "unrepresentative" of himself. "When things go bad I always look to my musical mentors and see what they have done in similar situations," Bowie said. The mentors in question were Neil Young and Bob Dylan. "They have both made a few disastrous albums, but they always end up coming back to the point of what they started in the first place." He and Young, he said, were two of the few musicians who rebelled against becoming "creatively pedestrian" just because they were married with kids.

It was Young who came to the rescue when Bowie was sounding somewhat lost in the nineties. The English singer was captivated by a performance in which Young and his bandmates stomped around stage in a small circle as if in a tribal trance. "Three old men dancing under the moon shaking their sex and bones" is how he described the scene. "It seemed to me that they were doing that, to catch back their dreams, to find their youth again, to not allow the energy to escape." For Bowie, wondering how a middle-aged man could be relevant in a young person's medium, the performance was a revelation. In response, he wrote "Dead Man Walking" – "a homage to rock and roll that is still young while we are all growing old".

Young was also impressed by Bowie. He had picked up on Ziggy Stardust in the early seventies when he said, "The change in music is starting to come with people like David Bowie and Lou Reed. They don't expect to live more than thirty years and they don't care. They got something." And in 1997, he invited Bowie to perform with him at his Bridge School charity event to help children with severe speaking and physical difficulties (Young's son Ben has cerebral palsy).

Bowie was as taken with Young in the flesh as he was on vinyl. "A pioneer loaded with integrity and disarmingly charming as a man," he said. Young's wife, Peggy, was equally impressed, recalling how Bowie was one of the few stars present who hung out to play with all the children backstage.

Sonic Youth

New York noise merchants Sonic Youth were pleasantly surprised to be asked to play at Bowie's 50th-birthday celebrations at Madison Square Garden but what truly impressed them was Bowie's way with children. "That he even knew who we were, was amazing to us," said guitarist Lee Renaldo. He shouldn't have been shocked – Bowie had described Sonic Youth as making "the most compelling music in the entire 1980s".

Singer Thurston Moore described the gig as being from "another realm of experience". But the one thing that stuck with Moore happened off-stage in a dressing room packed with world-famous artists. As Bowie left the room, he looked over at Moore's three-year-old daughter Coco and shouted, "Hi, Coco, I'm so happy you're here! Have a great time!" Moore was touched, not only because Bowie had remembered her name but because, Moore said, "She was the only one unaware of any hierarchy of celebrity in the room."

On stage, Sonic Youth were to join Bowie on "I'm Afraid of Americans", a song he had written with Trent Reznor.

Trent Reznor

Bowie had not witnessed an audience walking out on him since the sixties. But that changed when he went on tour with noise merchants Nine Inch Nails, led by singer and songwriter Trent Reznor. The two artists took it in turns to headline. But the majority of the black-clad crowd, some of whom were just 12 years old, had turned up to see Reznor's band. Unfamiliar with the "old" Bowie and perplexed by the "new" Bowie, when the singer walked out, the audience did, too. What went wrong? asked one TV interviewer. "I turned up," Bowie replied.

Bowie was already a fan of Reznor's banned video for "Happiness in Slavery", which featured graphic scenes of torture and death. But when he heard their "really brilliant" album *Downward Spiral* (1994), he was so impressed that he called up Reznor's management to suggest a joint tour. Reznor was just

Trent Reznor and Bowie, on set for "I'm Afraid of Americans" video, 1997.

coming to the end of a year on the road and was exhausted, but the opportunity to join his hero was one he dared not miss. "Yeah," he replied when Bowie asked him directly, "but no more than six weeks...please."

The show itself was unique. They took it in turns to headline and merged their bands so members of the headline act would gradually replace the support act. Reznor would end his set by singing a Bowie song, and Bowie would end with a Nine Inch Nails song. Reznor said that looking over to see his hero joining him on "Hurt" was one of the greatest moments of his life. They ended up working together on one of Bowie's best songs of the nineties, "I'm Afraid of Americans" (1997).

Reznor had been at the height of his drug addiction at the time of their tour, so when he bumped into Bowie some years later, the first thing he did was apologize for his behaviour and say that he was now clean. He did not even get to finish his sentence. "I got a big hug," Reznor said. "He said, 'I knew. I knew you'd come out of that.' I have goosebumps right now just thinking about it."

Henry Rollins

American punk legend Henry Rollins was backstage at a festival in the Netherlands when, in the distance, David Bowie walked by. As the two came level, Bowie abruptly stopped, turned 90 degrees, pointed directly at the former Black Flag singer and shouted across the sea of people, "Rollins!"

Treating it as an order, Rollins reacted like any soldier and quick-marched straight up to Bowie, "my right hand extended like a lance, not knowing what I'm going to say". But before Rollins could open his mouth, Bowie said, "Henry, you said something in a magazine last month that I found very interesting," and proceeded to quote Rollins back to Rollins.

"I went numb. 'You read an interview of mine? Are you kidding?'" Rollins said.

"I read all your interviews," Bowie continued, adding, "Now, last year in a magazine in Germany you also said this..."

"He proceeded to quote me from something he had translated from German," recounted Rollins during his one-man show *Keep Talking, Pal*. "All I wanted in life was a highway and a truck, so I thought, 'Kill me now because my life is never going to get better than this.'"

Bowie then invited Rollins to join him for lunch in the catering tent. As they walked in, hundreds of people went silent and stared.

"Good afternoon," said Bowie, addressing the seated crowd. "I don't want to disturb anyone's meal. Please carry on."

"He got a standing ovation for that," Rollins later said.

A few weeks later, Rollins got a call at home. "Henry, it's Lou Reed. David said you wanted to talk."

Moby

"This is the story I tell David Bowie fans, and it makes them want to kill me," begins Moby.

Moby lived right across the street from Bowie in New York, so close that the two would wave at each other from their respective balconies. One Saturday morning, Moby popped around to his friend's apartment, armed with two coffees and a guitar to rehearse some songs for a joint acoustic show. "I worked up my nerve and said, 'You know, we should really play "Heroes" – acoustic.' And he said, 'Well, I never have.'" The result was so good, not only did the song make the set, but Bowie went on to perform the version on tour. When the two had finished, Bowie turned to Moby and said, "Let me tell you a little secret. 'Heroes' was originally a cover version of 'Waiting for My Man'." "So, he just rewrote it," said Moby, "and turned it into, 'I…I will be king,' rather than, 'I…I'm waiting for my man.'"

Moby praised Bowie for the greatest act of showmanship he had ever seen. Back in the mid-seventies and halfway through a song, Bowie had collapsed on stage and then stayed there, motionless, for ten minutes. The audience was left shocked, then panicked and then confused. Bowie never did reveal to his friend that he had had exactly the same response when watching the same trick played by Little Richard, all those years ago (see page 19).

Oddly, Bowie was the opening act on their joint tour in 2002. The reality was not that Moby was the bigger star but that Bowie wanted to get home before the traffic.

Interpol

The same desire to get home early was true when Bowie went to see bands. Wanting to see his family, read a book or just get to sleep (he would get up around 5am), he would tend to approach bands before their show rather than after.

So it was that, one night, ten minutes before going on stage, Interpol heard a knock on their dressing-room door. Hungover from the night before, the band were in an irritable mood. Their tour manager shouted, "Can I help you?" in a tone of "Please, fuck off", recalled singer Paul Banks. "Then I saw him back away slowly, like he'd seen a spectre, and in walks Bowie."

Bowie told the band he was a big fan, and wanted to let them know early because he was shortly off to bed. His endorsement came just at the right time. The group were taking a battering in the press for supposedly being derivative.

"It was a very generous gesture," said Banks. "Fucking David Bowie likes us. Whatever.'"

Kate Moss

"It's fine, Bowie loves me. I don't care what others think." That was Kate Moss's reaction to a stream of unflattering depictions of her in the tabloids.

The heroin-chic supermodel's relationship with Bowie began when *Vogue* asked her in 2003 to wear some of the singer's early outfits. Incredibly, despite her "size zero" physique, she was too big for his famous powder-blue "Life on Mars?" suit. As a result, his now delicate jacket had to be painstakingly let out.

Later that year, Moss got to do a photoshoot with Bowie himself. When she told friends Stella McCartney and Liv Tyler about the person she was about to meet, both women, no strangers to rock gods, screamed in excitement. Moss summed up the session afterwards by saying, "I've just been clinging to David Bowie, naked. It doesn't get much better than that." The two became friends, although Bowie, she added, would never forget to tease her about the "snug fit" of that original photoshoot.

For a period, Moss became a target for the tabloids. Bowie, only too aware of how the press could hound certain celebrities, would always make sure to call her if a critical story appeared. "There are people who believe in you, that don't give a shit what people say," Moss told *The Edit* magazine. "He was one of them."

Beyoncé

Bowie came to Beyoncé's defence while giving a concert in New Jersey in 2004. He had just seen an American TV show called *Divas*, which revelled in applying that word to the American R&B singer. "They've watered down this word," Bowie told the crowd. "When I was in the seventies, a diva was a bitchy, mean-tempered cow who was also incredibly talented. One that ruled like an empress. She would have a plate of undercooked salmon and throw it out the window because it was on the wrong colour plate. That was a diva! Aretha Franklin was a diva. Joan Crawford was diva. Beyoncé? No. Lovely girl, I've met her. Couldn't be nicer. She is so sweet. A star, yes. But not a diva."

Beyoncé appreciated Bowie's support. When asked if she considered herself a diva like Diana Ross, she said, "That sounds cool because she's glamorous. But people don't mean it that way. They think I go around kicking people out of the group." With a touch of irony, Beyoncé later recorded a song called "Diva" (2008), in which she chants, "I'm a diva!" Bowie would have approved.

Tony Blair

Colombian pop singer Shakira and PR guru Alan Edwards were at Westminster talking to Chancellor Gordon Brown about debt relief when a civil servant walked in to announce that "Tony" needed to see the visiting pair urgently. Ushered along a maze of corridors and past a lengthy line of MPs, who gave the queue-jumpers outraged looks, the pair were escorted into the prime minister's room, where Blair got straight down to business.

Ignoring Shakira, Blair turned to Edwards and said, "Look

Alan, it's you I want to talk to. I've got to have an important conversation with you, it's something really serious...The new David Bowie album...is it being recorded in Switzerland or New York?" Despite Shakira shooting Edwards incredulous looks, the PR man felt compelled to answer; it was the prime minister of Britain, after all. "The only two times I saw Tony Blair starstruck were when he met David Bowie and when he met Barbra Streisand," said his adviser Alastair Campbell.

"I was actually starstruck three times," Blair said later. "The other time was with Paul McCartney." When the then prime minister invited Bowie to his official country residence, Chequers, for dinner, the thing which most struck him was the rock star's new, healthy lifestyle and, in particular, his choice of fruit juice over alcohol. "He was polite, charming and very disciplined in his personal habits because he'd been through enough in his youth to know that was sensible," said Blair.

Bowie was equally impressed with Blair. "I really like him a lot – we get on very well," he said. "It seemed ironic that a major priority on both our minds was the challenge of how to present new ideas." In fact, Bowie was so enthused by Blair's New Labour government that he considered making London his permanent home.

Nelson Mandela

But it was another politician whom Bowie most revered. "Nelson Mandela," Bowie said, when asked who he would most like to meet. And what would he ask the South African leader? "How he kept his sense of purpose for such a long time," Bowie replied.

The singer got to fulfil his dream in 1995. Normally, it would be Bowie who would be the one granting an audience. But this time the singer was the one being given just three minutes. Photographer Bruce Webber was there to capture the moment for *Vanity Fair* and recalled Bowie and Iman being "so excited" upon meeting the "gentle and sincere" 77-year-old. The couple went on to meet two other icons of the anti-apartheid movement, Archbishop Desmond Tutu and Miriam "Mama Africa" Makeba, on that trip.

The encounter with Mandela was so fleeting that it does not appear that Bowie had time to ask his burning question. However, coincidentally, the singer was himself once asked what his own sense of purpose was. "Just avoiding the catastrophe of success," he said.

Eddie Murphy

Comedian Eddie Murphy was another who admitted being starstruck around Bowie. Having been introduced by director Tony Scott, Murphy suggested an amble around Hollywood. Rather than coming on his own, the comedian turned up with a gaggle of minders and friends. Bowie loved his anonymity and revelled in his ability to disappear in public, armed with nothing more than a foreign-language newspaper or a quickly grown moustache, so he was not best pleased.

"I was always suspicious of people who say they need entourages because you don't," said Bowie. "Every time we took five paces down the street, there'd be the sound of about 40 footsteps following us. It was impossible."

As well as a comedian and actor, Murphy was also a musician. One year his soul band were invited to play at the Montreux Jazz

Festival in Switzerland. After the gig, Murphy retired upstairs to a small room where there was an old piano. After a while, he heard someone say, "I didn't know you played." It was Bowie. Despite their having hung out together, Murphy admitted he was completely thrown. "I'm a big Bowie fan. If I'm around someone like that, I'm starstruck," he said.

Keanu Reeves

When Bowie played a Halloween concert in Hollywood in 1996, he surprised everyone by asking a virtually unknown local band to be his support act. Unknown, that is, apart from the bassist, who had a side career as a Hollywood actor.

Dogstar's drummer, Rob Mailhouse, recalled getting a call from a booking agent saying, "You are not going to believe this but David Bowie has requested you guys to open for him."

Mailhouse did not believe it. "He doesn't need us," he told the agent. "What's going on here? Is this the Keanu Reeves thing? I was like, okay. Maybe he just wanted to meet Keanu." It seems highly unlikely that Bowie was desperate to meet the hero of *Bill & Ted's Excellent Adventure*, but in any case, the drummer had to know. On the night of the gig, he asked Bowie why he had picked Dogstar. "I heard some of your music. Pretty cool," Bowie replied. Another possible reason is that Bowie knew about the band because his old costume designer, Patricia Taylor, was Reeves's mother.

As for the gig, "The crowd were like, 'Who the fuck is this?'" recalled Mailhouse. "But it went really well."

Stereophonics

Bowie was famously supportive of his support bands, but his relationship with the Welsh rockers Stereophonics came with a fair amount of ribbing, too. "He would heckle us from the auditorium during our sound check," bassist Richard Jones recalled.

"He was just walking around bored most of the time, just trying to keep himself interested," said singer Kelly Jones. Nervous of boring their patron even further, the band would race through the sound check, playing no more than 30 seconds of each song. "Afterwards, Bowie would put his arm around my shoulder and walk with me and say, 'You know, if you extended a few of those songs you might be fucking onto something,'" recalled Jones.

One way to while away the hours was for the two bands to play soccer matches against each other. Bowie, no soccer player, would continue his heckling, this time from the touchline. "He'd lower a trophy down over our heads on a string when we lost the match, and comically mock our poor football skills," said Kelly.

The Stereophonics singer was especially touched by two things from that tour: the first was Bowie taking the time to read a story Kelly had written, and the second was dedicating "Life on Mars?" to him one night (Kelly had been begging for Bowie to play it all tour.) "He was a gentleman, he was brilliant," said Kelly.

Perry Farrell

The best story concerning Bowie and the Jane's Addiction singer is not about how they first got together, it is about how they fell out. One day, Perry Farrell left his phone in a cab. Rather than hand the phone in, the cabbie leafed through the contacts and stumbled upon the name "Bowie". Thinking, "Why not?", the driver texted, "Yo Bowie! What's up?" The inane stream of questions continued over the coming days, driving Bowie to despair. When he finally tracked down Farrell to ask what was going on, the New York singer explained and apologized. All would have been well except that Farrell went on to suffer a similar mishap. A keen environmentalist, he had been campaigning to stop a local river being polluted. Appealing to all his email contacts, he sent out a request for help, unaware of anything called "blind cc". Hundreds of people now had Bowie's personal email address.

"What are you doing?" Bowie emailed back, quickly. "Perry, please delete me."

Perhaps thinking Farrell was a liability, Bowie shut down contact. But in 2015 Farrell got an invite from producer Tony Visconti to take part in a musical event in Carnegie Hall celebrating the English singer.

"I thought, 'I'm going to get this thing right. I'm going to do the tribute and we're going to hang out. It's going to be great,'" recalled Farrell. However, just before plans could be finalized, Bowie died.

Beastie Boys
- - - - - - - - - - - - - - -

Farrell was not the only one to run afoul of Bowie when it came to email. Adam Yauch, singer and bassist with Beastie Boys, was once cornered by an upset Bowie backstage at the 2007 Webby Awards, the Oscars of the Internet. The singer had taken exception to Yauch not using "blind cc" on a mass email. On receiving his award, Yauch took the opportunity to say sorry:

"I'd like to apologize to David Bowie in front of everyone. I cc'd him on an email that I sent to a bunch of people and he was really mad at me." The Beastie Boy added, "I don't know what I was thinking." Ever humorous, Yauch then asked the audience if there was anyone present who might be able to fix his broken computer. Bowie was also in a playful mood when it came to his turn to receive his Lifetime Achievement award for UltraStar, his digital media company. "I only get five words?" he said. "Shit! That was five."

It is likely that the banter between the two was good humoured, as not only did they share a deep interest in Buddhism but Bowie was a regular performer at the Tibet House Benefit Concerts, which were organized by Yauch. In fact, when Bowie played "Space Oddity" at one of those concerts, he asked Yauch to play bass.

Marilyn Manson

Marilyn Manson had been waiting years for what he called his "Bowie moment", only to have it ruined by an actress seemingly high on drugs.

After a Bowie show in 2004 in Santa Barbara, Manson was invited backstage. He walked into the dressing room and was delighted to find himself alone with his hero. Bowie immediately reached out to feel the shock-rocker's tie. "Oh, Hedi Slimane," said Bowie, referring to its designer. "I felt like I was going to pee my pants like a little girl," Manson said.

Having been going through a rough patch with drug addiction, Manson decided to ask how Bowie had finally managed to kick his habit. "I just got bored with it," said Bowie. But before the conversation could develop, in came a garrulous TV actress who started talking loudly "about cocaine and toilets", as Manson recalled. "She was really overwhelming and she was fucking with my Bowie moment. I wanted her to be a boil and I'd lance it."

While the shock rocker was clearly influenced by and idolized Bowie, the latter was more equivocal. "Except for the breasts, I don't mind him. What Manson does is a strong statement, but a singular one and not very interesting."

Alexander McQueen

Bowie certainly knew his clothes designers, and one he was especially fond of was Alexander McQueen. The singer had been alerted to the enfant terrible of British design early on, and one day he phoned his studio in London's Hoxton. Worried the caller might be a creditor, McQueen initially put on a fake accent and pretended to be a secretary, saying, "'E's not 'ere. Does 'e owe you money?" When McQueen finally put the phone down, his colleague asked him who he had been speaking to. "Fucking David Bowie, innit," McQueen responded. "He wants me to do tour costumes... or something...'

The designer went on to create Bowie's Union Jack frock coat based on the singer's desire to update Pete Townshend's iconic sixties jacket. McQueen never got to meet Bowie face to face but they did take part in an engaging interview by phone for *Dazed & Confused* magazine. Bowie's first question was, "Are you gay and do you take drugs?"

"Yes, to both," McQueen replied. "Do you dress to the left or right?" McQueen asked.

"Both," the singer replied.

During the interview, Bowie revealed that he had never paid for any of his costumes until he met McQueen. He treated him differently because, he told the financially struggling designer, "You needed it!"

Jake Shears

The Scissor Sisters singer still kicks himself for blowing his "Bowie moment". After finishing a show in New York in 2004, Shears was told Bowie had been watching from the balcony. A long-time Bowie nut, he started hyperventilating: "Is he still here? Why didn't anybody say anything? How come no one told me? The show was fucking terrible!" On the verge of tears, Shears decided to make the best of a bad situation by putting on a fresh shirt to meet his "first and only favourite rock star". But Bowie never came. "He had seen my shitty show and left," wrote Shears in his memoir. "I was inconsolable. They say never meet your idols. I guess the only thing worse than meeting your idols is not meeting them."

Two weeks later he received an email: "Hi, I came to your show a few weeks ago. It sounded very good from where I was sitting. db." After three weeks and dozens of drafts, Shears managed to compose a reply: "Dear David Bowie, You mean more to me than any artist on earth. My favorite song you've ever written is 'Fantastic Voyage.' Thank you so much for coming to my show, but I really hope at this point that we never cross paths. There's not a lot in this world I keep sacred, but I would rather you just stay imaginary. Sincerely, Jake Shears."

Looking back at the correspondence years later, Shears said, "Now I realize that it was my insecurities that made me prickle. I felt like I didn't deserve to be so close to what I knew to be greatness. David Bowie, the man who gave me the idea and inspiration to perform in the first place, sent me a note to just tell me he liked my show, and I couldn't just see that for what it was. I wish I'd just replied with a simple, 'Thank you.'"

No doubt, the reason Bowie had not gone backstage afterwards was that he wanted to beat the traffic home.

PJ Harvey

PJ Harvey deliberately torpedoed her one and only chance to sing with her hero. Bowie had invited the Dorset singer, whom he described as "fabulous", to join him at the 1995 MTV Awards to sing "The Man Who Sold the World". But Polly Jean Harvey had her own ideas.

"Polly, being Polly, said she'd only do it if she could use her own band," said her guitarist, Joe Gore. "We even rehearsed a dirge-like version of the song, without David of course."

But Bowie refused to jettison his band and, exasperated by Harvey's conditions, eventually withdrew the offer. "We both had different ideas," he said. "It ended friendly enough but I doubt that we will get back together again."

It was only a month later that Harvey was asked by a music magazine to name the artist she most respected. David Bowie, she replied. Which made it even more surprising that she seemingly sabotaged the opportunity to work together.

TV on the Radio

Working with Bowie was not always the dream it may have seemed. In fact, to one young Brooklyn band, it became a curse. TV on the Radio were initially delighted when their older fan asked to record a song with them. The trouble was, journalists were to never let the band forget the fact. "I never want to be asked again what it was like to work with David Bowie," exasperated singer Kyp Malone would eventually say.

It all started at a filling station in the middle of nowhere in particular in Philadelphia. Guitarist David Sitek was filling up the band's beat-up old van when he got a call.

"Hello, this is David Bowie. I just want to say I love your daring and refreshing music." Sitek put the phone down. The phone rang again. "This is David," the caller managed to say before being cut off yet again. The phone rang a third time. "No, this is actually David." A disbelieving Sitek was finally convinced.

Bowie's hair stylist was a girlfriend of one of the band members, and had been playing TV on the Radio in the background while cutting the singer's hair. Bowie was so impressed, he asked her for Sitek's number. The two became friends, with the guitarist often dropping demos off at Bowie's New York home. Bowie liked one song, "Province", so much, the band suggested he sing on the track. Even though the collaboration came to overshadow their other work, and despite the incessant questions, all the band said their "Bowie moment" remained the highlight of their career.

Camille Paglia
- - - - - - - - - - - - - - - - -

Bowie would get used to having the phone put down on him. One of the problems of being so famous was that people rarely believed it was David Bowie on the end of the line. Not even if their name was Camille Paglia.

"Is it really David Bowie? And if it is, is it important?" That's what the no-nonsense cultural commentator shouted over to her assistant when Bowie kept phoning to ask her to appear on his record. Convinced it had to be a prank, she never took the calls herself, or returned them. "It was one of the biggest fiascos of my chequered career," she lamented.

The author's infatuation with Bowie began late one night in 1969, when the young student was listening to the radio in bed. The DJ paused before introducing one particular record, admitting that its peculiarity had so polarized the station's staff that there had been an argument about whether to play the song at all. Paglia's ears pricked up. What type of record could cause such division? Within seconds, she was transfixed by "the eerie, mesmerizing" sound of "Space Oddity". Here, she sensed, was the first true song of the seventies, a record which heralded the end of the peace-and-love counterculture and hinted at "a darker decade of disillusion and decadent hedonism".

Bowie entered her life again in 1971 when she was at Yale Graduate School, working on her PhD dissertation that would, eventually and belatedly, be published in 1990 as *Sexual Personae*. It was the only dissertation about sex in the whole of the graduate school that year, and, specifically, it was about androgyny. So, when Ziggy Stardust burst onto the scene, Bowie's daring gender-bending experiments seemed to Paglia "like the living embodiment of everything I had been thinking about". Ziggy convinced her she was right to ditch the arcaneness of the typical academic treatise for her new approach. "Who the hell needed Foucault when we already had a genius like Bowie?" she said. Bowie himself loved her work and was to include *Sexual Personae* in his 2014 list of 100 books that had most influenced him creatively. "No wonder he felt at home with my ideas," she said, "he was sensing himself mirrored back!"

In the mid-nineties, the real Bowie finally came into Paglia's life. Well, almost. Paglia's publishers told her the singer had called asking for her number. The author was convinced it was a joke. Someone of Bowie's stature, she reasoned, would never make such a call himself. "I laughed. I didn't believe it," she said. The calls kept coming but Paglia kept rebuffing them. "Oh boy, it's just some fan," she told her assistant. "It's ridiculous."

As Bowie recalled, "I nearly sampled Camille Paglia on this album [*Outside*] but she never returned my calls. She kept sending messages through her assistant saying, 'Is this really David Bowie and, if it is, is it important?' (laughs). I just gave up!"

Years later, Paglia was asked to contribute to the book that accompanied his retrospective *David Bowie Is* exhibition. This time, she agreed. For her, Bowie was more than a singer, songwriter and musician. He was a courageous performance artist. Bowie, she said, had taken the next major step, post-Warhol, in art history.

The Arctic Monkeys

The Arctic Monkeys were halfway through their set when some of the band's family members turned up at the small New York venue. Wanting to give them the best possible view, the tour manager moved towards the VIP tables. Noticing a man seated on his own, the manager asked him to move, and he did so without complaint. It was only after the show, when the same man appeared backstage, that it dawned on everyone who exactly had been told to vacate his seat. "He didn't say anything like, 'I'm David Bowie'," said frontman Alex Turner. "He just moved tables politely and then came to say hello afterwards." The band were too starstruck to speak. "We didn't know what to say to him, you know," said Turner. "We were just overwhelmed."

The Libertines

Libertines guitarist Carl Barât risked both ridicule and getting fired to meet David Bowie. Barât was working the door at the New London Theatre for the musical *Cats* when a rumour started that Bowie was to sing one of the songs on stage that night. Watching the rehearsals, Barât became so convinced that one of the performers in a cat mask was Bowie himself that he wrote a quick note inviting the singer "to come around to our squat for a cup of tea", and left it at the stage door for him. That evening, Barât asked the doorman if Bowie had received his message. "David Bowie?" replied the mystified bouncer. "In *Cats*?? Get the fuck outta here!"

A year later, Barât was still working at the theatre when the staff were all gathered together to be told a "very, very special" guest was arriving that night. "Special" on its own was Spice Girls level, so "very, very special" left everyone feeling wildly excited. But, they were all warned, if anyone tried to approach the VIP, they would be sacked on the spot.

That evening, with everyone in place and the theatre abuzz, in walked a resplendently suited Bowie. He paused in the lobby to put a cigarette to his lips and then patted his pockets searching for a light. Manning the nearby door, Barât, a fellow smoker, realized that this might be his one and only chance to meet his hero. Putting his job on the line, he rushed over, flicked his lighter and, in one deft movement, "lit the great man's fag".

"I somehow expected this moment to change my life for the better," recalled Barât. But just as Bowie looked up to see who had performed such a gracious feat, Barât heard his boss say, "Get back to your fucking post."

By 2004, the Libertines' star had risen and fallen. Barât was at the Isle of Wight Festival but as a spectator – his band had been on the bill to support Bowie but had once again self-destructed. Watching his stand-ins from the wings, thinking of what might have been, Barât began crying. As the tears rolled down his cheeks, he felt someone stand next to him, and then a hand rest on his shoulder. "You all right?" a voice asked. He looked up to see a concerned-looking man in a brown baseball cap. It slowly dawned on Barât that it was David Bowie, and he was being touched by "the hand of God".

"Yeah," said an overcome Barât. Several seconds of silence passed as Barât desperately tried to think of something more profound to say.

"Cheers," he eventually added, as meaningfully as he could.

Bowie smiled, and the two men turned to watch the rest of the set together in silence.

Following Bowie's death, Barât recounted his Bowie encounters to bandmate Pete Doherty.

"That's weird," replied the Libertines singer. "You know, he wanted to do something with us."

"You what?" said Barat

"Yeah. I told him to fuck off."

"You WHAT?"

"Yeah, he called my phone and said, 'Hi, is this potty Pete? This is David.' And I said, 'Fuck off, David,' and hung up."

Years later, a sanguine Barât said of his chance to work with Bowie, "It seems it just wasn't meant to be."

The Charlatans

The band who replaced the Libertines at that festival were the Charlatans. A tweet by their singer, Tim Burgess, reads as follows:

Backstage at The Isle of Wight Festival 2004…

Me (nervously): Hi, David, I'm the singer in the Charlatans. We're playing before you tonight.

Bowie (sweetly): I know, Tim. I know.

Life made

THE NEXT DAYS
2005–16

What happened to Bowie after his heart attack? Or was that heart attacks? The truth is, we really don't know. He disappeared, he briefly re-emerged, he disappeared again. There was talk that he might open the Olympics, that he had Alzheimer's and that he was dying. Then *The Next Day* (2013) came out. It was joyous. Bowie was making music again! Great music! And he was definitely alive! But he had noticeably aged. The video showed an old man, unadorned and unmade up, singing about his past. It was a farewell song, and it was a song about dying. "Where Are We Now?" was not sentimental or maudlin; it was beautiful and it was heartbreaking.

Then came more videos and songs, a play and another album. It felt like the crazy sprint you see from a marathon runner as they enter the stadium for the final lap. They have given everything but there they are, tearing up the last 100 metres. Then, just as it felt like old times with a new Bowie record always to look forward to, he died. It seemed impossible and inevitable. For decades, we had believed the contradictory thoughts that he couldn't possibly have survived and that he couldn't die. He had defied the odds so many times; surely it wasn't asking much for him to defy them this last one time. Bowie, typically, flouted our expectations again.

Arcade Fire

- - - - - - - - - - - - -

Author Molly Knight recalled going to New York's Tower Records to buy Arcade Fire's new CD, only to find that it was nowhere to be seen. Going up to the counter to complain, the assistant told her they had sold out. "Bowie bought them all," he said, by way of improbable explanation. In fact, Bowie was such a convert, he had bought every copy to give them to friends as presents.

Following his heart attack in 2004, Bowie disappeared from public view for over a year. When he did re-emerge, it was with Arcade Fire. Bowie had invited his band-of-the-moment to join him for a short set at a benefit event alongside the likes of Duran Duran and Gwen Stefani. It had been such a tame affair that some of the seated audience could be spotted with their heads down, buried in books. But then Bowie appeared with the Canadian band to sing "Wake Up". The previously lethargic crowd took the musicians at their word and rose to their feet in delight.

After the concert, Bowie invited all eight members to dinner as a thank-you. Arcade Fire's violinist Owen Pallett was left dumbfounded as half the group declined the offer. "Most of the band said they had other plans so it was literally me, Patrick, Win, Regine, Will and Jenny having dinner with Bowie," wrote Pallett on his website. "Bowie and I hit it off insanely and talked about Mishima and This Heat. We talked about his smoking habit. He told me he'd quit just a year before he had his heart attack." Pallett was especially taken by Bowie's cologne, Creed's Silver Mountain Water, which was way too ostentatious a scent, he said, for anyone but Bowie. He also recalled the singer's childish delight when the waiter provided him with his favourite pomegranate juice.

"Every report I'd heard about meeting Bowie suggests that the guy was really, really good at meeting people and making them feel a million bucks, but no words could really describe the man's complete generosity of spirit, intelligence and charisma," wrote Pallett. "The next day we were all in rehearsals and Bowie looked around and said, 'Where's Patrick?' Patrick had flown back to Toronto to get back to work at his job at The Power Plant. When I called Patrick on the break, Bowie tapped me on the shoulder and said, 'Can I say hello?' When they hung up Patrick turned to his co-workers and said, 'That was David Bowie. He just wanted to see how I was doing.'"

When Bowie died, the band paid him the ultimate accolade in terms of colour and loudness. They arranged a New Orleans-style parade with drums and trumpets, and a request to participants to wear "their best Bowie outfit or something more strange".

James Murphy

James Murphy was in the studio producing his friends Arcade Fire when in walked their guest vocalist. After a polite and brief hello, he recorded his track and left. The next day, the singer returned. But this time he walked straight past the band and right up to Murphy. "I'm so sorry, I had no idea it was you!" he apologized. "I just blanked. Of course it's you! I'm an enormous fan of your work."

Murphy was overcome. "David Bowie was, like, apologizing to me for not recognizing my greatness! I said, 'Well, if you know anything about me, you know I'm an enormous fan of your work because I steal from you liberally.' He leaned in and said, 'You can't steal from a thief, darling.' And I'm like, 'Wow! That's just in the holster? You just have that ready to go?' Someone so charming, it's invisible. So, if you manage to not have your head explode, you start a friendship."

The two ended up working together, and Bowie wanted Murphy to co-produce *Black Star* alongside Tony Visconti. But Murphy said he felt so unworthy, he limited himself to arranging some drum tracks in a corner before slinking off. "I was supposed to do a lot more, but I got overwhelmed," he said. "It takes a different kind of person than me to walk into that room and be like, 'I belong here.'"

When Murphy was debating whether to put LCD Soundsystem back together, it was David Bowie to whom he turned. "Does it make you uncomfortable?" Bowie asked him. When Murphy replied yes, Bowie said, "Good, it should." Murphy took the advice and the band reformed.

Ricky Gervais

"Do you like David Bowie?" is a common enough question. But it's not often followed by "Want to meet him, then?"

Ricky Gervais almost fell over when BBC boss Greg Dyke offered to introduce the comedian to his hero at a BBC party in honour of the singer. Dyke, who knew Gervais was a fan, pulled him through the throng. On the way, the gregarious BBC Director General spotted Salman Rushdie. 'Salman!' he shouted, beckoning the writer to follow.

Bowie recognized Rushdie, but it soon became clear he had no idea who Gervais was. A polite, if awkward, conversation followed over salad before the comedian made his excuses and left. In the meantime, Dyke, who knew Bowie loved British comedy, sang the praises of *The Office*. A week later, Gervais received an email.

Ricky Gervais and Bowie in New York City, 2007.

"I just watched *The Office*. I laughed. What do I do now? DB"

What Bowie did was appear as himself in one of the most unexpected cameos in British television history. Gervais was invited around to Bowie's New York apartment, shortly after the singer had undergone his heart operation. Bowie delighted in poking fun at the rumours of his health troubles. He went to the kitchen to make coffee and returned hunched over the tray and shuffling, like a doddery 90-year-old.

Gervais suggested Bowie write a song for a scene in *Extras*. "Something retro, like 'Life on Mars?'," he suggested. "Oh sure," replied Bowie. "I'll just knock off a quick fucking 'Life on Mars?', shall I?" The song they came up with was "Little Fat Man".

On 19 May 2007, Bowie appeared at Madison Square Garden. He pulled out a harmonica, played a single note and then sang, "Chubby little loser..." The surprised crowd, who were there to see Gervais, went wild. It was to be Bowie's last-ever performance.

Dom Joly

Dom Joly could not believe his luck when he spotted Bowie sitting on his own in an airport in Geneva. Sensing a once-in-a-lifetime opportunity, the comedian approached. But the nearer he got, the more his confidence ebbed away, and he soon found himself turning around and heading back to the magazine rack. He gathered his thoughts and tried a second time but exactly the same thing happened. Not to be defeated, he gave it a third go, this time getting within a few feet.

Most people would have given up by now, but Joly, writing in his autobiography, *Here Comes the Clown*, convinced himself it would be fourth time lucky. He was halfway towards his target when Bowie lowered his newspaper and looked up, having clearly been aware all along of his stalker's comings and goings. With no choice but to go forward, Joly stuck his hand straight out and marched ahead. Bowie took his hand. Joly's mind went blank. They continued to hold hands. Still, no words came. So, there they stayed, two strangers holding hands in a busy airport.

"For what seemed like an interminable period of time we stared at each other," recalled the comedian. Then, just as Joly found the words he wanted to say, Bowie said, "Excuse me," and walked away. "It took me five or six years to be able to tell this story," said Joly.

Echo and the Bunnymen

Guitarist Will Sergeant was so overcome on meeting Bowie he spilled his beer over the singer.

In the mid-nineties, former Bunnymen Sergeant and Ian McCulloch were supporting Bowie on tour in France with their new band, Electrafixion. Bowie had come to their dressing room to wish them luck. "I'd had a few beers and I was still holding this glass of Duvel, which was strong Belgian ale," Sergeant told *The Vinyl Guide* podcast. "He opened the door. My hand stopped working. Bowie was stood in front of me, my massive, total hero. I dropped the glass and it splattered everywhere." Sergeant was left speechless. On the following night, the guitarist went up to Bowie to apologize.

"Sorry for dropping my ale all over you," he said.

"I didn't even notice," replied the ever-urbane Bowie.

Relieved, Sergeant then came out with the real reason he had gone over, and handed over his Bowie records to be autographed – all 35 albums and 15 singles. Bowie signed every single one.

As for the notoriously cocky McCulloch, he said of Bowie, tongue in cheek, "Yeah, he met me a few times." McCulloch described Bowie as still looking amazing on that tour and remained a huge fan: "He was the greatest artist in any walk of art of the 20th century."

RuPaul

The world's most famous drag queen was having palpitations. Sitting near him at a dinner party was his hero. Finally, unable to stand it anymore, RuPaul made an excuse and hurriedly left to try to find a room in which to calm down. This being a large, swanky New York apartment, the room turned out to be a cavernous library. As RuPaul stood alone surrounded by walls of books, trying to catch his breath, he heard someone quietly enter and softly say, "Hi." It was Bowie. The singer had been worried that his fellow guest was unwell and had come to check up on him.

"We spoke for a little bit," said RuPaul. Bowie went back to the gathering, but RuPaul felt unable to return and sit next to a man he described as "a beacon of light" for challenging gender stereotypes. Instead, he skipped dinner, ran out the door and down the stairs, and out onto the sidewalk. "I had to let out the screaming and crying that followed," he said.

Val Kilmer

On meeting Bowie, some people resorted to running, others resorted to petting. Val Kilmer was at a rock concert when he realized that sitting in front of him was the man he had loved since boyhood. The *Batman* actor was possessed by an urge to do something. He just didn't know what. Language felt insufficient to convey the depth of his feelings so, instead of talking, Kilmer put his hands on his hero's shoulders and started to stroke him like a beloved pet.

"I haven't petted that many men in my life," the actor confessed, "but it was the only way I seemed to be able to express my joy."

Bowie, seemingly no stranger to such outpourings of emotion from people he hardly knew, allowed the petting to continue and, unfazed, simply turned around to smile. "He seemed not only to understand, but accept the strange offering of gratitude and recognition," said Kilmer.

Cheap Trick

That was not the only time Bowie demonstrated an impressive coolness despite some strange behaviour exhibited towards him, as Cheap Trick were to find out. At a celebrity function in Switzerland, the Illinois rockers spotted Bowie deep in conversation with Annie Lennox. Bassist Tom Petersson bet his bandmates he could get Bowie to talk to him. With the wager accepted, Petersson walked up behind the singer and gently took his hand. Bowie did not even bat an eyelid and carried on talking to Lennox.

"For like five minutes, I'm standing there," Petersson told DJ Howard Stern. "Finally, he turns around, looks at me and goes, 'Oh, you must have the wrong person.'"

Scarlett Johansson

Many people might be surprised to discover that Scarlett Johansson has not only had a successful recording career, but that Bowie has sung on one of her albums.

Johansson's crush on the singer began early but had nothing to do with his vocal talents. She was just two when *Labyrinth* was released, and she recalled being transfixed by the shaggy-haired, leotard-wearing Bowie, who played Jareth the Goblin King.

It was almost another 20 years before the two met backstage

after one of his concerts. "I couldn't tell him he was my first love," said Johansson, "because I couldn't actually speak when he shook my hand. The only time I've ever been like that before was when I met Bill Clinton."

Johansson recalled that she tried telepathically to invite Bowie to the studio where she was about to start recording her first album. Somehow, the message got through. Johansson's producer called her to say Bowie had "dropped by" and recorded backing vocals for two of her songs, both written by Tom Waits. Johansson was away filming in Spain at the time, but the realization Bowie was on her record thrilled her. "It was the best phone call I ever got," she said.

Hugh Jackman

Thirteen-year-old Hugh Jackman was thrilled. Not only had he bought his first concert ticket but his parents were allowing him out at night on his own. On the morning of the big day, Jackman bragged at school that he was off to see Bowie. One of the older children overheard and offered to pay double for the ticket. The youngster deliberated ever so briefly before taking the cash.

Twenty-five years later on the set of *The Prestige* (2006), the Australian actor got to meet Bowie. The two got on so well that Jackman decided the time was right to tell his ticket anecdote. It was a mistake. "All of a sudden, he looks at me and goes, 'Oh, so you're that kind of guy, are you?' And I said, 'No, no, no. I was 13. You know, 50 bucks was just too…' And actually, I've never seen him in concert since. That's one of the great regrets of my life." Bowie referred to his co-star, from that moment on, as "the scalper".

Christopher Nolan
- - - - - - - - - - - - - - - - - - - -

Nolan had already assembled a stellar cast for *The Prestige*. Along with Hugh Jackman, he had Christian Bale, Scarlett Johansson and Michael Caine. But he was missing one key person: the only actor he felt was right to play the mystical scientific genius Nikola Tesla. Such was the allure of working with the director of *Memento*, *Insomnia* and *Batman* that Nolan had never had to beg any actor to take a part in a film of his. This was to be the one and only time.

Bowie had already rejected the role, but the English director could think of no other suitable replacement. Compelled to try once more, Nolan flew to New York to plead his case face to face.

"In total honesty, I told David if he didn't agree to do the part, I had no idea where I would go from there. I would say I begged him," the director told *Entertainment Weekly*. It was, he said, the only time he had ever gone back to ask an actor a second time. Bowie was won over and agreed to take part in what would be his last major movie role.

Nolan has worked with the biggest names in film, from Al Pacino to Leonardo DiCaprio, but said Bowie had "a level of charisma beyond any". When the singer was due to film a scene, the whole crew would suddenly reappear, finding things to do around the set. Bowie, Nolan said, had a gift for making them feel at ease. "He was very gracious and understood the effect he had on people," he added.

Wim Wenders

Bowie was so desperate to work with German director Wim Wenders, he issued a come-get-me plea to a German news magazine. "No one offers me anything," he told *Der Spiegel* in 1993. "Come on, Wenders, offer me a part!" The journalist expressed disbelief that someone so famous could be sitting by the phone waiting for it to ring. "The roles I get offered are rubbish," insisted Bowie. "I don't want any part just to be in a movie. I'll say it again: Wim Wenders, get on the phone!"

Some 13 years later, Wenders finally did get on the blower, but Bowie was almost certainly hoping for a more challenging project than a Nokia promotional video. The company had just launched an online music service and wanted Wenders to direct the promo and Bowie to talk about his love of buying records. "Music Recommenders," Bowie intones, "helps navigate the undiscovered music that's out there."

Elvis Costello

Among Bowie's many talents was an ability to organize party games. In 2007, he and Elvis Costello found themselves sitting next to each other at a charity dinner. In the corner sat a demure house band playing instrumental arrangements of eighties hits. Their versions were so esoteric, people were struggling to identify the original. To break the ice, Bowie gave everyone at the table five chances to "name that tune".

"If the band had known the delight he took in counting us out as we failed," wrote Costello in his autobiography, "they might have thought better about their thankless task that night." Bowie was the only one who guessed every tune correctly. Costello continued, "Eventually, David leaned into me conspiratorially and said, 'Do you remember 1978? We were the only people having lunch in an Indian restaurant overlooking Central Park.'"

Costello nodded and replied, "You were sitting at the window with a girl."

"That's right," said Bowie, a touch of naughtiness creeping into his tone. "We were both entertaining young ladies and acting far too cool to speak to one another."

"Then we both broke up laughing," recalled Costello, "at the ridiculous memory."

Bowie loved Costello's music as well as his company. He was once asked if there were one song he wished he had written. "Shipbuilding," he replied, referring to the Costello-penned number. "Makes me want to cry. I think it's the most tragically beautiful song."

Dave Gahan

The scene could not be more ordinary: two dads waiting by the school gates to pick up their daughters. The only difference being that the two fathers in question were David Bowie and Dave Gahan. And, just like typical fathers, they stood there in silence, keeping themselves to themselves, exchanging only the merest nod of recognition.

"I never bothered him on the school run or when we were watching our children in the school play or anything," said Gahan. "We didn't really talk about music or anything. We were just two dads picking up our children."

The Depeche Mode singer recounted how charming Bowie

was right from the start. After one of Bowie's gigs, Gahan was told Bowie wanted to meet him backstage. "He said straight away, 'I know you'," said the flattered Basildon man.

Bowie was such a huge influence on Depeche Mode that his death led Gahan to burst into tears: "I don't think I was that upset about someone passing away in my whole life, to be honest. One thing I regret is never telling him how much his music meant to me." The singer arguably owes his whole career to Bowie. According to the band's folklore, the 18-year-old Gahan was singing "Heroes" in a Basildon scout hut when he was overheard by a passing keyboard player by the name of Vince Clarke.

Courtney Love

Telling someone to turn down the volume is not very rock and roll. So, imagine Courtney Love's surprise to discover that the neighbour asking her to "keep it down" was none other than David Bowie.

Love had moved into a plush new apartment in New York's SoHo area around 2011. She liked to play her music loud and she liked to start early. One morning around 9am, with Fleetwood Mac's *Rumours* blaring out, there was a knock at the door. Bernard, the doorman, asked her to turn down the decibels.

"Who could possibly object to *Rumours*?!" responded Love. Barnard pointed to the floor above and said, "The Bowie family."

Love complied and left flowers outside the Bowies' door, with a note saying, in case they hadn't noticed, "Hi, I've moved in!" She never did receive a reply, which surprised her given that she had been invited to Bowie's 50th-birthday party, and been described by Bowie himself as one of his favourite performers.

Paul Weller

According to the tabloids, Bowie and Paul Weller were involved in a long-running feud, which began when the Jam frontman was asked to give his verdict on Bowie receiving a Lifetime Achievement Award at the Brits in 2006. "Wrong," said Weller. "I like about three records of his. The rest is pish."

If Bowie was upset, he did not mention it. Either way, any hatchet was truly buried when Weller subsequently named his son Bowie. Upon hearing the news, the real Bowie sent a bouquet of flowers. Weller responded by saying how much he had grown to love Bowie's music and how, even in his youth, *Low* had been a constant in his life. Bowie emailed back a photograph of himself from his mid-sixties mod days, looking uncannily like the Jam singer in his heyday, with the words: "Can I have my haircut back now?"

Rufus Wainwright

A snatched conversation in a locked toilet stall while having a pee – such was the less than glamorous encounter between Rufus Wainwright and David Bowie in 2008.

Bowie had gone to see the singer perform in New York, sneaking in under cover of darkness. "When David goes to a show he insists that he enter the theatre during the blackout before the band comes on stage," so as not detract from the performance, recalled Wainwright's husband, Jörn Weisbrodt.

Afterwards, Bowie went backstage. "David wanted to avoid being seen too much, I guess, and followed Rufus to the bathroom. I did too," said Weisbrodt. "The meeting was short. I believe someone did pee in the stall."

Bowie told Wainwright how much he had loved his Judy Garland show in 2006. It was the only performance, Bowie said, that he had seen that whole year, presumably because of his heart trouble. "There was not all that much to talk about after exchanging ravishing compliments," said Weisbrodt. "How do you talk to a legend?"

Chris Hadfield

In 2013, floating in his tin can, far above the world, astronaut Chris Hadfield sky-rocketed to fame with his outer-space version of "Space Oddity". Having seen the video, Bowie messaged Hadfield to say he had really made the grade with "the most poignant version of the song ever done". The fact that Bowie loved the song "floored me", said the astronaut.

The battle to get the video online proved more difficult than the filming. NASA found itself in a legal minefield, unsure which country's licensing and copyright laws applied to something shot in space. In the end, Bowie himself stepped in to help resolve the legal confusion.

Bowie already had quite a track record within the astronomical community. British astronaut Tim Peake, who made sure Bowie was on his space-station iPod, once asked Stephen Hawking what one song would he take to space. "'Starman'," the physicist replied.

Britt Ekland

Britt Ekand and Bowie were once kicked off a plane. But this is no tale of rock and roll excess. Instead, it involved the Swedish model-actress and Bowie, the chihuahua.

Ekland always booked two seats on a flight, one for her and one for her four-legged friend, whom she had named after her favourite singer. But this time, when she boarded the Los Angeles to Stockholm flight, she was told the seats had been double booked. Treated like any other standard economy passengers, Ekland and Bowie were told to disembark and wait for the next flight.

Marion Cotillard

When the French Oscar-winner received an email titled "David Bowie & Marion Cotillard", she almost dragged it straight to the trash, believing it to be a prank. When she read the invitation, asking her to appear with Bowie in a video, she became convinced it was a prank. But gradually, as she pored over the message, she became "feverish" with excitement as it dawned on her that the real Bowie was really asking her to perform alongside him.

Cotillard went to New York to play a Mary Magdalen-type prostitute, alongside Bowie as a Christ-like figure and Gary Oldman as a drunken priest for "The Next Day". The *La vie en rose* star described herself as "intimidated and excited" at working alongside "my idol" (she had, years before, chosen to sing a Bowie song on French TV). When the video was briefly banned by YouTube for being controversial, she was delighted.

"I adore the whiff of scandal," she told French weekly news magazine *L'Express*. "And when it's created by David Bowie, it is an honour I carry with pride."

Tilda Swinton

When the young Tilda Swinton saw the cover of *Aladdin Sane*, she felt an immediate connection with the "gingery, boney, pinky, whitey" face. The 12-year-old would carry the album around with her as a constant reminder that she was not alone in her unusual looks. Not owning a record player, it was two years before she actually got around to playing the thing. "It took me years to admit it was the vision and not the sound which hooked me," she said.

She and Bowie were to become close friends many years later in New York. But the fact that Swinton had always seen Bowie as her "alien cousin" meant she never quite came to terms with the reality. "The moment that the phone rings and it's someone who calls themselves David Bowie...you never stop pinching yourself," she said.

Such is the similarity between the two that there is a Tumblr account dedicated to the belief that "Tilda and Bowie are one person". Bowie himself played with the lookalike visual gag in the video to "The Stars (Are Out Tonight)" which features the two of them as a married couple.

Bowie asked Swinton to give the address at the opening of the *David Bowie Is* exhibition at London's Victoria and Albert Museum, with the proviso she include the word "testicular". She did so by saying, "You brought us out of the wainscotting...Like so many loners and pretty things and dandies and dudes and dukes and duckies and testicular types."

Cillian Murphy

Back in the nineties, Bowie was asked by a fan online about a cap he once wore in a photograph. "Interesting thing about caps," Bowie replied, "there was a mob of unruly youths in the nineteenth century called The Peakies. They had sharp razors embedded in the peaks of their caps and would use them for slashing their victims." After Bowie described how the gang descended from the Mohocks, the sons of rich aristocrats who cut off their victims' noses and ears and made necklaces of them, another fan asked him how he knew about these groups. "From research I started doing around the time of *Diamond Dogs*, when I was trying to evolve a new type of street gang," he wrote. All of which helps explain why the *Peaky Blinders* TV series, inspired by Victorian-era gang culture, so fascinated him.

"We were friends and I sent him a cap from the first series as a Christmas present," said *Peaky Blinders* actor Cillian Murphy. In response, Bowie sent back a photograph of himself in the same cap with blades added. The singer said he had written some music which might work for the show. A copy of the album, still heavily under wraps, was taken by hand from New York to the UK, and the delighted production team picked the song "Black Star" for their next series. Bowie was invited onto the set, but his manager responded apologetically, "I'm afraid that won't be possible." A week later, Bowie was dead.

Coincidentally, three years earlier, at the start of the series, Murphy's character is filmed drawing a black star in his diary. "Why are you drawing that?" he is asked.

"Because this is the day someone dies," he replies.

Michael Cunningham

Bowie once wrote a sci-fi musical about a love affair between a marooned alien and a human who discovers a batch of unknown Bob Dylan songs in a trunk. Pulitzer Prize-winning novelist Michael Cunningham was sceptical when Bowie pitched the idea to him, and became even more so when Bowie suggested introducing a mariachi band. But he began to draft a script and collaborated daily with Bowie, who would compose short pieces of music on piano for the scenes.

In 2007, the writer of *The Hours* added that there was one final element Bowie had wanted to include in their musical – a reference to an American poet by the name of Emma Lazarus, a clue perhaps to understanding the musical Bowie eventually did write with Enda Walsh.

Enda Walsh

The Irish playwright Enda Walsh was escorted to the back of a New York apartment block where he was shown a "secret" elevator that took him down to the basement. The lift opened onto a long grey corridor at the end of which was an enormous concrete door. Walsh slowly pushed it open to reveal an "extraordinary" office and a man standing on his own. David Bowie walked up to his guest, embraced him and said, "God, you've been in my head for three weeks."

Bowie had spent the previous month reading everything Walsh had written and had decided he was the man to fulfil his long-held dream of writing a musical. Over the next 18 months, the two worked on a script about an alien trying to get home or, as Walsh put it, "about a man dying". Bowie addressed his illness at the outset, saying, "Look, I've got cancer, but we have work to do." After that, there was never any discussion about the disease. Sitting opposite each other, they would take turns reading the script, making changes and choosing songs.

"Occasionally, he picked up a guitar and started singing," recalled Walsh. "That was the only time I allowed myself to indulge in the oddity of being opposite David Bowie singing 'Life on Mars?'"

The show premiered a month before Bowie died. "I knew when we did *Lazarus* and we left that night, the opening night," said Walsh, "that I'd never see him again."

Billy Ritchie

In the last months of his life, Bowie sent out a number of what can only be considered goodbye emails. Some were to friends, and some were to those with whom he had lost contact. Most had little or no idea about his illness and certainly could not believe he was about to die. None realized this would be the last communication they would ever have with him. One of those whom Bowie reached out to in those final days was the man who had introduced him to Jimi Hendrix and who is credited as one of the founders of prog rock.

Billy Ritchie struck up a friendship with Bowie in 1967 when the Londoner heaped praised on the keyboard player after a joint gig in Dundee in 1967. Ritchie was also impressed with his fan. "I didn't take much notice of his band but I did take note of him," recalled Ritchie. "He seemed to have a style and an unusual attitude and confidence to go with it."

Bowie would seek out Ritchie whenever his band, 1-2-3, were in London and they would head off to the pub. "He was our number-one fan," said Ritchie, whose band had just been taken up by Beatles' manager Brian Epstein. "I wasn't dewy-eyed about David's admiration," said Ritchie. "I realized he was the kind of guy who was going to be at the centre of whatever was going on. There was that desperation to make something happen for himself too and, at that moment in time, we were it."

But the two fell out after a gig in Brighton in 1969 when both were on the bill. Despite "Space Oddity" having recently been in the charts, the long-haired, acoustic guitar-playing Bowie was still struggling. The crowd began booing, and he slunk off stage. Ritchie's fellow bandmates, Ian Ellis and Harry Hughes, saw Bowie backstage with a woman on his arm and approached to say hello. But he cut them dead. "He was like, 'Do I know you?'" recalled Ritchie, who was a few steps behind. "He then looked up and saw me. I said, 'Why don't you go and fuck yourself?' and I turned away." Ritchie's bandmates tried to patch things up, insisting Bowie was simply upset at the crowd's reception. Bowie tried to contact Ritchie several times after that, and even asked him to play piano on demo sessions for *Hunky Dory* and "Life on Mars?" Ritchie ignored the messages.

Then, close to 50 years later, in January 2016, Ritchie received an email from his erstwhile friend and his mind immediately went back to that encounter in 1969. "I really do think my harsh words in Brighton back then is why he remembered me," said Ritchie. "My quiet little theory is that he was hurt but I think he needed it. It was a kick up the backside. You have sometimes got to be prepared to say to a friend you are talking out of your arse."

Few of those who received these goodbye emails from Bowie have ever revealed their contents. That absence of information has fed speculation about Bowie's state of mind in those last couple of months. Did he know his death was imminent? Was he confident a new drug regime would give him more time? Or was it, perhaps, a mixture of the two – hoping for time while preparing for death? Ritchie is one of the only ones to reveal what Bowie said in those final days.

"The email was rather terse and puzzling," said the former keyboardist. "'*I just want you to know that those days together were very important,*' was all it said. It seemed to me, in my stupidity at the time, that he was having one of his pangs of conscience about the bumps in our history. It never even crossed my mind that he was saying goodbye.

"I had known he was ill but just sent him a 'Get well soon' message. I thought it was just a malady, something passing by. I didn't realize it was fatal until he was actually gone. So many regrets." Bowie died at home that Sunday.

Dave Grohl

"Fuck off!"

Dave Grohl had been hoping for a friendlier response after tentatively emailing Bowie to suggest a collaboration. The former Nirvana man had just written a song for a film soundtrack and, knowing Bowie from the singer's 50th birthday celebrations at Madison Square Garden, decided to contact the man himself.

"I've got to be honest, it's not my thing," Bowie replied. "I'm not made for these times."

Grohl thanked the singer for his time, and Bowie replied, "All right, now that's settled then, fuck off." Not being able to judge how serious Bowie was, Grohl decided he ought to send another email. "See you in another 16 years," he wrote, in reference to the birthday bash.

"Don't hold your breath…no more birthdays," replied Bowie. "I've run out of them. But that was a really fun night, wasn't it?"

ENDNOTES

1   On 20 September 1969, John Lennon told the rest of the band that he wanted to leave the Beatles, but this decision was not made public until April 1970, when Paul McCartney released a statement to the press in which he indicated that he would not be working with Lennon again. Bowie got into the Top 10 with "Space Oddity" on 12 October 1969.

2   One of Bowie's pupils was permanently dilated as a result of an injury in his youth, making that eye appear darker, a condition known as anisocoria. Little Richard had heterochromia, a colour difference of the iris.

3   Bowie's mime wasn't badly received in all quarters. "David Bowie received the longest and loudest applause of all the performers and he deserved it," wrote the critic for the *International Times*.

4   "The Gnome", a whimsical song about a wine-drinking gnome, appeared on Pink Floyd's debut album, *The Piper at the Gates of Dawn* (1967).

5   Writer Giles Tremlett argues in *David Bowie: Living on the Brink* that Bowie could well have been earning larger sums of money by this time, in which case the daily allowance of ten marks might have been a way of limiting Pop's ability to buy drugs.

6   Bowie's first bands, The Buzz and The Riot Squad, covered Zappa's "It Can't Happen Here" and "Who are the Brain Police?" in 1966–67. "I also made them cover Mother of Invention songs," Bowie says in David Buckley's *Strange Fascination*. "Not happily, I seem to remember, especially as my big favourite was 'It Can't Happen Here'. Frank's stuff was virtually unknown in Britain and relistening to that song I can see why he wasn't on any playlists."

7   American actor Martin Hewitt, also on the set for *Yellowbeard*, told me that he had a different memory of how Chapman injured his leg, which involved Bowie, Chapman and himself being involved in a collision with a local taxi after the three of them had driven into town looking for, he said, "something that shall remain secret".

8   Ōshima also knew Bowie could act. He had previously seen him in *The Elephant Man* and been impressed.

SELECT BIBLIOGRAPHY

Bennett, Alan, *Keeping on Keeping On*, Profile Faber, 2016

Bowie, Angie, *Backstage Passes: Life on the Wild Side with David Bowie*, Cooper Square, 1993

Bowie: The Last Interview and Other Conversations (The Last Interview Series), Melville House, 2016

Bowiewonderworld.com (great resource for interviews)

Buckley, David, *Strange Fascination: David Bowie: The Definitive Story*, Virgin, 2005

Caine, Michael, *What's It All About?*, Random House, 1993

Cann, Kevin, *David Bowie. Any Day Now. The London Years: 1947–1974*, Adelita, 2010

Cassidy, David, *Could It Be Forever?: My Story*, Headline, 2012

Everett, Rupert, *Red Carpets and Other Banana Skins*, Little, Brown, 2016

Faithfull, Marianne, with Dalton, David, *Faithfull: An Autobiography*, Little, Brown, 1994

Finnegan, Mary, *Psychedelic Suburbia: David Bowie and the Beckenham Arts Lab*, Jorvik Press, 2016

Fried, Stephen, *Thing of Beauty: The Tragedy of Supermodel Gia*, Pocket Books, 1993

Gillman, Loni and Peter, *Alias David Bowie*, Hodder & Stoughton, 1986

Griffin, Roger, *David Bowie: The Golden Years*, Omnibus Press, 2016

Harris, Bob, *Still Whispering after All These Years*, Michael O'Mara Books, 2015

Harry, Debbie, *Face It: A Memoir*, HarperCollins, 2019

Hynde, Chrissie, *Reckless*, Ebury Press, 2015

Idle, Eric, *Always Look on the Bright Side of Life*, Weidenfeld & Nicolson, 2018

Iman, *I am Iman*, Universe, 2001

John, Elton, *Me: Elton John Official Autobiography*, Pan Macmillan, 2019

Jones, Dylan, *David Bowie: A Life*, Random House, 2017

Jones, Dylan, *When Ziggy Played Guitar: David Bowie and Four Minutes that Shook the World*, Random House, 2012

Jones, Grace, *I'll Never Write My Memoirs*, Simon & Schuster, 2015

Jones, Lesley-Ann, *Hero: David Bowie*, Hachette, 2017

Jovanovic, Rob, *The Biography of Kate Bush*, Little, Brown, 2015

Lancaster, Phil, *At the Birth of Bowie*, John Blake, 2019

Lauryssens, Stan, *Dalí and I: The Surreal Story*, Macmillan, 2008

Leigh, Wendy, *Bowie: The Biography*, Galley Books, 2014

Light, Alan, *What Happened, Miss Simone?* Canongate, 2016

Lydon, John, *Anger is an Energy: My Life Uncensored*, Dey Street, 2016

Lynskey, Dorian, *The Ministry of Truth: A Biography of George Orwell's 1984*, Picador, 2020

O'Leary, Chris, *Pushing Ahead of the Dame*, David Bowie Song by Song, online

O'Leary, Chris, *Rebel Rebel: All the Songs of David Bowie from '64 to '76*, Zero Books, 2015

Palin, Michael, *Diaries 1969–1979: The Python Years*, Weidenfeld & Nicolson, 2006

Peel, John, *Margrave of the Marshes*, Bantam Press, 2005

Pegg, Nicholas, *The Complete David Bowie Updated*, Titan Books, 2016

Pitt, Ken, *David Bowie: The Pitt Report*, Omnibus Press, 1985

Pop, Iggy, and Wehrer, Anne, *I Need More: The Stooges and Other Stories*, Karz-Kohl, 1982

Porter, Darwin, and Prince, Danforth, *Carrie Fisher & Debbie Reynolds: Princess Leia & Unsinkable Tammy in Hell*, Blood Moon Productions, 2018

Mendelssohn, John, *Gigantic: The Story of Frank Black and the Pixies*, Omnibus, 2004

Morrissey, *Autobiography*, Penguin Classic, 2013

Rees, Paul, *Robert Plant: A Life*, Harper, 2014

Reynolds, Simon, *Shock and Awe: Glam Rock and Its Legacy*, Faber, 2016

Robinson, Lisa, *There Goes Gravity: A Life in Rock and Roll*, Riverhead, 2015

Rogan, Johnny, *Ray Davies: A Complicated Life*, Vintage, 2016

Sandford, Christopher, *Bowie: Loving the Alien*, Hachette Books, 1996

Schaffner, Nicholas, *A Saucerful of Secrets*, Dell, 1992

Sounes, Howard, *Notes from the Velvet Underground*, Doubleday, 2015

Spitz, Marc, *David Bowie: A Biography*, Crown, 2009

Stewart, Rod, *The Autobiography*, Century, 2013

Thian, Helene Marie, *Moss Garden: David Bowie and Japonism in Fashion in the 1970s, An Essay on David Bowie*, Critical Perspectives, Routledge, 2015

Townshend, Pete, *Who I Am*, HarperCollins, 2012

Trynka, Paul, *Starman: David Bowie*, Sphere, 2010

Turner, Tina, *Tina Turner: My Love Story*, Century, 2018

Visconti, Tony, *Bowie, Bolan and the Brooklyn Boy*, HarperCollins, 2007

Wilcken, Hugo, *David Bowie's Low*, Bloomsbury, 2014

Zanetta, Tony, and Edwards, Henry, *Stardust: The Life and Times of David Bowie*, Michael Joseph, 1986

ATTRIBUTIONS

Early Years, 1947–69

– – – – – – – – – – – – – –

Queen Elizabeth II
"Oh, hello, little boy": Bowie talking
to Dominic Mohan of *The Sun*,
12 September 2003

Tommy Steele
"My son is going to be…": letter by
Kristina Paulsen, Bowie's cousin, to
The Economist, 23 January 2016

Arthur Haynes
"I went over three mornings…" : from
a discussion between David Bowie
and Alexander McQueen for *Dazed &
Confused*, No. 26 (1996)

Brian Jones
"Piss off!": Paul Trynka, *David Bowie:
Starman*, Sphere, 2011
"I made a better Keith Relf…": "David
Bowie Verbatim", *The Daily Telegraph*,
31 January 2016

Peter Frampton
"There's this Jones chap…": Frampton
talking to PCAudiolabs on YouTube at
youtube.com/watch?v=X9iEnVjlN1E
"Wait a minute, that's Peter!": Frampton
talking to Absolute Radio for "Bowie:
The Definitive Story", 2013
"I can never thank him…": Interview with
Frampton for *M: Music & Musicians*,
2013
"Smoke! Smoke!": Frampton's memoir,
Do You Feel Like I Do?, Hachette, 2020

Little Richard
"It filled the room…": David Buckley,
*Strange Fascination: David Bowie:
The Definitive Story*, Virgin, 2005
"I think he's dead": George Underwood
in Dylan Jones, *David Bowie: A Life*,
Penguin, 2017
"I got to play with piano with him" and
"…different-coloured eyes": Bowie
talking on VH1 TV, 1996
"I always wanted to be Little Richard":
Paul Trynka, *David Bowie: Starman*;
Bowie also said elsewhere that "I wanted
to be a white Little Richard at the age
of eight."

365

Stevie Wonder
Phil Lancaster talking to the author.
Also from his *At the Birth of Bowie: Life with the Man Who Became a Legend*, John Blake, 2019

Ray Davies
"He used to hang out with us": Jeanette Ross, Ray Davies's partner at the time, talking to the David Baddiel podcast, *Stalking Time for the Moon Boys*, Episode 13
"How shall we do this?": Ray Davies speaking to Adrian Deevoy, *Event* magazine, Mail Online, August 2017
"I've never heard a Kinks song...": from Bowie's sleeve notes for a 50th-anniversary box set, *The Essential Kinks*, Legacy Records, 2014
"To say a few words about my friend": members of the audience discussing the concert online at iorr.org, an international Rolling Stones fans website, 12 January 2016 www.iorr.org/talk/read.php?1,2286695,page=10

James Brown
"Let's just wait and see...": Carlos Alomar talking in Buckley, *Strange Fascination*

Pete Townshend
"You're trying to write like me": Phil Lancaster talking to the author
"They both said, I'm going to do this" and "That single should do all right": from Pete Townshend's autobiography, *Who I Am*, HarperCollins, 2012

Sonny Boy Williamson
Bowie joining Williamson on stage: from bowiewonderworld.com
Robert Plant stealing Williamson's harmonica: from Stephen Davis, *Hammer of the Gods*, William Morrow & Co, 1985

John Lee Hooker
"Everybody was picking...": interview Bowie gave to Timothy White for the blog site jackthatcatwasclean, 19 September 2007
"Look at those hands": Trynka, *David Bowie: Starman*

Marc Bolan
Tony Visconti speaking to the author
Dustbin shopping: from Kevin Cann, *David Bowie: The London Years*, Adelita, 2010
"David would say...": Ken Pitt, *The Pitt Report*, Music Sales, 1983
"We were all green..." and "he was stellar": Bowie interview with Paul Du Noyer, pauldunoyer.com
Rolan quotes: from an interview with David Wigg, *Daily Mail*, 12 August 2011

John Peel
"With your inimitable...": *This Is Your Life* tribute to Peel, ITV, 24 January 1996
"We kept David alive...": "RadioRadio", BBC Radio 1, a profile of John Peel, 1986
"Below that of an Australian sitar..." and "Hey, asshole...": from Peel's autobiography, *Margrave of the Marshes*, Chicago Review Press, 2007

Jonathan King
"I thought he was very sweet...": from Wendy Leigh, *Bowie: The Biography*, Gallery 2014
"Fat shit": from Susan Black, *Rock Venom: Insults, Abuse and Outrage*, Omnibus Press, 2008

Simon Napier-Bell
"The sheer sleaziness...": from Napier-Bell's own website, 2005. Tony Visconti assures me Bowie would never have agreed to any such transaction.

Mandy Rice-Davies
Phil Lancaster talking to the author

"If I hadn't been married..." and "I'd love to come...": from Leigh, *Bowie*
Elton John
Meeting in La Giaconda: from *The Daily Telegraph*, 1 April 2016. Elsewhere, Elton said Bowie, Bolan and he would go to gay clubs together, but it is unclear how close their friendship was in these early days.
"Gus is a great producer... " and "Other people can sing about...": from Angie Bowie, *Backstage Passes*, Cooper Square, 2000 (first published 1993)
"Fat Reg" reference: *Rolling Stone*, 7 October 1976
"We used to hang out together" and "He wasn't my cup of tea": *Evening Standard*, 12 February 2016
"That was a cunty thing...": Joe Hagan, *Sticky Fingers: The Life and Times of Jann Wenner and Rolling Stone Magazine*, Knopf, 2017
"A whole new school of pretensions": Bowie's interview with *Playboy*, September 1976
Dana Gillespie
From Dana Gillespie, "David Bowie and Me", *The Guardian*, 23 February 2013
Lindsay Kemp
"It was a fabulously..." and "Love at first sight": from Lindsay Kemp, "David Bowie and Me", *The Guardian*, 13 February 2013
"He was completely at home": Trynka, *David Bowie: Starman*
"His day-to-day life...": Buckley, *Strange Fascination*
Marcel Marceau story: from Keith Emerson's Facebook page, 12 January 2016
Lionel Bart
Mary Finnigan quotes: from *Psychedelic*

Suburbia: David Bowie and the Beckenham Arts Lab, Jorvil, 2016
"With a rent boy in tow, or snuggled up to David": Trynka, *David Bowie: Starman*
"the evocative aroma of the chip shop": from David Stafford and Caroline Stafford, *Fings Ain't Wot They Used T'Be*, Omnibus Press, 2011
Electric Light Orchestra
Bev Bevan quotes: from "Drummer Bev Bevan says David Bowie paved way for The Move, Wizzard and ELO" by Graham Young, *Birmingham Mail*, 11 January 2016
Paul McCartney
Bowie told to stop playing "Young Americans": attributed to May Pang (1983), who was present, and recounted in Roger Griffin, *David Bowie: The Golden Years*, Omnibus, 2016
Bowie and McCartney sifting through chart books: from Steve Hoffman Music Forums blog, forums.stevehoffman.tv/threads/the-next-david-bowie-album.492685/page-3
"McCartney shits": interview Bowie gave to Belgian magazine *HUMO*, 1995
The story about a young Bowie turning up at McCartney's home was told by the Beatle to Dylan Jones and appears in *David Bowie: A Life*.
Alfred Lennon
Phil Lancaster talking to the author. A fuller version can be found in his book *At the Birth of Bowie*.
John Paul Jones
"Come over and..." and "What a dreadful irony": from Bowie's interviews with *Playboy* magazine, September 1976
Eric Clapton
Bowie recounted the story of his brother's

breakdown to the *NME*, 27 March 1993 and to Paul Trynka
In *Spider from Mars: My Life with Bowie*, St Martin's Press, 2007, drummer Woody Woodmansey writes on p68: "I was impressed when he told me he'd had guitar lessons from Eric Clapton."
"The song took me…": from "Backstage News", markconnorstv.com, 2013 (available on YouTube)
Jimi Hendrix
Billie Ritchie talking to the author
Vince Taylor
"I thought of Vince Taylor and wrote…": *Cracked Actor: A Film about David Bowie*, dir. Alan Yentob, *Omnibus*, BBC, 1975
"Part of the stew": *Arena* interview with Tony Parsons, 1993
"The happiest days…": Steve Leggett's Vince Taylor biography on music.com
Syd Barrett
"Wow, he's a bohemian…": from Nicholas Schaffner, *A Saucerful of Secrets*, Dell, 1992
"I only met him…": from an interview for *Rock* by Martin Hayman, October 1973
"He was the first I'd seen…": from Julian Palacios, *Syd Barrett and Pink Floyd: Dark Globe*, Plexus, 2010
"… toes tapping": Barrett talking to Chris Welch of *Melody Maker*
"Had Barrett continued…": from Buckley, *Strange Fascination*
"A major regret… diamond indeed": from a statement Bowie released on Barrett's death
Bob Harris
"Remember this night…" and "Mark my words…": Harris talking to Bowie TV on YouTube, 10 December 2019

Ridley Scott
"Apparently, yeah… as I am": "Bowie takes readers' questions", Clark Collis for the now-defunct *Blender* magazine, August 2002
Lionel Blair
The story appears in "I Rejected David Bowie" by Mike Pattenden, *Daily Mail*, 26 March 2016
Freddie Mercury
Alan Mair talking to the author (Mair was with the Beatstalkers and went on to form the Only Ones)
Noddy Holder story: from *The Guardian*, 26 November 2015
Ealing College meeting appears in Mark Blake, *Is This the Real Life? The Untold Story of Queen*, Da Capo, 2011
"I doubt it": from an interview of unknown origin, requoted by David Thomas in *Mojo* magazine, August 1999
"Of all the more theatrical…": from an article by Jeffrey Ressner in *Rolling Stone*, No. 621 (9 January 1992)

Haddon Hall, 1969–73
- - - - - - - - - - - - - - - -

Mick Ronson
"There was something about… sheep too!" and "I'm not sure about this": from Marc Spitz, *Bowie: A Biography*, Aurum Press, 2010
"I just sat and watched …": from Kevin Cann, "Play Don't Worry", *Starzone*, Autumn 1984
"They were going…": from *Beside Bowie: The Mick Ronson Story*, dir. Jon Brewer, 2017
Peter Gabriel
Visconti talking to the author
"The stage was very small…": Anthony Phillips in Daryl Easlea, *Without*

Frontiers: The Life and Music of Peter Gabriel, Omnibus, 2014
Tony Banks quotes: from Rob Hughes, "The Gig that Invented Glam", *Loudersound*, 20 December 2014
"We were sort of ahead...": interview with Gabriel, *NME*, October 1973
Windsurfing anecdote: from CBC News cbc.ca/news/canada/british-columbia/david-bowie-remembered-vancouver-1.3399379

Alice Cooper
"He was just an average boy...": *Popular 1* magazine, August 1994
"It looked good...": Trevor Bolder speaking to the Bowie website 5years.com
The bizarre golfing threesome is from the Bowie biography Christopher Sandford, *Loving the Alien*, Hachette, 2009

Gene Vincent
Kevin Cann speaking to the author
"Gene was very impressed...": Kevin Cann, *Any Day Now*
"Floating around on Ebay..." and "position number one": from David Bowie, *Moonage Daydream: The Life and Times of Ziggy Stardust*, Genesis Publications, 2002,
"I went on to explain...": Jones, *David Bowie: A Life*

Moondog
"He told me something...": Bowie speaking in 2003, quoted on www.thevikingof6thavenue.com

Lou Reed, Not
"Lou replies thoughtfully...": David Bowie, "David 53 Interviews David at 23", *Canadian National Post*, October 1999.
Bowie has given various versions of the story. Yule remembers the meeting somewhat differently: "England was one of the prime sources of rock 'n' roll back then, of course, and we were all Anglophiles to some degree. So I remember this English kid coming backstage, and I was holding forth as if I was somebody, feeling very self-important as the leader of this band. He came in, and obviously assumed I was Lou Reed, and so I had to explain that Lou wasn't there."

"It got my mind really working...": from Dylan Jones, *When Ziggy Played Guitar*, Random House, 2012

Lou Reed
"I played it and thought...": from "Bowie Rules NYC", a piece Bowie wrote for *New York* magazine, 18 September 2003
"Lou was going through a bad patch": *NME*, 1 December 2000
"His imagistic lyrics...": from Simon Reynolds, *Shock and Awe: Glam Rock and Its Legacy*, Day Street Books, 2016
"Don't ever say that...": interview with Alan Jones, *Melody Maker*
"It was... romance": interview with Tony Zanetta for Thinwhiteduke.net, 27 September 2016
"Without it...digging a ditch": interview with Ian Fortnum, *Classic Rock*, 29 October 2016
"He is a very dear friend...": from David Wildman, "Holy Crap, David Bowie!", *Weekly Dig*, December 2003
"David and I are still friends...": Reed talking about David Bowie in *Rolling Stone*, published online 3 December 2010
"No, I think... last person...": interview with Bowie in 1993, quoted in Nicholas Pegg, *The Complete David Bowie*, Titan Books, 2016

Iggy Pop

"Nobody else came, nobody" and "He talked about Iggy…": from Trynka, *David Bowie: Starman*

"We trooped into…": Bowie speaking to Clark Collins for *Blender* magazine, August 2002

Iggy smashing a beer bottle over his head appears in Christopher Sandford, *David Bowie: Loving the Alien*, Da Capo, 1998. Throwing water over Iggy: Marc Spitz, *David Bowie: A Biography*, Crown, 2009

"You're not going to like…": from Loni and Peter Gillman, *Alias David Bowie*, Hodder & Stoughton, 1986

"This guy saved me from annihilation…": *New York Times*, 14 January 2016

The car crash story: told to the author by Kevin Cann (it happened in Los Angeles)

Andy Warhol

"He walks away…Andy hated it": from Bill DeMain, "The Freakiest Show", *Classic Rock*, April 2011

"Andy noticed David's shoes…": Angie Bowie, *Backstage Passes*

"You have such nice shoes": from Pegg, *The Complete David Bowie*

"Reptilian": told to the author by Craig Copetas

"I just thought…half the time": from *Quad City Times*, May 2004 (bowiewonderworld.com)

"The meeting was kind of tense…": Tony Zanetta quoted in Trynka, *David Bowie: Starman*

The story about the shoes is from Bowie talking on BBC Radio 1 to Mary Anne Hobbs, 8 January 1997

"Like everyone else…": interview with Mike Jollet, "Such a Perfect Day", *Filter*, No. 6 (July/August 2003)

"It was a very sad little bag with all these contents" and "I've always felt more emotive than Andy": from Bowie talking to Duke of Hazard, *Vox*, 1995

Rick Wakeman

"The finest selections of songs…": from Rick Wakeman, *Say Yes! An Autobiography*, Hodder & Stoughton, 1995

The call from Chris Squire appears in an interview with *Classic Rock*, 13 September 2016

"I played my plodding version": Wakeman interview on the official Bowie website davidbowie.com

The Dudley Moore story appears on davidbowie.com (it appears Bowie may have asked a few pianists to play on a demo of "Life on Mars?" Billy Ritchie of 1-2-3 told the author that he, too, had been asked)

Ian Curtis

The story of Curtis going backstage: from Stephen Morris, *Record Play Pause: Confessions of a Post-Punk Percussionist: The Joy Division Years: Volume I*, Constable, 2019

Quotes from Curtis's sister: from *The Life of Ian Curtis: Torn Apart*, dir. Lindsay Reade, *Omnibus*, BBC, April 2006

Marc Almond

"I was bleeding…": Almond told the story on *Loose Women*, ITV, 10 March 2017

"It was one of the most magical things that has happened to me": from "Marc Almond on Bowie, TV and Joining Holy Holy", on davidbowie.com, 7 January 2014

Boy George

"Fuck off" and George's delight at being acknowledged: from an interview he gave to Heidi Parker, dailymail.com, 12 January 2016

"Best line of the seventies" and talking about *EastEnders*: from George's interview with Piers Morgan for *Piers Morgan's Life Stories*, Season 14, Episode 3, 2009

Steve Jones

"I was like the phantom...massive fan": from *Jonesy's Jukebox*, Steve Jones's radio show on 95.5 KLOS, 26 April 2016

"We got a full range...": Paul Cook speaking on "The Sex Pistols: Fact or Fiction?", *Loudwire* interview, on YouTube, November 2017

"I get on very well...": "Bowie: The Fashion Rocks Q&A", interview with Dave Itzkoff, *Lucky* magazine, 2005

Hall & Oates

"I saw him backstage...took a Quaalude... never seen anything like that": from an interview with John Oates in *Something Else*, 19 August 2014

"This guy put the bar...": interview with John Oates by Phillip Gutgesell, *MAT Magazine*, 5 September 2017

""We thought we better get some amps": from the Daryl Hall and John Oates official YouTube site: youtube.com/channel/UCSRoN5Sxu5M-jc0JXt3E-xg

Sylvester

Carl Sandburg (1878–1967) was an American poet. The fact that many readers may ask, "Who?" is perhaps the best response to Wasserman's attempt to damn Bowie with faint praise. Sylvester claiming he hung out with Bowie was told to the author by Sylvester's biographer Joshua Gamson. For more on Sylvester, read Gamson's excellent *The Fabulous Sylvester: The Legend, the Music, the 70s in San Francisco*, Picador, 2006.

Chrissie Hynde

Chrissie Hynde, *Reckless*, Ebury Press,

2015. Hynde's is just about the best autobiography written by a rock star. She recounted the same story on *The Fearne Cotton Show*, BBC Radio 2, 23 July 2016.

Placido Domingo

From Gillman and Gillman, *Alias David Bowie*.

Kansai Yamamoto

Woken by a friend: told to Sheryl Garratt of *The Daily Telegraph*, 17 March 2013

Angie Bowie's quotes: from her autobiography, *Backstage Passes*

Buying a busman's handbag was told to Erin Donnelly of *Elle* magazine, 1 November 2013

Bandō Tamasaburō V

Quotes: from Helene Thian, "Moss Garden: David Bowie and Japonism in Fashion in the 1970s", in *David Bowie: Critical Perspectives*, ed. Eoin Devereux, Aileen Dillane and Martin Power, Routledge, 2016

Chris Difford

Quotes are from Difford's website chrisdifford.com

Elvis

"I hobbled down..." and "If looks could kill...": from Buckley, *Strange Fascination*.

"I could see him thinking... sit the fuck down" and "I would have loved to have worked with him...": *Blender*, 2009

Dwight Yoakam's story appeared out of the blue when he spoke to Kelli Skye Fadroski of the *Orange County Register*, 21 January 2016

Bryan Ferry

Ferry feeling aggrieved: attributed to Simon Reynolds in his book *Shock and Awe*

Bowie being supportive: David Buckley, *Strange Fascination*

"Too poppy... don't like the idea..." and "so many sounds...": from an interview with Ferry for *GQ* by Jacques Braustein, 3 May 2011

"I have met him...": David Bowie talking for his 50th Birthday Live Chat on bowiewonderworld.com, 8 January 1997

"We got our own back": Manzanera talking to the *Daily Mirror*, 1 December 2010

"If Bowie had said in '73" : from Ferry talking to *The Quietus*, 18 November 2010

Brian Eno

"A short, balding brain with a feather boa and remarkably silly clothes": from his 50th Birthday Live Chat on bowiewonderworld.com, 8 January 1997

Talking about existentialism and Philip Glass: from Griffin, *David Bowie: The Golden Years*

"When everything changed" is a comment Bowie made to Kate Moss, who recounted the story to Dylan Jones

"My favourite collaborations...": from an interview with Mark Thompson of *The Japan Times*

"God, he must be smart": an Eno quote that appears in Hugo Wilcken, *David Bowie's Low*

Ian Hunter

"He just walked in... so grateful": from Dave Simpson, "All The Old Dudes", *The Guardian*, 13 June 2001

"Very seldom in your life...": from Spitz, *Bowie: A Biography*

"I would never have given...": from Robert Chalmers, "Ian Hunter: The truth about Mott the Hoople", *The Independent*, 5 June 2011

"Dracula" quote: from Gillman and Gillman, *Alias David Bowie*

"Don't tell me...": from a Bowie interview given to Jérôme Soligny with French-language magazine *Rock & Folk*, December 1998

Jethro Tull and Steeleye Span

Ian Anderson's quotes: from jethrotull.com, under "David Bowie"

Nigel Pegrum's quotes: from the "David Bowie Downunder" newsfeed on Facebook, 28 July 2017

Cliff Richard

Richard's unflattering quotes about Bowie appear in Travis Elborough, *The Long-Player Goodbye: The Album from Vinyl to iPod and Back Again*, Soft Skull, 2009

"I was never a great fan": from Bowie speaking to *Event*, Mail Online, 16 January 2016

"What a terrible loss...": from Richard's Facebook page

Jacques Brel

"I couldn't give a fuck...": from Jérôme Soligny, *David Bowie*, Albin Michel, 1996 (French-language book)

B-52s

The story of Wilson screaming appears in Griffin, *David Bowie: The Golden Years* and at sanluisobispo.com/entertainment/music-news-reviews/article39118887.html

"There was a little party...": from an interview by Kate Pierson with SiriusXM Entertainment

"Faggot": from Shannon Carlin, "Kate Pierson on the Music That Made Her", *Pitchfork*, 25 February 2020

New York Dolls

"They have the energy...": from Reynolds, *Shock and Awe*

"Who does your hair?": from Lee Martin, *The Lipstick Killers*, No Exit, 2009

Canal Street altercation: from Nina Antonia, *The Makeup Breakup of The*

New York Dolls: Too Much, Too Soon, Omnibus, 2011

Cyrinda Foxe
Quotes from Cyrinda Foxe-Tyler, *Dream On: Livin' on the Edge with Steven Tyler and Aerosmith*, Berkeley, 2000

Sweet
Andy Scott's quotes: from "Everyone Attack!", *Record Collector*, recordcollectormag.com/articles/sweet
Bowie swearing at Chinn: from Pegg, *The Complete David Bowie*

Todd Rundgren
"I've heard of you…" and "Yes, I am…": from Legs McNeil and Gillian McCain, *Please Kill Me: The Uncensored Oral History of Punk*, Penguin, 1997
"I do remember someone crying…" and his dislike of the cut-up technique: from Rundgren speaking to *The Guardian*, 1 May 2013

Jim Morrison
Kennealy quotes: from her website, lizardqueen.livejournal.com
Densmore wanting Bowie as their frontman: from an interview in *Rolling Stone*
"We don't see enough": *NME* in conversation with Brett Anderson
"Morrison meets industrial…": from George A Paul, "Bowie Outside Looking In", *Axcess*, Issue 3, No. 5 (1995), pp. 60–2

Michael Palin
All quotes from Michael Palin, *The Complete Michael Palin Diaries*, Weidenfeld & Nicolson, 2015

Bob Hope
Story from Kevin Cann's *David Bowie: A Chronology*, Vermillion, 1983

Peter Cook
"There was deliberate footsie…": from Judy Cook with Angela Levin, *Loving Peter: My Life with Peter Cook and Dudley Moore*, Piatkus, 2009
"Peter Cook's without a doubt…": from Bowie interview by Jay Matthews, "Drum 'n' Bass Oddity", *NME*, February 1997

Mick Jagger
"The Stones were so funny…": Bowie on *Parkinson*, BBC 1, 20 September 2002
"Nothing but cocaine": Simon Napier-Bell, *Black Vinyl White Powder*, Ebury, 2002
"They used to pick up…": Bebe Buell, *Rebel Heart*, St. Martin's Press, 2001
"I used to dream of being Mick Jagger": Sandford, *Bowie: Loving the Alien*
Angie Bowie's quotes: from her *Backstage Passes*
"I believe David was madly in love with Jagger": Laura Jackson, *Heart of Stone: The Unauthorized Life of Mick Jagger*, John Blake, 1998
"I just want to piss Mick off a bit": Alan Parker, guitarist, speaking to *Uncut* magazine, April 2014
Pete Townshend: quoted from Andrew Loog Oldham, *Stoned*, Vintage, 2003
"Mick was silly…": Cameron Crowe for *Playboy* magazine, 1975
"Mick believes in music…": Leigh, *Bowie: The Biography*
"He was so relaxed…" and "Favourite memory": from *Rolling Stone*, January 2016

Marianne Faithfull
Quotes from Marianne Faithfull with David Dalton, *Faithfull: An Autobiography*, Little Brown, 1994

Twiggy
Quotes from Twiggy speaking to BBC 5 Live on *The Danny Baker Show*, 10 March 2018

Carrie Fisher
Quotes from Darwin Porter and
Danforth Prince, *Carrie Fisher & Debbie
Reynolds: Princess Leia & Unsinkable
Tammy in Hell*
Lulu
"I'm not going to sing with Lulu": from
Edward Willett, *Jimi Hendrix: Kiss the
Sky*, Enslow, 2006
The hotel lobby and disappearance: from
Lulu's autobiography *I Don't Want to
Fight*, Time Warner, 2003
"He was uber cool...": *Uncut*, March 2008
"Long and slim...": *Event* magazine, Mail
Online, 1 March 2015
Salvador Dalí
Amanda Lear's comments to the author
"Ggguudda morning ...": from Stan
Lauryssens, *Dalí & I: The Surreal Story*,
Thomas Dunne, 2008
Dalí and Bowie staring at each other in a
lift: told to the author by Kevin Cann
William Burroughs
The story of Bowie's meeting with
Burroughs and Gyssin was told to the
author by Craig Copetas, the *Rolling
Stone* reporter who introduced them.
Copetas is now an author based in Paris
whose most recent book is *Mona Lisa's
Pyjamas: Diverting Dispatches from
a Roving Reporter*. His original article
appears in *Rolling Stone*, 28 February
1974
Jean Genet
Story from the author's interview with
Craig Copetas. The eventual encounter
appears in Cann, *Any Day Now*.
George Orwell
The rejection from Sonia Brownell:
from Bowie speaking in 1993, source
unknown; also quoted in Buckley,
Strange Fascination.

"For someone who married a socialist...":
Bowie speaking to the press, date
unknown; requoted in Chris O'Leary,
*Rebel Rebel: All the Songs of David Bowie
from '64 to '76*, Zero Books, 2015
Arthur C Clarke
A description of the evening appears in
Angie Bowie, *Backstage Passes*
Clarke's belief in life on Mars appears in
Popular Science, 17 December 2001
Ray Bradbury
Quotes are on the website for the Center
for Ray Bradbury Studies, California:
https://bradbury.iupui.edu/pages/
bradburys-office/index.php
Rod Stewart
Vodka pancake: from 25 March 2012
post on Shidobee, the most popular
Rolling Stones website, quoting a past
associate of the band
Stewart's comments about not being
seen as intellectual were made to *Rolling
Stone* in 2015
George Harrison
"I pulled up his hat...": Graeme Thomson,
*George Harrison: Behind the Locked
Door*, Music Sales, 2013
"I hope he wasn't offended...": Radio KHJ
930 AM, 21 December 1974
Bowie quotes: from 2003 *Reality* tour
press conference

**Fear and Foaming in Los Angeles,
1974–1976**
- - - - - - - -

Elizabeth Taylor
"I was so excited...": from Leigh, *Bowie:
The Biography*
Daily chats about things like colonic
irrigation: Sandford, *Loving the Alien*,
and Leigh, *Bowie: The Biography*
The Blue Bird reference: from *The Cut*,

1 February 2015
"We managed to persuade her to stay":
Terry O'Neill quotes appear in Nellie
Eden, "The First Time David Bowie Met
Elizabeth Taylor", refinery29.com,
13 January 2016
Waiting five hours: from Michelle Doyle,
"Sixties Revisited: Interview with Terry
O'Neill", V&A blog, 26 July 2018
"That endeared me...": Cameron Crowe,
Rolling Stone, 12 February 1976

John Lennon
"Mutant crap...": from Mick Brown,
"A Star Comes Back to Earth", *The Daily
Telegraph*, 14 December 1996
"It's big red, and I want it..." and
"There was nothing that didn't interest
him...": Bowie interview with Michael
Kimmelman, *The New York Times*,
14 June 1998
"He's great. But you don't know which
one...": Bowie talking to Andy Peebles,
BBC Radio 1, December 1980
"What the hell...": May Pang quoted in
Leigh, *Bowie: The Biography*
"So, the night after John was killed":
interview with Bowie, InetheStudio.com,
Redbeard's blog
"Like a little kid": from Ava Cherry
Bowie second on Chapman's list:
mentioned in Sandford, *Loving the Alien*
Many of Bowie's fond reminiscences are
from his speech to Berklee College of
Music on 8 May 1999, when he received
an honorary doctorate.

Aretha Franklin
"I could kiss...": Franklin at the 17th
Annual Grammy Awards, 1 March 1975
"See, Dave, America loves ya...house
on fire": from Bowie's commencement
speech to Berklee College of Music,
May 1999

Nina Simone
Quotes from Alan Light, *What
Happened, Miss Simone?* Canongate,
2016

Frank Sinatra
Bruce Robb's quotes: from a talk with the
author
"They said, 'Look...Anka to do...'": Cann,
David Bowie: The London Years
"No limey faggot...": quoted in Griffin,
David Bowie: The Golden Years
"They asked him to step down...": Rory
MacLean writing in *The Guardian*,
13 January 2016
It is worth noting that the only two
Sinatra Christmas songs that Bowie
could realistically have sung at that time
would have been "A Baby Just Like You"
and "Christmas Memories". Neither of
the dates associated with the recording
of those songs chimes with the dates
at Cherokee Studios, which possibly
means the final mix was recorded later
or the backing tapes were ditched. It is
definitely worth an intrepid Bowie fan
tracking this story down further!

Bob Dylan
"I think he hates me..." and "I talked at
him for hours...": from an interview with
Cameron Crowe, *Playboy*, September
1976
"Everything great about America..."
interview with Mikel Jollett, *Filter*
magazine, July/August 2003
"I think he's a prick...": interview with
Chris Charlesworth, March 1976
"It was at that period...": Bowie speaking
to *Melody Maker*, 1976
Bowie telling Dylan where he was going
wrong: from Cann, *David Bowie: The
London Years*
"His music has such resonance...":

interview with Michael Kimmelman, *New York Times*, 14 June 1998

"Garden Party": Q&A with Bill Flanagan, bobdylan.com, 22 March 2017

Richard Pryor

"What's the white dude ..." and "He was fearless...": Carlos Alomar talking to Dylan Jones in *David Bowie: A Life*

"You have to have a lot of cojones...": in "What's It Like to Play Guitar With David Bowie" by Jean Pelly in *Pitchfork*, 14 January 2016

Rudolf Nureyev

Quotes are from Stuart George, Bowie's former bodyguard, speaking to *The Sun*, 6 April 2016

Bette Midler

Angie Bowie quotes: from her *Backstage Passes*

Record executive quote: from Christopher Andersen, *Mick: The Wild Life and Mad Genius of Mick Jagger*, The Robson Press, 2012

"I had a nightmare...": from Mark Bego, *Bette Midler: Still Divine*, Cooper Square, 2002

"Ticket prices...": from a CBS TV interview in 1984; available on YouTube: youtube.com/watch?v=OWVqKi_VUfY

Ronnie Spector

Ronnie Spector quotes: from her *Be My Baby*, Harmony, 1990

David Cassidy

Quotes from Cassidy's autobiography *Could It Be Forever? My Story*, Headline, 2012

Christopher Lee

Quotes from "Get Ready to Rock", Lee's interview with Joe Geesin, 21 March 2007

A Mystery Hollywood Star

The original story appeared in Leigh, *Bowie: The Biography*. Following

publication, Loretta Young's family challenged the story on Linda Lewis's Facebook site and on cinephiled.com in an interview with Danny Miller, 28 January 2016

Raquel Welch

Bowie mentions Welch's intention to join Mainman in his weekly diary published in *Mirabelle*, 8 February 1975

Michael Jackson

"Copped the walk...": from Griffin, *David Bowie: The Golden Years*

"You don't get much feedback...": Bowie interview with Jo Whiley, BBC Radio 1, August 1997

Bowie being taught the robot dance: from *Rock 'n' Soul Songs*, January 1975

Luther Vandross

Quotes from Kalamu ya Salaam, "The Sensitive Luther Vandross", kalamu.com; interview initially published in *The Black Collegian Magazine*, February 1982

Bruce Springsteen

Description of Bowie first seeing Springsteen: from an interview with Bebe Buell by Rosemary Feitelberg for *WMD: Women's Wear Daily*, 12 January 2016

"I was out of my wig...": Bowie talking to Scott Isler for the now defunct *Musician* magazine in 1987. The two singers sharing stories about stage jumpers also appears here.

Tony Visconti's comments made to the author

"He was very shy...made out of wax": Bowie's sleeve notes for *One Step Up/Two Steps Back: The Songs of Bruce Springsteen*, a 1997 various artists Bruce Springsteen tribute album

Alien spaceship story: recorded by Mike McGrath in *Distant Drummer*,

26 November 1974 [alternative, now-defunct, newspaper published in Philadelphia]

Gia Carangi
Quotes from Stephen Fried, *Thing of Beauty: The Tragedy of Supermodel Gia*, Simon & Schuster, 1993

Norman Rockwell
Bowie speaking to Cameron Crowe for *Playboy*, September 1976

Cher
Quotes from George Schlatter and Bowie appear in Josiah Howard, *Cher: Strong Enough*, Plexus, 2014
Lisa Robinson observed in *Cream*: "Cher was obviously ecstatic doing a number with someone relevant, hip and her own age"; also quoted in Howard, *Cher*

Kenneth Anger
"I blotted it out..." and "David started getting more...": from Trynka, *David Bowie: Starman*

Jimmy Page
"He was quite generous...": interview with Mary Anne Hobbs, BBC Radio 1, 8 January 1997
"I don't think it's a hit": from Trynka, *David Bowie: Starman*
The story of exorcising the house is from Zanetta and Edwards, *Stardust: The David Bowie Story*
"There was a battle of wits...": from Gillman and Gillman, *Alias David Bowie*

Robert Plant
Bob Harris quotes: from Paul Rees, *Robert Plant: A Life*, HarperCollins, 2014

Glenn Hughes
"I was hallucinating 24 hours a day...": from Spitz, *Bowie: A Biography*
Hughes quotes: from Glenn Hughes with Joel McIver, *Glenn Hughes: The Autobiography*, Foruli, 2011

Peter Sellers
Pool stains remark: from Wilcken, *David Bowie's Low*
"They don't have parties...": told to "The Thin White Duke" at thinwhiteduke.net, 21 September 2016

Sly Stone
Quotes from "My Work Is Done Here", an interview with Bowie by David Quantick for *Q* magazine, October 1999

Ozzy Osbourne
The AA meeting story: from Kory Grow, "Ozzy Osbourne: David Bowie's Death 'Knocked the Shit Out of Me'", *Rolling Stone*, 13 January 2016
"The good thing about AA...": from Paul Lester, "Thirty Minutes with Moby", *The Guardian*, 26 September 2013

Slash
Quotes from a 2012 interview with Slash on Australian radio network Triple M

Nicolas Roeg
Story of Bowie being late: from Reynolds, *Shock and Awe*
"This is what I wanted to do": from Wilcken, *David Bowie's Low*
"It would have been a wonderful score": Roeg speaking in 1993; requoted in Nicholas Pegg, *The Complete David Bowie Updated*, Titan Books, 2016

Christopher Isherwood
"Young Bowie...": from Wilcken, *David Bowie's Low*

Berlin and Switzerland, 1977–81

Kraftwerk
"I wanted to be in the swim": interview with Paul Du Noyer, pauldunoyer.com
"Look at them!": Wilcken, *David Bowie's Low*
"Car always lasts longer": from a 1978

interview, requoted on davidbowie.com
Kraftwerk rejecting being a support
act: from Tim Barr, *Kraftwerk: From
Düsseldorf to the Future with Love*,
Ebury, 1998
"He was so fanatical…": from "David
Bowie, Iggy Pop, Madonna & Asparagus:
Kraftwerk 1976", *The Quietus*,
30 August 2012
Neu!
"I was completely seduced…": from
Wilcken, *David Bowie's Low*
Rother quotes are from "Michael
Rother Interview" by Paul Klotschkow
for *Leftlion* [monthly arts and culture
magazine for Nottingham, April 2017]
Edgar Froese
"A shared a love of…": Bianca Froese-
Acquaye, on Tangerine Dream's official
Facebook page
"Just to get rid of the depression…":
Wilcken, *David Bowie's Low*
"Horrific time…": from an interview
with Elmar Schütze, *Berliner Zeitung*,
14 January 2013
"There was no choice…": from an
interview with Pascale Hugues,
Hannah's Dress, Polity Press, 2017
The story of Froese hanging around
for hours and eventually walking out:
Reynolds, *Shock and Awe*
Conny Plank
Loving German cereal and ashtrays in
aisles: from an interview with Stephan
Plank by Chris May for *The Vinyl Project*,
21 August 2018
"My father was quite all right…": from
Daniel Dylan Wray, "My father, Conny
Plank", loudandquiet.com, 13 November
2017, originally published in Issue 90
Tony Visconti
All quotes told to the author

Robert Fripp
"Do you think you could play some
hairy…": fripp.com
"This was Bowie .. why not?": Jones,
David Bowie: A Life
"I became sucked back…": interview
with Rob Hughes, *The Daily Telegraph*,
31 October 2014
Tony Visconti quotes given to the author
Devo
"You bet" and "I'm thinking we should
see…": from Mothersbaugh's interview by
Daniel Maurier with Bedford + Bowery,
5 December 2017
"This can't be real" quotes: from Beatie
Wolfe, "My LA: Mark Mothersbaugh
Talks Life in the City of Angels and
His Friendship with David Bowie",
Evening Standard, 13 January 2020
Marlene Dietrich
Bowie trying and failing to get Dietrich
to have some photographs taken with
him: told to the author by the scriptwriter
Joshua Sinclair
"It made an enormous impression…" and
"Oh my God, it was incredible": Bowie
interview with Nicky Horne on Capital
Radio, 1979
Kim Novak
"Splendid woman… married, though":
interview with Michael Watts, *Melody
Maker*, February 1978
"David Bowie and I…still resists":
Novak's personal website, plus.google.
com/+KimNovakArtist
Rainer Werner Fassbinder
"He was with…": interview with
Kurt Loder, "David Bowie, Stardust
Memories", *Rolling Stone*, 23 April 1987
Romy Haag
Quotes from Alina Mae, "VIP Lounge",
The Exberliner, 29 May 2014

agnès b
Interview with Stephanie Eckhardt for *W* magazine, 24 March 2017

Bing Crosby
"I won't do that song": *American Masters: Bing Crosby Rediscovered*, PBS, Larry Grossman interview, 14 December 2014
"He looked like an orange": from *Q* magazine article by David Quantick, October 1999
"You may think it strange": a special message recorded by Bing Crosby for his UK fan club, 6 October 1977

Charlie Chaplin
Oona Chaplin quotes: from *The Sunday People* interview, 11 May 1981
Christmas story: from Sandford, *Loving the Alien*
Bowie's quotes: feelingmyage.co.uk/2017/05/bowie/

Roger Moore
Hanif Kureishi speaking to Dylan Jones in *David Bowie: A Life*

Sean Lennon
Interview with Sean Lennon by Alan Light, *Mojo*, July 2016

Yoko Ono
Breakfast rebuke story: from Sandford, *Loving the Alien*

Frank Zappa
Quotes from Adrian Belew's Facebook page, posted 12 January 2016
Bowie covered Zappa's "Who are the Brain Police?" in 1966–7.

John Lydon
Quotes from John Lydon's interview with the author

Sid Vicious
Lydon quotes: from John Lydon, *Anger is an Energy: My Life Uncensored*, Simon & Schuster, 2015, and Sid Vicious's memoir

Mr Rotten's Scrapbook, Concert Live Publishing, 2015
"Mindless twerp... nothing romantic...": from *Rolling Stone*, April 1987
"Sid was near catatonic...": interview by Rob Hughes and Stephen Dalton for *Uncut*, April 2001

Glen Matlock
Quotes from Matlock talking to Eric Blair, available at YouTube.com/watch?v=tOPOEizEoUM, and from his interview with *The Sunday Times*, 19 July 2020

Siouxsie Sioux
Bowie's quotes: from *The Jonathan Ross Show*, BBC Radio 2, 2 August 2003

Bob Geldof
Quotes from Bob Geldof, "Bowie Smiled", *Daily Mail*, 16 January 2016
Story of the massage: from Geldof's interview on *The Six O'Clock Show*, Virgin Media One, Ireland, 4 March 2020

Debbie Harry
"Can I fuck you?" and the Jimmy Destri quotes: from Spitz, *Bowie: A Biography*
"To have flirtations..." and Iggy Pop's quote: from Dick Porter and Kris Needs, *Blondie: Parallel Lives*, Omnibus, 2012
"Flattered...": from Debbie Harry, *Face It: A Memoir*, HarperCollins, 2019
"Without this visionary...": part of a statement released by Debbie Harry after Bowie died

The Ramones
All the information was supplied by author and journalist Jari-Pekka Laitio Ramone, the fount of all Ramone knowledge, who has written three books on the band and runs the world's largest Ramones website ramonesheaven.com. His surname (it's real) provides just a little clue as to his deep allegiance to the band.

David Byrne
"I don't fit in here…" and the Castro story: from Stacey Anderson, "David Byrne on the Music That Made Him", *Pitchfork*, 29 March 2018
"Are you going to be eating that cheese?": from an article by Chris Frantz of the Talking Heads in the *New York Post*, 11 January 2016

Jim Kerr
"Bowie was trying to change…": from an interview with Kerr by Jane Stevenson, *Toronto Sun*, 23 April 2018
Memories of recording at the studio in Wales: from an interview with Kerr by Greg Prato for *Songfacts*, 9 January 2015

John Bonham
Story is from Angie Bowie's book; it also appears in an article by journalist Steve Pafford on his website stevepafford.com

Tom Verlaine
Story told by Tony Visconti

G E Smith
The story is from Smith's appearance on CTWIF Podcast Shorts, 14 January 2020, https://www.youtube.com/watch?v=hNv2Up_iTIA
For the various theories behind the meaning of the little green wheels, there is a fun thread at reddit.com/r/DavidBowie/comments/him8we/what_are_little_green_wheels_in_ashes_to_ashes/

Human League
"It was like Jesus…": from Brian Hiatt, *A Portrait of Bowie: A Tribute to Bowie by His Artistic Collaborators and Contemporaries*, Cassell, 2016
"People forget…": from Phil Oakey's interview with Dave Simpson, "Riot in Steel City", *The Guardian*, 28 November 2008

"We were just four lads…": from Dave Simpson, "Time Machine: When the Human League Met Bowie", a blog at electronic sound.co.uk

Giorgio Moroder
The sound of the future story: from Bowie's own sleeve notes to his *Sound and Vision* compilation
Metropolis quotes: from an interview with Bowie for *Movieline* magazine, April 1992

Commercial High to Critical Low, 1981–89
- - - - - -

Jon Bon Jovi
Thai Rath story: from the Bangkok news website BK, https://eu.app.com/story/entertainment/2016/01/13/thai-newspaper-gives-bon-jovi-song-david-bowie/78760444/
Bon Jovi's quotes: from *Paste* magazine, 16 January 2009

Joan Jett
"John DeBella's Best Joan Jett Interviews" on *The John DeBella* Show on 102.9 MGK, or wmgk.com

Gary Numan
"I was gutted… wanker": from an article by Simon Price, *The Quietus*, September 2013
"Before then, I thought…insecure patch": from an article by Fiona Sturges, *The Independent*, 27 January 2003
"He's not only copied me… cloning…": Bowie speaking to Paula Yates, *Record Mirror*, 1979
"If he were asked…": Bowie speaking to the press in 2000, requoted by David Buckley in *Strange Fascination*
"Later, he said some nice things…": Numan interview in *Uncut*

Princess Margaret
Story told to the author by Edward Bell
Edward Bell
From the artist talking to the author. The stories are given a much fuller outing in Bell's own unique book *Unmade Up: Recollections of a Friendship with David Bowie*, Unicorn, 2017.
Steve Strange
"I've been watching you...": Strange speaking to Dave Owens, *Wales Online*, 13 February 2015
The old man walking the dog story: posted by assistant director Michael Dignum on Facebook, 11 January 2016. Bowie recounted the story to him while shooting the video for "Miracle Goodnight" in October 1993.
Hazel O'Connor
O'Connor has recounted the story several times. To see her talk about it, go to youtube.com/watch?v=1Vv4f7uuEAY, which is the Cherry Red Records site; or read it in an article by Gemma Jarvis for *East Anglian Daily Times*, 17 February 2020.
John Cleese
Quotes from Martin Lewis speaking at the Secret Policeman's Film Festival, 2009. Reprinted *Huffington Post*, huffpost.com/entry/30-years-of-mocking-and-r_b_215404
Graham Chapman
"Do you know who we are?": from The Pythons, *The Pythons' Autobiography*, Orion, 2005
The collision story: from "One mad night, travels with my ass", Eric Idle's blog at ericidle.com, posted 4 December 2011
Eric Idle
Bowie's role in a *Life of Brian* prequel is from *The Complete Michael Palin*

Diaries by Michael Palin, Weidenfeld & Nicolson, 2015
"I didn't know how to respond ...": from Eric Idle, *Always Look on the Bright Side of Life*, Weidenfeld & Nicolson, 2018
Richard Curtis
Richard Curtis, "Behind the Lines", *The Guardian*, 16 November 2003
Kate Bush
Bush's foreword to *MOJO Classic 60 Years of Bowie Special Birthday Tribute*, *Mojo* special edition, 2007
Prince
"You should have been there...": from thedawn.com, Prince's own website set up in 1996 but now defunct. However, if you go to http://prince.org/msg/7/149350, you can find a thread of the mythic/made-up collaboration between Prince and Bowie; this line from Novabreaker stands out: "You don't remember the first round of the fan cent questions (this was an era when e-mail was still a novelty invention) for at the original dawn.com website? One of the questions was 'Would you ever consider a collaboration with David Bowie?' And his own answer was, 'You should have been there.'"
"He's probably the most eclectic...": from "David Bowie: Stardust Memories", interview by Kurt Loder for *Rolling Stone*, 23 April 1987
"In terms of the more exhibitionist...": from Chris Hall, "David Bowie at 40", *The Observer*, April 1987
"I only met him once... ": Paisley Park Piano and a Microphone concert, 21 January 2016
Donnie Simpson's quotes are from an interview with the author.
Abbie Hoffman
Quotes from an interview with writer

Chris Norris, found at bychrisnorris. com/music/golden-years

Catherine Deneuve

"It allowed me to meet…" and "He's rather shy…", translated from an interview Deneuve gave to *Le Soir illustré* in 1983: from the French website "Extracts from Interviews with Catherine Deneuve", http://toutsurdeneuve.free.fr/Francais/ Pages/Carriere_Films/Les_predateurs "I'm not a midinette" translated from French: Deneuve speaking to Frédéric Bonnaud and Serge Kaganski under the title "Les Inrockuptibles 1996", and also found on the above website. This is a great source for anyone interested specifically in Deneuve's comments to the French press over the years.

Susan Sarandon

"Yeah!": from *Watch What Happens Live with Andy Cohen*, Bravo TV, April 2016 "She's great…": from Virginia Campbell, "Bowie at the Bijou", *Movieline*, 1 April 1992 Paean to Sarandon: from *Mojo*, March 1997 "I was very fortunate…": *Larry King Live*, uploaded to YouTube, 6 May 2016 "He's worth idolizing…": from an interview with Andrew Ryan, *The Globe and Mail*, 31 July 2014

Pete Murphy

Murphy quotes from an article by Chris Alexander in *Fangoria*, an American horror-film fan magazine, 11 January 2016 "I wish we'd done Ziggy": from an interview with Murphy by Leigh Salter for *Beat*, beat.com.au/peter-murphy/ guestlisted.blogspot.co.uk/2013/12/

Pete Burns

Boy George wrote about the story when he and Bowie featured together on BowieNet Live Chat, 27 February 1999

John McEnroe

There are a couple of slightly different versions of this story, as there are with quite a few Bowie stories. For McEnroe's memory of this occurrence, read his *You Cannot Be Serious*, Putnam, 2002. Bowie quotes here are from an interview with Bill DeMain for *Performing Songwriter*, September 2003

Nile Rodgers

Naked on the beach: from an article Rodgers wrote for *Rolling Stone*, 12 January 2016 Billy Idol vomiting: from Buckley, *Strange Fascination* "I want you to make hits…flop with you": from an interview with Leah Greenblatt, for EW.com, 13 September 2018

Stevie Ray Vaughan

The story of the hostile reception: from Damian Fanelli, "Stevie Ray Vaughan Gets Booed at 1982 Montreux Jazz Fest", *Guitar World*, 8 February 2016 Hanging out with Bowie: described by writer Alan Paul at alanpaul.net A riveting read on the bust-up and much more terrific detail can be found in Alan Paul and Andy Aledort, *Texas Flood: The Inside Story of Stevie Ray Vaughan*, St. Martin's Press, 2019 Vaughan accusing Bowie of bullshit: from an interview Vaughan gave on New Zealand TV in 1986. It can be found here: www.ultimateclassicrock.com/ david-bowie-lets-dance-video-stevie-ray-vaughan/ "What the fuck…": from Sandford, *Loving the Alien* Bowie talking about them buddying up again: from his January 1996 interview with *Guitar Magazine*

Tina Turner
The story of how Bowie saved Turner's
career: from Tina Turner, *My Love Story*,
Century, 2018
"Get some balls": from "David Bowie
Remembered", quotes from fellow stars
for *The Guardian*, 17 January 2016
Nagisa Ōshima
"I don't like acting…": from Roger
Pulvers, "Ōshima was in a realm of his
own", *The Japan Times*, 19 January 2013
"The last thing…" and "I've spent more
time…": from Sandford, *Loving the Alien*
"Best-dressed…": Bowie speaking to a
press conference in Tokyo in 1983.
Bowie also spoke to *Rolling Stone*
magazine in "Straight Time" by Kurt
Loder, 12 May 1983.
"One of the highlights…": from "Dear
Friends" by David Bowie, 1983, on
bowiewonderworld.com
Ryuichi Sakamoto
"I was struggling…every song": interview
with Dominic Maxwell for *The Times*,
27 June 2018
"Great musician…": from live chat
hosted by Hollywood Online,
website 1 July 1994, as transcribed on
bowiewonderworld.com
David Sylvian
Sylvian seeing Bowie and Bolan at a
nightclub: from the comments section of
Sylvian's Facebook page, 11 January 2016
Bowie being rejected by a bouncer: from
Simon Napier-Bell, *I'm Coming to Take
You to Lunch*, Ebury Press, 2006
Takeshi Kitano
Kitano's quotes are translated from a
Japanese TV show in which he appeared,
with Sakamoto and Ōshima, alongside
Bowie in 1983, available at youtube.com/
watch?v=ac45Ic57-gU

Masayoshi Sukita
Sukita having only a few hours to get
ready for the photoshoots: from James
Hadfield, "The Shoot Must Go On",
Japan Times, 17 May 2018
Bowie quotes: from his introduction to
Sukita and Bowie's *Speed of Life*, Genesis
Publications, 2012
Extra details are from the author's
interview with Sukita.
Rupert Everett
"The mystical…": from Rupert Everett,
Red Carpets and Other Banana Skins,
Abacus, 2007
"The frustrating thing…": interview with
Chris Heath for *US Weekly*, June 1999
Rent boy story: from "Middle Class
Boy to Rent", article on Everett in *The
Independent*, 13 July 1997
Icehouse
Kathy McCabe, "Icehouse Reveal
Their Unique Music Bond with David
Bowie", News Corp Australia Network,
12 January 2016
Thompson Twins
Matt Wardlaw, "Tom Bailey, Who
Plays the Kent Stage Next Week, Gets
Conceptual on His New Solo Album",
Clevescene.com, 22 August 2018
Suggs
Falling off a stage and underwear
blowing away: from a Suggs interview
with Paul Simper for *The Sun*,
23 October 2017
"I like your lyrics…": from an interview
with Adrian Devon for *Event* magazine,
Daily Mail, 28 January 2017
The Beat
As told to L Khan by Dave Wakeling,
http://englishbeat.net/the-beating-
heart-of-bowie-is-rebel-music-
ripdavidbowie/

Kevin Rowland
The quotes are from a recording of Bowie's concert at the Hippodrome d'Auteuil, Paris (Source 2 VHS), 6 August 1983, and also www.davidbowieworld.nl, which has a bootleg of the evening.

Psychedelic Furs
The backstage antics: from "David Bowie fan Bruce Butler recalls…", an interview with Cameron Adams for news.com.au on 13 January 2016
"We were just arguing…": from an article by Dave Everley at loudersound.com, 7 August 2017

Rosie O'Donnell
Bowie appeared on her TV show in March 1997
Iman's quotes appear in Leigh, *Bowie: The Biography*

John Foxx
"David Bowie fan Bruce Butler recalls meeting his hero", news.com.au, 13 January 2016
"Of course, he really…": from an article by Paul Lester at loudersound.com, 28 November 2017

Noel Edmonds
Carl Wilkinson, "Live Aid in Their Own Words", *The Observer*, 17 October 2004

Princess Diana
"I was in tears": from Andrew Morton, *Diana: Her True Story in Her Own Words*, Michael O'Mara Books, 1992

Sting
"We were totally captivated…": Sting in *People* magazine, 12 January 2016
"I would like to have been Sting": Bowie talking to Charlie Rose on ABC television in 1998

Mel Giedroyc
Giedroyc recounted the story on BBC One's panel game *Would I Lie to You?*, Series 8, Episode 3, first aired 3 December 2016

Keith Haring
From an interview in *SKY Magazine*, May 1990

Tim Pope
"David Bowie and Me", interview with Tim Pope by Dave Simpson, *The Guardian*, 23 February 2013

Keith Richards
Trivial Pursuit: from recollections of Hanif Kureishi as told to Dylan Jones for *David Bowie: A Life*
"It's all pose… not a big fan": from "Bowie's 30 Best Songs", *Uncut*, May 2008
"I'm not an actor…": *Sabotage Times*, 27 February 2018

Werner Herzog
Information on *Cobra Verde*: from a 1987 interview with Jean-Pierre Lavoignat, included in Eric Ames (ed.), *Werner Herzog Interviews*, University Press of Mississippi, 2015
"Depth of a neon light bulb…": from Paul Cronin, *Werner Herzog: A Guide for the Perplexed: Conversations with Paul Cronin*, Faber & Faber, 2014

Carl Perkins
Bowie and Goldblum jamming: from an interview given by Goldblum to *Glastonbury Free Press*, 30 June 2019

Martin Scorsese
"I had seen his…": from Ruben V Nepales, "A Chat with Martin Scorsese about Music, for a Change", *Philippine Daily Inquirer*, 18 March 2020
"With somebody like…": from "Action Painting", a Bowie interview by Chris Roberts, *Ikon* magazine, October 1995

Steven Spielberg
Michael Jackson being considered and

Bowie turning down the role: from "Hook Trivia" on *IMDb.com*

Jim Henson

"Jim Henson's *Labyrinth* Returns to Theaters and Set to Become a Musical", interview with Henson's son, Brian, by Simon Thompson, *Forbes.com*, 17 April 2018

Froud's comments from *The Making of Labyrinth*, available at https://www.youtube.com/watch?v=GlbqC1D4WHU

Derek Jarman

The story appears in Pegg, *The Complete David Bowie Updated*. Edward Bell has a slightly different recollection, told to the author.

Bowie's denial: from Robert Phoenix, "Bowie's Head", *Dirt*, 5 October 1999

Raymond Briggs

Quotes from his appearance on BBC Two's *Newsnight*, filmed around 1987; the video is widely available on YouTube and Facebook

Alan Bennett

Alan Bennett, *The Alan Bennett Diaries*, Faber & Faber, 2016

Michael Caine

Yacht quotes: from Michael Caine, *What's It All About?*, Random House, 1993

"Fuck me, Eric…": from Eric Idle, *Always Look on the Bright Side of Life*, Weidenfeld & Nicolson, 2018

"He's bouncing about…": from *Parkinson*, BBC TV, 18 October 2003

Patsy Kensit

Interview with Gerard Gilbert for *The Independent*, 4 January 2017

Mickey Rourke

"Method rapping": from The Glass Spider Tour press conferences (Amsterdam), 30 March 1987

"My biggest up…I was so encouraged…": from *Q* magazine, June 1989

"I really shouldn't have bothered…": from Chris O'Leary's site *Pushing Ahead of the Dame*, online at https://bowiesongs.wordpress.com/about/

Axl Rose

"I'm going to kill you": from *Slash: The Autobiography*, It Books, 2008

"Bowie and I… situation and stuff" and the chat with Jagger and Clapton: from Mick Wall, "Stick to Your Guns", *Kerrang!*, 21 and 28 April 1990

Grace Jones

The whole story is based on an interview with Pee-wee Herman conducted by Geoff Edgers, titled "Sorry Bob Hope", *The Washington Post*, 21 December 2015. The suggestion that Bowie wrote the backing track seems highly unlikely, especially when you hear how bad it is.

The Berlin Wall

Bowie quotes here are from an interview with Bill DeMain for *Performing Songwriter*, September 2003

Artistic Reinvention, 1991–2001

- -

Jeremy Irons

Irons speaking to publicize the film *La Corrispondenza* in Italy, 11 January 2016, at https://jeremyirons.net/2016/01/11/jeremy-irons-in-rome-to-promote-the-correspondence/

Iman

Antolin quotes from *The Independent*, 14 February 2016

Bowie quote from *Hello!* magazine, 19 September 2000

Piers Morgan

Good Morning Britain, ITV, 11 January 2016

Christie Brinkley
Shared on Brinkley's Instagram
David Lee Roth
"All flowing blond hair...admired them":
from Lisa Robinson, *There Goes Gravity:
A Life in Rock and Roll*, Riverhead, 2015
""He had never put down an anchor...":
from PodKats! (via Blabbermouth), and
requoted in *Ultimate Classic Rock*,
23 January 2020
Pixies
Kim Deal getting stuck in the toilet: from
John Mendelssohn, *Gigantic: The Story
of Frank Black and the Pixies*, Omnibus,
2004
Bowie having "Jones" on his credit card:
from Santiago speaking to Dylan Jones
for *David Bowie: A Life*
Robert Smith
"I think my opening gambit...": from
an interview with Dorian Lynskey, *The
Guardian*, 7 June 2018
Other quotes: from Smith's interview
with David Bowie on XFM in 1995
Scott Walker
Quotes from "Happy Birthday David
Bowie", BBC Radio with Mary Anne
Hobbs, 1997
"The one that killed me...": from Triple J
Radio interview with David Bowie,
16 March 1997
Harvey Keitel
Veronesi quotes: translated from Italian
from *La Repubblica*, 6 August 1998, and
"Veronesi: Bowie era ironico come un
Toscano", *Il Tirreno*, 11 January 2016,
which includes Pieraccioni's story
The Legendary Stardust Cowboy
Bowie quotes from BowieNet,
live chatroom, reappearing at
bowiewonderworld.com
"I don't care for dobro...": Jeff Gage, "The

Real-Life Legendary Stardust", *Vice*,
25 May 2017
Coldplay
"Not one of your best...": Coldplay
interview with David Renshaw for *NME*,
2 December 2014
Champion's comment: Jeff Gage, "How
David Bowie Turned "Down Coldplay",
The Guardian, 20 January 2016
The Smashing Pumpkins
Midnight Chats show on the *Loud and
Quiet* podcast, Episode 35,
www.loudandquiet.com/podcasts/billy-
corgan-midnight-chats-episode-35/
The Prodigy
"There's no other band...": *Raygun*,
March 1997
Howlett's quotes: from Tim Noakes,
"Liam Howlett: Lord of the Dance",
Dazed magazine, 4 July 2014
"We started doing festivals...": David
Bowie Daddy Cool interview with Paul
Sexton, *The Times*, 14 November 2003
Goldie
Goldie, *All Things Remembered*, Faber
& Faber, 2017
"A Celebration of Bowie", an evening at
Sonos Studios, London, 17 November 2017
Björk
"I always wondered...": Björk Facebook
post, 10 January 2016
Bodyguards picking up eggs: from *GQ*
interview with Björk, 2011
Carolyn Asome, "Oscar Gowns That
Changed the Red Carpet", *The Daily
Telegraph*, 27 February 2016
Madonna
"Conventional in the extreme": from US
TV interview in 1991, requoted O'Leary,
Pushing Ahead of the Dame
"A vicious put-down...': from O'Leary,
Pushing Ahead of the Dame

"Oh no, not you two": from Billy Idol, *Billy Idol: Dancing with Myself*, Simon & Schuster, 2015

"She's quite miraculously gathered…": from "Madonna Special", BBC Radio 1, March 1998

"I've been hanging out with Sean…": from a Bowie interview in 1989, requoted O'Leary, *Pushing Ahead of the Dame*

Annie Lennox

"It's not an easy song…": Annie Lennox speaking at a launch for her book *Nostalgia* at Barnes & Noble in New York, 21 October 2014

"Eurythmics Live by Request" show, 19 January 2000.

Françoise Hardy

Trafic.musique, presented by Guillaume Durand, France 2 TV, November 2003

"J'ai rencontré David Bowie en 2003", interview in French with Françoise Hardy by Sophie Delasseoin for *L'Obs* magazine, 19 January 2016

David Lynch

Bowie's quotes are from Lawrence Schubert, "Back to Earth", *Detour* magazine, March 1997

"Someone must have made him…": Daniel Dylan Wray, "David Lynch on Bowie", *Pitchfork*, 19 September 2017

Ben Stiller and Owen Wilson

Quotes from "Como David Bowie Topou Fazer *Zoolander*?", an interview with Stiller and Wilson for Paplpop, a Portuguese entertainment website, uploaded to YouTube, 3 March 2016

Russell Crowe

"I was his coke dealer": from an interview with Russell Crowe, *The Gladstone Observer*, 1 December 2014

Tony Parsons

"He was the only musician…": from Tony Parsons, "Life Was Never Cosy around Bowie", *The Sun*, 11 January 2016

Sean Combs

"Courage to change my names": @Diddyone, Twitter, 11 January 2016

"What exercise machine do you use?": *New York Daily News*, 29 July 2001

Lenny Kravitz

Audition is from a podcast for *Rolling Stone* with Kravitz, 28 February 2017

"This man changed my life": from Kravitz's Facebook page

Hanif Kureishi

Hanif Kureishi, "My Friend", *The Guardian*, 12 August 2017, and also a similar article by Kureishi in *The Times*, 12 January 2016,

"We were shitting…": from Jones, *David Bowie: A Life*

Stephen King

Talking to Marlow Stern for the *Daily Beast*, 16 February 2016

William Boyd

Reference to bringing a friend and the Greek newspaper: from Boyd's own journal, quoted in *The Guardian*, 12 January 2016

"Daniel in lions' den": from Jones, *David Bowie: A Life*

"Nobody special" and "Snazzy tics": from an article in *The Independent* by David Lister, 24 September 1994

Balthus

"The Last Legendary Painter: Balthus with David Bowie", *Modern Painters*, Vol. 7, No. 3 (Autumn 1994)

"Most rewarding…" and "Whoa, that's me": Pegg, *The Complete David Bowie*

"Show my mettle": article by Moon Zappa and Brian Eno, *Raygun*, October 1995

Damien Hirst

Minotaur: from Buckley, *Strange*

Fascination
"Never happened before..." and "We had
a ball...very pure thing": from Michael
Kimmelman, "TALKING ART WITH/
David Bowie: A Musician's Parallel
Passion", *The New York Times*, 14 June
1998
"I loved that...": from damienhirst.com/
news/2016/bowiecollector
Tracy Emin
"I'm so sorry to interrupt you": *The
Leisure Society with Gemma Cairney*,
BBC 6 Music
"Elastic lips..." and "Within 30
minutes..." and "That's art": from *Modern
Painters*, Vol. 10, No. 3 (October 1997)
Willem de Kooning
"Oh, fuck visitors": *David Bowie: The
Last Interview and Other Conversations*,
Melville House, 2016
Roy Lichtenstein
"Most painters think...": *The Interview*,
January 1998
"I enjoyed the heck...": Pegg, *The
Complete David Bowie Updated*
Jeff Koons
Looking for the look: from "*Whitewall*
Icons: Jeff Koons in Conversation with
Stephanie Seymour", *Whitewall*,
11 May 2017
Bowie quotes: from Bowie interview
with Koons, *Modern Painters*, Vol. 11.
No. 1 (Spring 1998)
Jean-Michel Basquiat
Girlfriend's quotes from Ekow Eshun,
"Bowie, Bach and Bebop: How Music
Powered Basquiat", *The Independent*,
25 September 2017
Mudd Club quote: from Richard Boch,
doorman at the Mudd Club (1979–80),
speaking to Miss Rosen for Dazeddigital.
com, 15 September 2017

"Burning immediacy" and "relates to
rock": from David Bowie, "Basquiat's
Wave", *Modern Painters*, Vol. 9, No. 1
(Spring 1996)
Laurie Anderson
Interview in *Female First*, 12 June 2016
REM
BBC 6 Music's Matt Everitt for "The First
Time", 26 May 2017
Glenn Branca
Daniel Maurer, B+B Newsroom, by
Bedford + Bowery, 11 October 2013,
available at bedfordandbowery.com/
category/bb-newsroom-2/
Denis Leary
Jimmy Kimmel Live!, uploaded to
YouTube, 22 July 2015
Michael Parkinson
"When he died...": from "Parky's People",
Norfolk Mag, norfolkmag.co.uk,
21 March 2016
"It's those genuine musical...":
from Robert Sandall, "Parky the Hit
Maker", *The Daily Telegraph*,
18 December 2003
Terry Wogan
Terry Wogan, *Is It Me?*, BBC Books,
2001
Liam Gallagher
"I must have coughed": from *Later with
Jools Holland*, 4 August 1996
Punch-up story: from Pegg, *The
Complete David Bowie*
Damon Albarn
"For 24 hours...": interview by Stephen
Dalton for *The Quietus*, 24 March 2012
Other quotes from his appearance on
TV5 France with Bowie, 2003
Jarvis Cocker
Cocker speaking to Chris Evans on
Channel 4's *TFI Friday* show, 1996

Brett Anderson
Steve Sutherland, "Bowie and Brett: One Day All This Could Be Yours", *NME*, 20 March 1993

Morrissey
"Smiling keenly..." and "The 12-year-old in me...": Morrissey, *Autobiography*, Penguin Classics, 2013
"Put it this way...": *Select* magazine, May 1994
"One night...": "The Importance of Being Morrissey", TV documentary, dir. Tina Flintoff, 2002
"Oooh, it's soo grand": from Sutherland, "Bowie and Brett"
"I left the tour because...": Spitz, *Bowie: A Biography*
"David wouldn't budge...": Q&A fan site truetoyou.net, 2014
"I'll tell you what happened...": Bowie speaking to Scottish TV journalist Billy Sloan the day after Morrissey walked out
"Card from Bogarde...": article by Andrew Harrison in *Select*, 1994
"The tour didn't work because...": *Hot Press*, June 2008

Neil Young
Kooks: John Peel Radio 1 show, 3 June 1971
"When things go bad...": *Kansas Star* in 2004
Neil Young's quotes on Reed and Bowie made to music press in 1973, as reported in Rob Sheffield's *On Bowie*, Dey Street Books, 2016 and Chris O'Leary's site Pushing Ahead of the Dame
"... find youth again": article by Massimo Cotto in *Amica* magazine, No. 14 (4 April 1997)
"A pioneer loaded with integrity...": Pegg, *The Complete David Bowie*
Pegi Young's comments: from her

Facebook page posted 13 January 2016 ·
"... creatively pedestrian...": "Still Hip After All These Years?", *The Daily Telegraph*, 16 November 2003

Sonic Youth
Thurston Moore, "Coco: A letter to Pitchfork", January 2016

Trent Reznor
"No more than six weeks..." and "I got a big hug...": Bowie and Reznor interviewed by Kurt Loder for *MTV News*, uploaded to YouTube 13 January 1995
"I turned up...": Interview with Bowie and Reznor for *USA Today* on opening day of tour, 14 September 1995

Henry Rollins
Keep Talking, Pal, Henry Rollins one-man show, toured 2018, dir. Brian Volk-Weiss, available on Amazon Prime

Moby
"This is a story..." ("Heroes" story): SiriusXM, 4 July 2018
"Get home before the traffic...": from Moby "David Bowie's *Low* Turns 40" at Billboard.com, 14 January 2017

Interpol
Jada Yuan, "David Bowie's Gift to Young Bands: His Fandom. Interpol's Paul Banks Remembers", *Vulture*, 25 January 2016

Kate Moss
Jacket let out and snug fit: "Kate Moss Joins Shaun", BBC Radio 6 Music's Shaun Keaveny show, 8 June 2016
"Clinging naked...": *Q* magazine, October 2003
"There are people..."; from an article by Ajesh Patalay in *EDIT* magazine, 22 June 2012
Liv and Stella screamed: from http://microsite.bauermedia.co.uk/q4music/duets/interview.shtml

Beyoncé
Bowie concert, New Jersey, 2004
Beyoncé's diva quotes: *CosmoGirl*, 2001
Tony Blair
Blair speaking to the author
Alan Edwards, "On Bowie, Jackson and
Working with the World's Biggest Stars",
Media Masters podcast, 28 January
2016, https://www.mediamasters.fm/
alan-edwards/
Nelson Mandela
Interview with David Bowie by Philip
Young for *The Journal* [daily newspaper
based in north-east England], 1995
Eddie Murphy
"I was always suspicious…": from Sean
Egan (ed.), *Bowie on Bowie: Interviews
and Encounters*, Chicago Review Press,
2015
"I'm a big Bowie fan": from Jeff Weiss, "A
Long Q&A with Eddie", Billboard.com,
6 February 2015
Keanu Reeves
Article by Jane Harkness for looper.com,
5 April 2019
Stereophonics
"He would heckle…": Richard Jones
speaking to Edwin Gibson, *The Argus*,
3 November 2017
"He was bored…interested": interview
by Eamonn Forde for *The Big Issue*,
13 November 2017
"Afterwards, Bowie would…" and "He'd
lower a trophy…": from Kelly Jones
talking to Nathan Bevan, Wales Online,
11 January 2016
Perry Farrell
Interview with Farrell on build.com TV,
13 June 2019
Beastie Boys
The Webby Awards, 2007
Marilyn Manson

WTF with Marc Maron, podcast
"Except for the breasts…": Chris Norris,
"Ashes to Ashes", www.bychrisnorris.com
Alexander McQueen
"David Bowie vs Alexander McQueen",
Dazed & Confused, No. 26 (1996)
Jake Shears
Jack Shears's autobiography, *Boys Keep
Swinging*, Omnibus, 2018
PJ Harvey
"We both had different…": BowieNet Live
Chat, November 1998
"Polly, being Polly…": from Joe Gore,
"My Brushes with Bowie", tonefiend.com,
11 January 2016
TV on the Radio
Gas station story: *NME*, 3 August 2007
"By end 2007…": from an article by David
Sitek in *Rolling Stone*, 28 January 2016
Camille Paglia
"It was one of the biggest…" and "eerie,
mesmerizing" and "No wonder…":
interview with David Daley, salon.com,
12 January 2016
"Oh boy, it's just some fan," and
"ridiculous": from "Conversations with
Tyler Cowen" at the George Mason
University, 25 April 2016
"Who the hell needed Foucault…" and
"I nearly sampled…": from Dominic
Wells, "David Bowie and Brian Eno",
Time Out, 23 August 1995
Arctic Monkeys
Jo Whiley, BBC Radio 2, June 2018
The Libertines
"Song Stories" evening with Barat,
Rostam and Goldie to honour Bowie,
held by Sonos, recorded live at Sonos
London, 17 November 2017
The Charlatans
Tim Burgess's Twitter page

The Next Days, 2005–2016

Arcade Fire
Molly Knight, author of *The Best Team Money Can Buy*, tweeted, "I didn't know he had gifted copies to all his friends. The next day I went to Tower Records on Lafayette to buy the CD. The guy told me they were told out. 'Bowie bought them all.'"
Band quotes: Owen Pallett's Facebook page

James Murphy
"I'm so sorry...": from *The Best Show*, 9 August 2017
"I was supposed to do more": "Future Sounds": interview with Annie Mac, BBC Radio 1, 6 July 2017
"Does it make you uncomfortable?": Lauren Laverne, BBC 6 Music, 11 July 2017

Ricky Gervais
Interview with Ricky Gervais by Mark Jefferies for *Daily Mirror*, 12 September 2013, and *Q* magazine, No. 335 (1 May 2014)

Dom Joly
Dom Joly's autobiography, *Here Comes the Clown: A Stumble through Show Business*, Simon & Schuster, 2015

Echo and the Bunnymen
Sergeant speaking to *The Vinyl Guide*, Episode 82, 5 June 2017, via YouTube

Rupaul
E Alex Jung, "Real Talk with Rupaul", *Vulture*, March 2016

Val Kilmer
Kilmer's Facebook page, posted 11 January 2016

Cheap Trick
The Howard Stern Show, 6 April 2016

Scarlett Johansson
"I couldn't tell him...": *Live* magazine, 11 September 2006
"It was the best phone call...": Andy Greene, "How Scarlett Johansson and David Bowie Got Together", *Rolling Stone*, 13 February 2008

Hugh Jackman
Jackman recounts the story at Femalefirst.co.uk, 10 March 2007, and indielondon.co.uk in an interview with Rob Carnevale

Christopher Nolan
"But he was very gracious...": from *Desert Island Discs*, BBC Radio 4, with Christopher Nolan
"In total honesty...": from Madison Vain, "Christopher Nolan Pays Tribute to David Bowie, the Actor", *Entertainment*, 19 January 2016

Wim Wenders
Bowie's quotes made to *Der Spiegel*, 12 April 1993
Details about the promotional video are from prosoundnetwork.com/archives, 31 October 2006

Elvis Costello
Elvis Costello, *Unfaithful Music and Disappearing Ink*, Blue Rider, 2015

Dave Gahan
"I never bothered ...": Jo Whiley, BBC Radio 2, 28 March 2017

Courtney Love
"Who could possibly object to *Rumours*?!": Jones, *David Bowie: A Life*

Paul Weller
"Pish": Weller speaking to the press after the awards ceremony
The email exchange: from an article in *The Sun*, May 2008

Rufus Wainwright
Luminato Festival Facebook page

(Weisbrodt was the artistic director), posted 11 January 2016

Chris Hadfield
Chris Hadfield's Facebook page

Britt Ekland
Story from Ekland's Instagram feed, 5 June 2017

Marion Cotillard
From an article by Paola Genone in *L'Express*, 9 December 2013, translated from the French

Tilda Swinton
Swinton's speech for the *David Bowie Is* exhibition at the Victoria and Albert Museum, London, 22 March 2013

Cillian Murphy
Bowie's comments on The Peakies from BowieNet conversation with fans on 31 October 2000, transcript available at bowiewonderworld.com

"We were friends": from an article by Roz Laws for the *Birmingham Mail*, 5 May 2016

"I'm afraid that won't...": interview with Steve Knight by Louisa Mellor for *Den of Geek*, 9 November 2017

Michael Cunningham
Michael Cunningham, "Stage Oddity", *GQ*, 9 January 2017

Enda Walsh
"God, you've been...": from an article by Jennifer Ryan, *The Irish Times*, 17 March 2017

"We never ever discussed him being sick...": from an article by Peter Stanford, *The Daily Telegraph*, 24 October 2016

Billy Ritchie
Interview with the author

Dave Grohl
Grohl tells the story while touring Bowie's LA haunts in a video shot for *Playboy*, 18 February 2016, available on YouTube

INDEX

PICTURE ACKNOWLEDGEMENTS

The publishers would like to acknowledge and thank the following for providing images for publication in this book:

28 ITV/Shutterstock; 36 Shutterstock; 72 Photo © Mick Rock 1972, 2021; 79 © Sukita; 93 Photo © Mick Rock 1972, 2021; 109 Terry O'Neill/Iconic Images; 123 Terry O'Neill/Iconic Images/ Getty Images; 149 CBS via Getty Images; 161 Steve Schapiro/ Corbis via Getty Images; 174 Rolf Adlercreutz/Alamy Stock Photo; 176, 180 Christian Simonpietri/Sygma via Getty Images; 195 Bob Gruen; 222 Jean-Claude Deutsch/Paris Match via Getty Images; 227 Chuck Pulin/Splash News; 229 Bob Gruen; 243 Dave Hogan/Hulton Archive/Getty Images; 264 Time Life Pictures/DMI/The LIFE Picture Collection via Getty Images; 279 Trinity Mirror/Mirropix/Alamy Stock Photo; 284 Dave Hogan/Hulton Archive/Getty Images; 291 Jonathan Becker/ Contour by Getty images; 312 Kevin Mazur/WireImage/Getty Images; 340 Gary Gershoff/WireImage

AUTHOR'S ACKNOWLEDGEMENTS

Thanks to Kevin, aka "Agent" Pocklington, for his enthusiasm and insight, Tony Visconti for his time and generosity of spirit, and Kevin Cann for the benefit of his unparalleled Bowie knowledge.

Thanks to Billy Ritchie for his wonderful turn of phrase, Alan Mair for possibly my favourite Bowie story and Craig Copetas, a natural-born storyteller. Dana Gillespie's *Weren't Born A Man* is one of the most entertaining autobiographies I've read and I was delighted when she made time to speak to me. It was a privilege to hear all about those early years from Phil Lancaster, whose *At the Birth of Bowie* filled a previous hole in the Bowie story. Thanks to Edward Bell, whose *Unmade Up: Recollections of a Friendship with David Bowie* is a unique treasure. It was an honour to hear back from Amanda Lear, another true original. My gratitude also goes to John Lydon, Tony Blair, Donnie Simpson, Helene Thian and Sukita.

Thanks to producer Bruce Robb, who had me in stitches as he described Sinatra and Bowie peeking round corners trying to snatch glimpses of each other while pretending to be above that sort of thing. I also want to say a big thank you to Tony Zanetta, who happily answered all my questions despite having had to answer them a hundred times before. And thanks to Jari-Pekka Laitio-Ramone, the font of all Ramones knowledge, whose decision to change his surname remains the yardstick by which all true music fans should be judged.

I'm indebted to the many great Bowie writers out there, especially Kevin Cann, Paul Trynka, Dylan Jones, David Buckley, Wendy Leigh, Nicholas Pegg, Marc Spitz, Roger Griffin, Christopher Sandford, Hugo Wilcken and Chris O'Leary.

I'm grateful to Brendon Le Page, Lawrence Pollard and Chris Hencken, friends who not only read the drafts but actually finished them, and Alex Stetter, whose editorial judgements and corrections were always spot on. I'm also thankful to friend and Beatles author Dave Rowley, who showed that it was possible to write books about people so famous you thought there could be nothing new to say about them, and Simon Glass, my fellow traveller in music across the decades. And my eternal thanks to Candy, Susie, Robin and those at Carlisle Road in Eastbourne who played me *Hunky Dory* and *Scary Monsters*, and gave me the gift of David Bowie.

Finally, love and thanks to Elijah, Nathaniel, Petroc, Reuben, Becky and my Mum, for indulging me in a distant hope.